COMPUTER TEST BANK
WITH TEST BANK
CD-ROM

Prentice Hall
Needham, Massachusetts
Upper Saddle River, New Jersey
Glenview, Illinois

COMPUTER TEST BANK

PRENTICE HALL
WORLD EXPLORER

2001 printing

Printed in the United States of America.

ISBN 0-13-434245-3

8 9 10   04 03 02 01

About the Computer Test Bank

The *Computer Test Bank* for *World Explorer* gives you unparalleled flexibility in creating tests. You can design tests to reflect your particular teaching emphasis. You can use the *Computer Test Bank* to create tests for different classes or to create alternative forms of the same test. You can also create tests for one chapter or for any combination of chapters, as well as for unit, midterm, and final examinations.

QUESTION ORGANIZATION

The *Computer Test Bank* provides printed test questions for all chapters and final exams, including:
- matching
- fill-ins
- multiple choice
- completion
- essay
- skill/short answer

AVAILABLE IN BOTH WINDOWS AND MACINTOSH FORMATS

The dual-platform Test Bank CD-ROM allows both Windows and Macintosh users to access the Test Bank on a single CD-ROM.

FLEXIBLE TEST-MAKI

The *Computer Test B* *or World Explorer* allows you to crea *sts easily* and conveniently. You can *t* exactly the questions you wan *or add* You can design tests for *ch test.* different ability levels, or you *ts of* add questions based on c *ct or* emphasized in class. You *ou Computer Test Bank* to create d *e* for different classes or alternate *s* the same test. The *Computer Tes* allows you to tailor tests to meet and local course requirements an the appropriate content, skills, an thinking into your testing progr there is no need to cut and paste graph, or chart that students need to a test item. When you select a te linked to an illustration, the Comput Bank will automatically prin illustration along with the question.

HELP IS JUST A TELEPHONE CAL AWAY

Stuck at any point? Simply call our toll-free HELP hotline (1-800-234-5TEC) for continuous and reliable support.

If you do not h... ...access to a computer or would like the convenience of designing your own tests without typing a word, you may want to... ...advantage of our free Dial-A-Test® Service. Available to all users of *World Explorer*, Dial-A-Test® is simple to use. At t... ...t is an example of a filled-out form.

HERE'S ... IT WORKS

1. ...he questions you want from C...made Chapter Test Questions.

2. ...he numbers of the questions in ...er you want on a Dial-A-Test® ...Form (see page v for a master ...ou may photocopy). Be sure to ...de the chapter number on the form. ...example, in the case of test question ...taken from Chapter 1, mark the ...er form with the designation 1,17.

...se a separate Dial-A-Test® order ...orm for each original test you request. You may use one form, however, to order multiple versions of the same original test.

If you would like another version of your original test with the questions scrambled, or put in another sequence, simply check the box labeled *Scramble Questions* on the order form. If you would like more than one scrambled version of your original test, note this on your order form or inform the Dial-A-Test® operator. Please note that Prentice Hall reserves the right to limit the number of tests and versions you can request at any one time, especially during the busier times of the year when midterms and finals are given.

5. **Choose the method** by which you would like to order your original test and/or multiple versions of your original test. To order by telephone, call toll free 1-800-468-8378 between 9:00 A.M. and 4:30 P.M. Eastern Standard Time and read the test question numbers to our Dial-A-Test® operator. Use the Dial-A-Test® Code 135 for *World Explorer*. To order by mail, send your completed Dial-A-Test® order form to the address listed below. Now you may also FAX your order to 1-614-771-7365.

–ORDER FORM–
CTS

DIAL-A-TEST®
PRENTICE HALL SCHOOL DIVISION
CUSTOMIZED TESTING SERVICE
TOLL-FREE NUMBER 800-468-8378 (H O-T-T-E-S-T)

–ORDER FORM–
CTS

You may **call** the PH Dial-A-Test® toll-free number during our business hours (9:00 A.M.-4:30 P.M. EST).
Now you may also FAX your order to 1-614-771-7365 anytime.

DIAL-A-TEST®
PRENTICE HALL SCHOOL DIVISION
4350 EQUITY DRIVE
COLUMBUS, OH 43228

FOR PH USE		DATE REC.	DATE SENT
__ PHONE __ MAIL __ FAX			

EXACT TEXT TITLE/VOL. _____ World Explorer _____ **© DATE** __1998__
CODE __135__

CUSTOMER INFORMATION
NAME _____ Ellen Mack _____
SCHOOL _____ Riverside High School _____
ADDRESS _____ 700 River Road _____
CITY __ Wells River __ STATE __TN__ ZIP __38578__
PHONE __ 208-555-2717 __ EXT. __34__

DATE BY WHICH TEST IS NEEDED __11/30/97__

TEST USAGE (CHECK ONE)
__ SAMPLE __ QUIZ __X__ CHAPTER TEST
__ UNIT TEST __ SEMESTER TEST __ FINAL EXAM

VERSIONS (SEE REVERSE-INSTRUCTION. #4)
(CHECK ONE)
__ 1. ORIGINAL __ 2. SCRAMBLE QUESTIONS

TEST IDENTIFICATION (This information will appear at the top of your test.)
_____ Ellen Mack _____
_____ History, Period 2 _____
_____ Chapter 1, Test _____

EXAMPLE: Mr. Holtman
History Period 5
Chapter 1 Test

1	1,3	26	1,74	51		76		101		126		151		176
2	1,5	27	1,80	52		77		102		127		152		177
3	1,6	28	1,81	53		78		103		128		153		178
4	1,9	29	1,82	54		79		104		129		154		179
5	1,11	30	1,83	55		80		105		130		155		180
6	1,12	31		56		81		106		131		156		181
7	1,14	32		57		82		107		132		157		182
8	1,17	33		58		83		108		133		158		183
9	1,18	34		59		84		109		134		159		184
10	1,21	35		60		85		110		135		160		185
11	1,32	36		61		86		111		136		161		186
12	1,34	37		62		87		112		137		162		187
13	1,35	38		63		88		113		138		163		188
14	1,38	39		64		89		114		139		164		189
15	1,40	40		65		90		115		140		165		190
16	1,41	41		66		91		116		141		166		191
17	1,45	42		67		92		117		142		167		192
18	1,47	43		68		93		118		143		168		193
19	1,55	44		69		94		119		144		169		194
20	1,57	45		70		95		120		145		170		195
21	1,66	46		71		96		121		146		171		196
22	1,67	47		72		97		122		147		172		197
23	1,69	48		73		98		123		148		173		198
24	1,70	49		74		99		124		149		174		199
25	1,71	50		75		100		125		150		175		200

---

6. **You may order** up to 100 questions per test by telephone on our toll-free 800 number or up to 200 questions per test by mail.

7. **Please allow a minimum of two weeks** for shipping, especially if you are ordering by mail. Although we process your order within 48 hours of your call or the receipt of your form by mail, mailing may take up to two weeks. Thus we ask you to plan accordingly and expect to receive your original test, any alternate test versions that you requested, and complete answer keys within a reasonable amount of time.

8. **Tests are available all year.** You can order tests before the school year begins, during vacation, or as you need them.

9. **For additional order forms** or to ask questions regarding this service, please write to the following address:

Dial-A-Test®
Prentice Hall School Division
4350 Equity Drive
Columbus, OH 43228

DIAL-A-TEST®
PRENTICE HALL SCHOOL DIVISION
CUSTOMIZED TESTING SERVICE
TOLL-FREE NUMBER 800-468-8378 (H O-T-T-E-S-T)

You may **call** the PH Dial-A-Test® toll-free number during our business hours (9:00 A.M.-4:3̶ ̶ ̶ ̶EST).
Now you may also FAX your order to 1-614-771-7365 anytime.

DIAL-A-TEST®
PRENTICE HALL SCHOOL DIVISION
4350 EQUITY DRIVE
COLUMBUS, OH 43228

FOR PH USE	DATE REC.
__ PHONE __ MAIL __ FAX	_____

EXACT TEXT TITLE/VOL. _____ PH World Explorer _____ © **DATE** __1̶9̶
CODE ___135___

CUSTOMER INFORMATION
NAME _____
SCHOOL _____
ADDRESS _____
CITY _____ STATE ___ ZIP ____
PHONE _____ EXT. _____

TEST USAGE (CHECK ONE)
__ SAMPLE __ QUIZ **X** CHAPT̶
__ UNIT TEST __ SEMESTER TEST __ FINAL

VERSIONS (SEE REVERSE-INSTRUCTION. #4)
(CHECK ONE)
__ 1. ORIGINAL __ 2. SCRAMBLE QUESTIONS

DATE BY WHICH TEST IS NEEDED _____

TEST IDENTIFICATION (This information will appear at the top of your test.)
_____
_____   EXAMPLE: Mr. Holtman
_____   History Period 5
_____   Chapter 1 Test

1 ____	26 ____	51 ____	76 ____	101 ____	126 ____	151 ____	176 ____
2 ____	27 ____	52 ____	77 ____	102 ____	127 ____	152 ____	177 ____
3 ____	28 ____	53 ____	78 ____	103 ____	128 ____	153 ____	178 ____
4 ____	29 ____	54 ____	79 ____	104 ____	129 ____	154 ____	179 ____
5 ____	30 ____	55 ____	80 ____	105 ____	130 ____	155 ____	180 ____
6 ____	31 ____	56 ____	81 ____	106 ____	131 ____	156 ____	181 ____
7 ____	32 ____	57 ____	82 ____	107 ____	132 ____	157 ____	182 ____
8 ____	33 ____	58 ____	83 ____	108 ____	133 ____	158 ____	183 ____
9 ____	34 ____	59 ____	84 ____	109 ____	134 ____	159 ____	184 ____
10 ____	35 ____	60 ____	85 ____	110 ____	135 ____	160 ____	185 ____
11 ____	36 ____	61 ____	86 ____	111 ____	136 ____	161 ____	186 ____
12 ____	37 ____	62 ____	87 ____	112 ____	137 ____	162 ____	187 ____
13 ____	38 ____	63 ____	88 ____	113 ____	138 ____	163 ____	188 ____
14 ____	39 ____	64 ____	89 ____	114 ____	139 ____	164 ____	189 ____
15 ____	40 ____	65 ____	90 ____	115 ____	140 ____	165 ____	190 ____
16 ____	41 ____	66 ____	91 ____	116 ____	141 ____	166 ____	191 ____
17 ____	42 ____	67 ____	92 ____	117 ____	142 ____	167 ____	192 ____
18 ____	43 ____	68 ____	93 ____	118 ____	143 ____	168 ____	193 ____
19 ____	44 ____	69 ____	94 ____	119 ____	144 ____	169 ____	194 ____
20 ____	45 ____	70 ____	95 ____	120 ____	145 ____	170 ____	195 ____
21 ____	46 ____	71 ____	96 ____	121 ____	146 ____	171 ____	196 ____
22 ____	47 ____	72 ____	97 ____	122 ____	147 ____	172 ____	197 ____
23 ____	48 ____	73 ____	98 ____	123 ____	148 ____	173 ____	198 ____
24 ____	49 ____	74 ____	99 ____	124 ____	149 ____	174 ____	199 ____
25 ____	50 ____	75 ____	100 ____	125 ____	150 ____	175 ____	200 ____

Contents

Contents continued

Contents Continued

World Explorer

LATIN AMERICA

BOOK 1

Chapter 1 ■ *Latin America: Physical Geography*

A. KEY TERMS

Complete each sentence by writing the letter of the correct term in the blank. You will not use all the terms.

a. hydroelectricity
b. tributary
c. Pampas
d plateau
e. El Niño
f. isthmus
g. elevation

1. _____ Central America is a narrow strip of land, or _____, that lies between Mexico and South America.

2. _____ Argentina's prized cattle graze on plains called the _____.

3. _____ The Amazon has hundreds of rivers and streams that flow into it, each of which is called a(n)_____.

4. _____ Down the center of Mexico is a(n) _____, or large, mostly flat, highland area.

5. _____ The height of land above sea level is called _____.

Match the descriptions with the terms. Write the correct letter in each blank. You will not use all the terms.

a. plateau
b. diversify
c. tributary
d. elevation
e. Pampas
f. isthmus
g. hydroelectricity

6. _____ a narrow strip of land that has water on both sides and joins two larger bodies of land

7. _____ a region of plains in Argentina and Uruguay; grazing ground for Argentina's prized cattle

8. _____ a large, mostly flat, highland area

9. _____ a river or stream that flows into a main river

10 _____ the height of land above sea level

B. KEY CONCEPTS

Write the letter of the correct ending in the blank provided.

11. _____ The whole of Latin America is located in the
    a. Northern Hemisphere.
    b. Southern Hemisphere.
    c. Western Hemisphere.
    d. Eastern Hemisphere.

12. _____ Mexico's Central Plateau is an important region because it
    a. is a mountainous region where few people live, but minerals are mined.
    b. contains most of the country's most important cities and best farmland.
    c. is a place where active volcanoes and earthquakes make life difficult.
    d. has a climate that is pleasant and therefore attracts many tourists.

13. _____ The soil in the farmland in Mexico and Central America is made fertile by
    a. decomposing leaves from trees.
    b. water from the Caribbean.
    c. melting snow.
    d. volcanic ash.

14. _____ Some Caribbean islands are formed from the tops of underwater mountains while others are formed from
    a. earthquakes and hurricanes.
    b. the skeletons of tiny sea animals.
    c. active volcanoes.
    d. high, flat plateaus.

15. _____ When the price of copper goes down, how does that affect the economy in Chile?
    a. The economy is not affected.
    b. The price of copper never goes down.
    c. The economy suffers.
    d. The economy improves.

16. _____ The types of crops grown by farmers in the Andes is influenced in large part by
    a. elevation.
    b. latitude.
    c. longitude.
    d. pampas.

17. _____ Farmers who live in the humid subtropical climates of Argentina, Uruguay, and Paraguay may grow
    a. bananas and coconuts.
    b. potatoes and coffee.
    c. corn and sugar.
    d. wheat and apples.

18. _____ One of the uses of rivers in Central America is to produce
    a. hydroelectricity.
    b. nuclear power.
    c. wind power.
    d. solar energy.

19. _____ The drop in oil prices in the 1980s probably helped to convince Venezuela to
    a. import more oil.
    b. increase its use of hydroelectricity.
    c. diversify its economy.
    d. stop pumping oil.

20. _____ All of the following are regions of Latin America except
    a. the United States and Canada.
    b. Mexico and Central America.
    c. the Caribbean.
    d. South America.

21. _____ The long mountain chain that runs along the side of South America is called the
   a. Rockies.   c. Andes.
   b. Sierra Nevada.   d. Sierra Madre.

22. _____ Some Caribbean islands are coral islands formed from
   a. tops of underwater mountains.   c. a long isthmus.
   b. skeletons of tiny sea animals.   d. high, flat plateaus.

23. _____ The Amazon River Basin is home to
   a. the rolling highlands called pampas.
   b. South America's gauchos.
   c. the largest tropical rain forest in the world.
   d. the world's biggest volcano.

24. _____ One statement that can be made about climate in Latin America is that throughout
   the region it is
   a. always hot and rainy.   c. very much the same.
   b. usually cold and frosty.   d. different from place to place.

25. _____ Among the factors that affect climate in Latin America are
   a. earthquakes, hurricanes, and volcanoes.
   b. elevation, the Equator, and wind patterns.
   c. vegetation, elevation, and earthquakes.
   d. El Niño, elevation, and earthquakes.

26. _____ Two South American countries that produce coffee as a key crop are
   a. Brazil and Colombia.   c. Paraguay and Argentina.
   b. Mexico and Cuba.   d. Nicaragua and Chile.

27. _____ To reduce their reliance on one natural resource or crop, many Latin American
   nations have begun to
   a. increase exports.   c. depend more on oil.
   b. reduce imports.   d. diversify their economies.

28. _____ Trade and travel among the regions of South America has been affected by
   a. natural resources and vegetation.
   b. high mountains and dense rain forests.
   c. the Caribbean Sea and the Pacific Ocean.
   d. Argentina and Venezuela's relationship.

C. CRITICAL THINKING

Answer the following questions in the space provided, on the back of this paper or on a separate sheet of paper.

29. Drawing Conclusions: Support or refute this conclusion: South America is a region of great variety and many contrasts.

30. Identifying Central Issues: Why has relying on one crop or resource presented a problem for many Latin American nations? How have these nations been trying to solve this problem?

31. Recognizing Cause and Effect: Identify three factors that affect climate in Latin America. Also, give one example of how climate affects the vegetation of a region.

32. Identifying Central Issues: Give one example of how reliance on a single crop or natural resource has hurt the economy of a Latin American country.

D. SKILL: USING REGIONAL MAPS TO SHOW CLIMATE

Use the map below to answer the following questions. Write your answers on the lines provided.

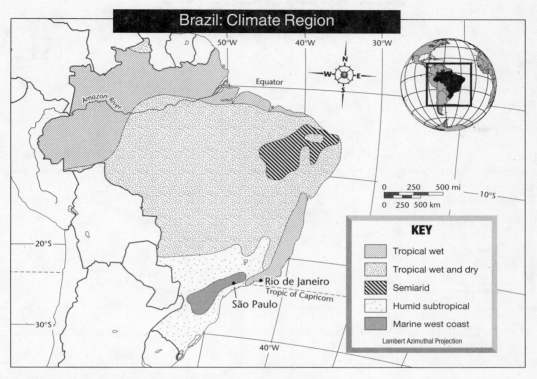

33. Which climate region covers the most territory in Brazil? _____

_____

34. In what climate is Rio de Janeiro located?_____

_____

35. Where do you think it is generally colder, in northern Brazil or southern Brazil? Why? _____

_____

36. What is the climate around the Amazon River?_____

_____

37. How do you think the equator affects the climate around the Amazon? _____

_____

Use the map below to answer the following questions. Write your answers on the lines provided.

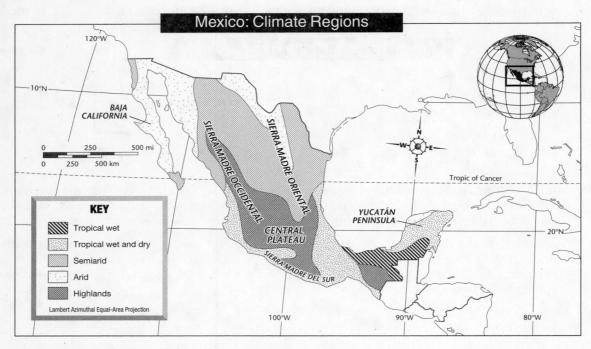

38. What part of the country has a highlands climate? _____

_____

39. What are the climate regions on the Yucatán Peninsula?_____

_____

40. Where are the driest parts of Mexico located?_____

_____

41. Where are Mexico's mountains located? _____

_____

42. What are the climate regions on the peninsula of Baja California? _____

_____

ANSWER KEY

1. f	2. c	3. b	4. d	5. g
6. f	7. e	8. a	9. c	10. d
11. c	12. b	13. d	14. b	15. c
16. a	17. d	18. a	19. c	20. a
21. c	22. b	23. c	24. d	25. b
26. a	27. d	28. b		

29. Students should agree with the statement. They should support their answer with concrete examples that show how the region is diverse. A good example would contrast the wet, dense Amazonian rain forest with the dry, barren Atacama Desert.

30. Students should recognize that lack of economic diversity has left Latin American nations vulnerable to world price fluctuations. A drop in price in a country's major export sets off an economic crisis in that country. For this reason, many Latin American nations have been trying to build new industries and grow new crops.

31. Students should identify the three factors of elevation, wind patterns, and distance from the equator. They could discuss how climate affects the vegetation that grows in the rain forest.

32. Students could use such examples as oil in Venezuela or copper in Chile to illustrate how one-crop/one-resource economies can be risky.

33. tropical wet and dry

34. tropical wet

35. southern Brazil; southern Brazil is farther from the Equator and has a cooler climate according to the map.

36. tropical wet and tropical wet and dry

37. closer to the Equator the climate tends to be warmer and moister

38. the Central Plateau

39. arid and tropical wet and dry

40. in the northern portion of the country.

41. down the eastern and western sides of the country

42. arid and semiarid

A. KEY TERMS

Complete each sentence by writing the letter of the correct term in the blank. You will not use all the terms.

a. criollo	b. hieroglyphics
c. rural	d. aqueduct
e. caudillo	f. mestizo
g. urban	h. encomienda
i. campesino	

1. _____ Someone who was born in Latin America, but had Spanish parents or grandparents is called a(n) _____ .

2. _____ The power to demand taxes or labor from Native Americans was called a(n) _____ .

3. _____ The Mayas recorded their history using signs and symbols that were part of a writing system called _____ .

4. _____ Many Latin Americans are moving from _____ regions of Latin America to the cities.

5. _____ The Incas used a(n) _____ to carry water from a lake to fields many miles away.

Match the descriptions with the terms. Write the correct letter in each blank. You will not use all the terms.

a. campesino	b. criollo
c. conquistador	d. hieroglyphics
e. mestizo	f. quipu
g. aqueduct	h. hacienda
i. encomienda	j. caudillo

6. _____ a military officer who gained power in Latin America after independence

7. _____ a pipe built to carry water from a far-away river or lake to fields

8. _____ a writing system that uses signs and symbols

9. _____ a knotted string that the Incas used to record information

10. _____ the power given by Spain to settlers to demand taxes or labor from Native Americans

B. KEY CONCEPTS

Write the letter of the correct ending in the blank provided.

11. _____ The Aztecs built a great civilization in the area now called
    a. Guatemala.
    b. the Andes.
    c. the Valley of Mexico.
    d. the Yucatán Peninsula.

12. _____ Which of the following are accomplishments of the Incas?
    a. pyramids
    b. floating gardens
    c. hieroglyphics
    d. roads and aqueducts

13. _____ All of the following contributed to the Spanish victory over the Aztecs except that
    a. disease wiped out many of the Aztecs.
    b. Native Americans in the region resented paying tribute to the Aztecs.
    c. the Spanish had horses and superior weapons.
    d. the Spanish had more soldiers.

14. _____ Spain's two most important colonies in the Americas were
    a. New Spain and Peru.
    b. Lima and Peru.
    c. Mexico and Central America.
    d. Mexico City and Lima.

15. _____ One result of the population explosion in Latin America is an increase in
    a. foreign investment.
    b. people moving to cities.
    c. the price of oil.
    d. people moving to rural areas.

16. _____ The first European colony in the Americas to win independence was
    a. Mexico.
    b. Cuba.
    c. Haiti.
    d. Brazil.

17. _____ Two leaders who contributed to independence in South America were
    a. Miguel Hidalgo and José Morelos.
    b. José de San Martín and Simon Bolivar.
    c. Toussaint L'Ouverture and Hernardo O'Higgins.
    d. Simon Bolivar and Prince Ferdinand

18. _____ Most of the caudillos who ruled Latin American countries after independence
    a. cared a great deal for the well being of the people of their countries.
    b. tried to unite South America.
    c. believed in liberal and democratic reform.
    d. were concerned mainly with getting rich and holding power.

19. _____ Which of the following statements about foreign companies in Latin America was true?
    a. Foreign companies often controlled the economies of Latin American countries.
    b. Foreign companies paid high wages to Latin American workers.
    c. Foreign companies offered good working conditions and opportunities to Latin American workers.
    d. Foreign companies used most of their profits to help strengthen Latin american economies.

20. _____ Copán and Tikal were cities that were part of
   a. Aztec civilization.
   b. Mayan civilization.
   c. Spanish civilization.
   d. Incan civilization.

21. _____ The city of Tenochtitlán was the center of which ancient civilization?
   a. Spanish civilization
   b. Mayan civilization
   c. Incan civilization
   d. Aztec civilization

22. _____ Incan civilization was located along the western coast of
   a. South America.
   b. the Yucatán Peninsula.
   c. Mexico.
   d. Central America.

23. _____ The Line of Demarcation was an imaginary line that divided control of the territory in the Americas between which two countries?
   a. England and France
   b. Spain and Portugal
   c. Incas and Aztecs
   d. Mayas and Spain

24. _____ Brazil was once a colony of which European country?
   a. England
   b. France
   c. Spain
   d. Portugal

25. _____ When the price of oil rose in the 1980s, many Latin American countries
   a. made a great deal of money.
   c. drilled for oil.
   b. borrowed money from wealthy countries.
   d. tried to develop other energy sources such as solar energy.

26. _____ All of the following are foods or animals that came to Europe from the Americas except
   a. maize.
   b. chocolate.
   c. potatoes.
   d. horses.

27. _____ Under Simón Bolívar's leadership, independent Colombia, Venezuela, Ecuador, and Panama became joined in a federation called
   a. the United States of South America.
   b. Gran Colombia.
   c. New Spain.
   d. the Incan empire.

28. _____ In recent times, many Latin American countries have tried to control foreign investment by
   a. allowing foreigners to invest as much money as they wish.
   b. forbidding any foreign investment.
   c. keeping foreign companies from buying too much land.
   d. forming free trade associations.

C. CRITICAL THINKING

Answer the following questions in the space provided, on the back of this paper or on a separate sheet of paper.

29. Making Comparisons: Compare the falls of Mayan, Aztec, and Incan civilizations. How were their falls similar? How were they different? Give an example of how an aspect of each civilization survives today.

30. Recognizing Cause and Effect: What world events inspired Haiti's fight for independence? What effect do you think Haiti's fight had on other parts of Latin America?

31. Recognizing Cause and Effect: List and explain at least two reasons why a relatively small band of Spanish soldiers were able to conquer much of Latin America and the people who lived there.

32. Identifying Central Issues: Describe how foreign investment affected Latin America in the early- to mid-1900s. How did foreign investment in Latin America change later in the century?

D. SKILL: USING A TIME LINE

Look at the time line and read each statement below. Then write the letter of the correct time period(s) in the blank provided. Some statements may require more than one letter.

Important Events in Latin American History

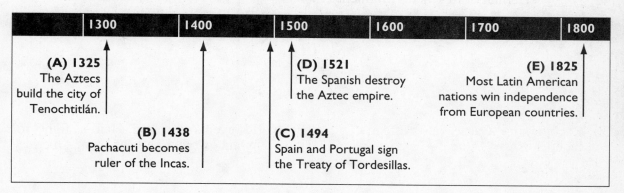

33. _____ Spain and Portugal sign the Treaty of Tordesillas.

34. _____ The Aztecs build the city of Tenochtitlán.

35. _____ Most Latin American nations win independence from European countries.

36. _____ Pachacuti becomes ruler of the Incas.

37. _____ The Spanish destroy the Aztec empire.

Look at the time line and read each statement below. Then write the letter of the correct time period(s) in the blank provided. Some statements may require more than one letter.

Important Events in Latin American History

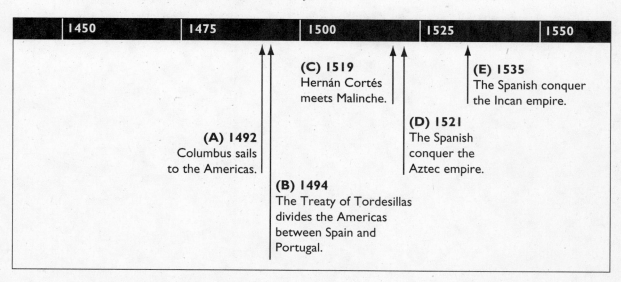

38. _____ The Spanish conquer the Aztec empire.

39. _____ The Treaty of Tordesillas divides the Americas between Spain and Portugal.

40. _____ Columbus sails to the Americas.

41. _____ The Spanish conquer the Incan empire.

42. _____ Hernán Cortés meets Malinche.

ANSWER KEY

1. a	2. h	3. b	4. c	5. d
6. j	7. g	8. d	9. f	10. i
11. c	12. d	13. d	14. a	15. b
16. c	17. b	18. d	19. a	20. b
21. d	22. a	23. b	24. d	25. b
26. d	27. b	28. c		

29. The reason for the fall of the Mayan civilization is unknown. The Incan and Aztec civilizations were conquered by the Spaniards. Today, millions of Mayas still live in Mexico, Belize, Guatemala, Honduras, and El Salvador. Many Aztec foods are still eaten today. Many descendants of the Incas speak Quechua, the Incan language.

30. The war the colonists of North America fought with Britain and the uprising of the French people against their royal rulers inspired Haiti's fight for independence. Haiti's fight probably inspired other people in Latin America to want their independence.

31. Students should list two of the following three reasons. The Spanish had guns, cannons, and horses—things the Native Americans did not have. The Spanish carried diseases that had the effect of wiping out many people. Finally, Spaniards had help from some Native Americans. These Native Americans were angry with other Native Americans because of local rivalries.

32. In the early- to mid-1900s, foreign investment controlled or affected most of the business in Latin America. Later in the century, Latin American nations tried to limit foreign investment.

33. C	34. A	35. E	36. B	37. D
38. D	39. B	40. A	41. E	42. C

Chapter 3 ▪ Cultures of Latin America

A. KEY TERMS

Complete each sentence by writing the letter of the correct term in the blank. You will not use all the terms.

       a. immigrant
       b. injustice
       c. indigenous
       d. subsistence farming
       e. ethnic group
       f. diversity
       g. Carnival
       h. maquiladora

1. _____ The name for a group of people that can be distinguished by race, language, religion, and cultural tradition is a(n) _____ .

2. _____ A term used to describe a person who is a descendant of a region's first inhabitants is _____ .

3. _____ There is much variety, or _____ , among the people of Central America.

4. _____ When farmers grow just enough for their families it is called _____ .

5. _____ A U.S.-owned border factory, called a(n) _____ , is located in Mexico near the U.S./Mexican border.

Match the descriptions with the terms. Write the correct letter in each blank. You will not use all the terms.

       a. import
       b. maquiladora
       c. immigrant
       d. diversity
       e. emigrate
       f. export
       g. indigenous
       h. subsistence farming
       i. ethnic group
       j. injustice

6. _____ a term describing people who are descendants of a region's first inhabitants

7. _____ to buy goods from other countries

8. _____ a person who lives in another country after leaving his or her own country

9. _____ another word for variety

10. _____ a U.S.-owned factory located in Mexico near the U.S./Mexican border

B. KEY CONCEPTS

Write the letter of the correct ending in the blank provided.

11. _____ In Belize, the official language is English, but in most Central American nations the official language is
    a. Portuguese.
    b. Spanish.
    c. French.
    d. a Native American language.

12. _____ One effect of rapid urbanization in Mexico is
    a. an increase in jobs.
    b. a shortage of housing.
    c. a decrease in emigration.
    d. an increase in the rural population.

13. _____ The world's largest community of Japanese outside of Japan live in the Brazilian city of
    a. Rio de Janeiro.
    b. Honduras.
    c. São Paulo.
    d. Huaynamota.

14. _____ The first people to live on the Caribbean islands were
    a. Ciboney.
    b. Spanish.
    c. African.
    d. mestizo.

15. _____ Two Carribean countries that share one island are
    a. Haiti and the Dominican Republic.
    b. Jamaica and Cuba.
    c. Trinidad and Tobago.
    d. the Bahamas and Cuba.

16. _____ Carnival is an event that is celebrated in many parts of Latin America to mark
    a. independence day.
    b. Christmas.
    c. the New Year.
    d. the start of Lent.

17. _____ The main idea of the story about how people in the Andes Mountains use totora reeds is that
    a. people use the resources offered by their environments to survive.
    b. totora reeds can be used for many different purposes
    c. some Native Americans live on floating islands on Lake Titicaca.
    d. many people from the Andes are moving to the cities.

18. _____ Which country has the greatest effect on Latin America culture?
    a. Italy
    b. France
    c. Germany
    d. Spain

19. _____ On the pampas of Argentina, many people make their living as
    a. bankers.
    b. cattle ranchers.
    c. factory workers.
    d. street vendors.

20. _____ In most Central American nations, the official language is
    a. English.
    b. French.
    c. Portuguese.
    d. Spanish.

21. _____ A main reason why Mexicans and Central Americans emigrate to the United States is to
   a. work in maquiladoras.
   b. find jobs.
   c. move to cities.
   d. escape earthquakes.

22. _____ The island of Hispaniola is divided into the countries of the Dominican Republic and
   a. Haiti.
   b. Cuba.
   c. Jamaica.
   d. Puerto Rico.

23. _____ The split of cultures on the island of Hispaniola is caused by
   a. natural geographic barriers that encouraged separate development.
   b. a difference in religious beliefs.
   c. European nations that dominated the region.
   d. immigration from various regions of the world.

24. _____ All of the following are types of Caribbean music or instruments except
   a. steel drums.
   b. calypso.
   c. Carnival.
   d. reggae.

25. _____ The three cultures that have had the most influence on Latin American culture are
   a. Spanish, French, and British.
   b. Native American, African, and European.
   c. Native American, Asian, and European.
   d. Asian, Spanish, and African.

26. _____ One reason the countries in the northern portion of South America share some cultural characteristics with the Caribbean islands is because they have
   a. a coastline on the Caribbean.
   b. mountainous landscapes.
   c. a similar ethnic makeup.
   d. the same religious beliefs.

27. _____ One difference between the populations of Chile and Brazil is
   a. most Brazilians live in the rain forest, while most Chileans live in the mountains.
   b. most Chileans are Roman Catholic, while most Brazilians are Protestant.
   c. most Chileans live in cities, while most Brazilians live in rural areas.
   d. most Chileans are mestizos, while Brazilians are very ethnically diverse.

28. _____ While workers on small farms generally grow just enough to meet their needs, on large farms, workers grow enough crops to
   a. feed cattle.
   b. subsist.
   c. export.
   d. import.

C. CRITICAL THINKING

Answer the following questions in the space provided, on the back of this paper or on a separate sheet of paper.

29. **Making Comparisons:** Choose two of the three regions of Latin America. Think about what you know about the culture of these two regions. What are two similarities and two differences in their cultures? Explain the reasons for these similarities and differences.

30. **Predicting Consequences:** How might the cultures of Latin America be different if the Spanish and Portuguese had never arrived? What kind of culture do you think would dominate the region today?

31. **Recognizing Cause and Effect:** Explain why there is so much variety in the culture of the Caribbean islands.

32. **Drawing Conclusions:** How are the cultures in South America like the cultures in Mexico? How are they different?

D. SKILL: DISTINGUISHING FACTS FROM OPINIONS

Read each of the sentences below. In the blank provided, write "Fact" if the statement is a fact and "Opinion" if the statement is an opinion. On the lines below each statement explain why the statement is a fact or an opinion.

33. _____ Mexico and Central America make up one region of Latin America.

_____

34. _____ Jamaica offers tourists the best beaches in the Caribbean.

_____

35. _____ Pablo Neruda is South America's most talented poet.

_____

36. _____ More than 20 languages are spoken in Guatemala.

_____

37. _____ People move to cities because they are looking for a better life.

_____

38. _____ Elvia Alvarado, who helps campesinos, is a good person.

_____

39. _____ In Guatemala, about half the people are mestizo and half the people are indigenous.

_____

40. _____ Most people in Latin America are Roman Catholic.

_____

41. _____ Jamaican jerk pork is the tastiest food you can find in the Caribbean.

_____

42. _____ Most of the soil in the Caribbean islands is fertile.

_____

ANSWER KEY

1. e	2. c	3. f	4. d	5. h
6. g	7. a	8. c	9. d	10. b
11. b	12. b	13. c	14. a	15. a
16. d	17. a	18. d	19. b	20. d
21. b	22. a	23. c	24. c	25. b
26. a	27. d	28. c		

29. Students should choose two regions and explain two similarities and two differences in their cultures. They might say that all the cultures of Latin America show native American influences, that the Christian religion is very influential throughout Latin America, and that many people in all three regions speak Spanish. Differences they might list include that many Brazilians speak Portuguese and that the Caribbean region's culture has been influenced by Africans.

30. Answers will vary. Students may say that indigenous cultures would have been more dominant. In that case, there would probably not be a single dominant language or religion throughout Latin America. Rather, all areas or countries might be more distinct in their languages or religions. Or they may say that the cultures of other colonial powers, such as England or France, would have had more influence in Latin America. Then perhaps English or French would be spoken throughout Latin America today.

31. Spanish, Dutch, French, and English colonists came to the Caribbean islands in hopes of making money from the region. They brought enslaved Africans to work on plantations. These many backgrounds gave the region a variety of cultures.

32. Many cultures in South America and Mexico are influenced by Native American backgrounds as well as the Spanish conquerors. Some cultures in South America are different, though. For example, many Brazilians speak Portuguese, and indigenous people in the Andes speak Quechua and other languages.

33. Fact (It is something that can be proven or verified.)

34. Opinion (It cannot be verified.)

35. Opinion (It cannot be verified.)

36. Fact (It is something that can be proven or verified.)

37. Fact (It is something that can be proven or verified.)

38. Opinion (It cannot be verified.)

39. Fact (It is something that can be proven or verified.)

40. Fact (It is something that can be proven or verified.)

41. Opinion (It cannot be verified.)

42. Fact (It is something that can be proven or verified.)

Chapter 4 ■ *Exploring Mexico and Central America*

A. KEY TERMS

Complete each sentence by writing the letter of the correct term in the blank. You will not use all the terms.

       a. ladino
       b. migrant farmworker
       c. strike
       d. political movement
       e. plaza
       f. squatter
       g. lock
       h. malaria

1. _____ A person who travels from one area to another farming other people's land is called a(n) _____ .

2. _____ To raise and lower a ship as it passes through the Panama Canal, a(n) _____ is used.

3. _____ A person who settles on someone else's land without permission is called a(n) _____ .

4. _____ A rich, Guatemalan landowner is a(n) _____ .

5. _____ A work stoppage, or _____ , can be used as a form of protest.

Match the descriptions with the terms. Write the correct letter in each blank. You will not use all the terms.

       a. strike
       b. squatter
       c. migrant farmworker
       d. ladino
       e. malaria
       f. lock
       g. plaza
       h. smog

6. _____ a person who settles on someone else's land without permission

7. _____ in Guatemala, a rich landowner

8. _____ a section of a canal that has a double pair of huge gates

9. _____ a person who travels from one area to another farming other people's land

10. _____ a work stoppage

CHAPTER 4

B. KEY CONCEPTS

Write the letter of the correct ending in the blank provided.

11. _____ A reason why many people move from small villages to Mexico City is to
    a. work as migrant farmworkers.   c. reduce their commute to work.
    b. become squatters.   d. earn more money.

12. _____ In a typical rural village in Mexico, you might expect to find that most people living on farms get their food by
    a. growing their own food.
    b. buying what they need at large supermarkets.
    c. buying what they need at small markets.
    d. gathering nuts and wild berries.

13. _____ Mexico City is considered a megacity because it
    a. has a large university and good school system.
    b. is a place where people from the countryside come to find work.
    c. contains many migrant farmworkers.
    d. contains a large portion of Mexico's population.

14. _____ Which of the following statements about Guatemala is true?
    a. All people in Guatemala are of French ancestry.
    b. Most people in Guatemala are of Native American ancestry.
    c. All people in Guatemala are of Spanish ancestry.
    d. People in Guatemala are of Caribbean ancestry.

15. _____ Most land in Guatemala belongs to
    a. a few rich families.   c. Mayan farmers.
    b. foreign companies.   d. national parks.

16. _____ The Panama Canal allows ships to travel between the Pacific Ocean and the
    a. Mediterranean Sea.   c. Indian Ocean.
    b. Atlantic Ocean.   d. Gulf of Mexico.

17. _____ Why did the United States first need to negotiate with Colombia to build the Panama Canal?
    a. Colombia was a neighboring country.
    b. Part of the canal would be located in Colombia.
    c. Panama was part of Colombia.
    d. Panama did not have a diplomatic mission in the United States.

18. _____ Which of the following statements describes a challenge builders of the Panama Canal had to solve?
    a. The water in the canal was frozen for most of the year.
    b. Many people who worked on the project became ill with malaria and yellow fever.
    c. Workers had to dig several miles beneath the Earth's surface.
    d. There were not enough workers in the Caribbean.

19. _____ Which of the following statements explains why it was necessary to build locks in the Panama Canal?
   a. There is a lot of traffic around the Panama Canal.
   b. Parts of the canal are at sea level, but other parts are above sea level.
   c. Ships move very quickly as they travel through the canal.
   d. Ships tend to drift out of the canal's path.

20. _____ The main reason Mexicans are moving from rural areas to the cities is to find
   a. farmland.
   b. squatters.
   c. employment.
   d. night classes.

21. _____ One effect of the population increase in Mexico is
   a. an increase in the size of cities.
   b. a decrease in disease.
   c. an increase in the use of modern farm equipment.
   d. a decrease in pollution.

22. _____ Mexico City's pollution problem is made worse by its
   a. farmland.
   b. mass transit system.
   c. squatters.
   d. geography.

23. _____ How did the Spanish conquest in the 1500s affect many Native Americans?
   a. Their lives improved.
   b. They died from hunger, exposure, and disease.
   c. They joined the Spanish army.
   d. They received farmland.

24. _____ To raise and lower ships from one elevation to another, the Panama Canal uses a system of
   a. elevators.
   b. locks.
   c. locomotives.
   d. artificial lakes.

25. _____ Which of the following words best describes the role of the United States in Panama's fight for independence?
   a. supportive
   b. uninterested
   c. uninvolved
   d. neutral

26. _____ One obstacle to the building of the Panama Canal was removed when scientists discovered that malaria was carried by
   a. vaccinations.
   b. yellow fever.
   c. locks.
   d. mosquitoes.

27. _____ In the original treaty signed by the United States and Panama, the United States was given control of the Panama Canal
   a. forever.
   b. for 99 years.
   c. for 150 years.
   d. until 1999.

28. _____ The ancestry of most of Guatemala's population is
    a. French.
    b. Native American.
    c. African.
    d. Portuguese.

C. CRITICAL THINKING

Answer the following questions in the space provided, on the back of this paper or on a separate sheet of paper.

29. Drawing Conclusions: Based on your reading, think of one option poor campesinos have once they decide to leave the countryside. What are the advantages and disadvantages of the option?

30. Expressing Problems Clearly: Name two geographic obstacles and one political obstacle that stood in the way of the construction of the Panama Canal. How did engineers and politicians overcome these obstacles?

31. Expressing Problems Clearly: List at least two challenges that you believe Mexico will face as more people move to the cities. Suggest a possible solution to one of the challenges on your list.

32. Distinguishing Fact from Opinion: What are the causes of problems the Mayas and other Native American groups face in Guatemala? How are people trying to solve these problems?

D. SKILL: PREVIEWING A READING SELECTION

Use your previewing skills to study the partial table of contents from a geography textbook. Then answer the following questions in the space provided.

33. In which chapter and section would you find information about Brazil's economy? _____

_____

34. What is the subject of Chapter 10? _____

_____

35. In which chapter and section might you find information about mestizos in Mexico? _____

_____

36. In which chapter and section might you find information about Guatemala? _____

_____

37. In which chapter and section would you read about Mexico's Central Plateau? _____

_____

Use your previewing skills to study the partial index from a book about Central America. Then answer the questions below in the space provided.

Coffee, 24, 31, 39, 40 illus., 41, 46, 48, 51, 54, 67
Colombia, 11, 14, 54, 75
Columbus, Christopher, 10, 54
Comayagua (river and city in Hond.), 36
Greytown (Nic.), 44–45
Guatemala, 3, 6, 7, 9, 11, 13, 19, 26, 28–29, 31–33, 58, 61, 66, 68, 71–72, 74, 81
Guatemala City, 28, 32, 72
Guaymi Indians, 9
Ladinos, 26
Land, 1, 2 map, 3
Land reform, 41–43, 77–79
Land Reform, Basic Law of, 41
Palm oil, 79, 80 illus.
Panama, Republic of, 3, 9, 10–14, 16, 19, 23, 25, 56, 63, 66–69, 72, 75–79
Panama Canal, 14, 15 illus., 18, 54, 56, 57 illus., 58, 78
Panama Canal Zone, 14, 56
Panama City (Pan.), 58, 69
Yaviza (Pan.), 58, 75
Yellow fever, 56
Yucatán Peninsula, 7, 9, 11

38. On which pages would you look to find out about land reform in Central America? _____
_____

39. On which pages could you find an illustration of the Panama Canal? _____
_____

40. On which page could you find out about one of the diseases that caused a problem during the construction of the Panama Canal? _____
_____

41. Do you think you could find out when Christopher Columbus sailed to the Americas in this book? Why or why not? _____
_____

42. Do you think coffee is an important agricultural resource in Central America? Why? _____
_____

ANSWER KEY

1. b	2. g	3. f	4. a	5. c
6. b	7. d	8. f	9. c	10. a
11. d	12. a	13. d	14. b	15. a
16. b	17. c	18. b	19. b	20 c
21. a	22. d	23. b	24. b	25 a
26. d	27. a	28. b		

29. Students will probably say that campesinos can move to a city. An advantage to the city is that they might be able to find a job. A disadvantage is that they often end up becoming squatters, living in temporary housing made of scrap metal.

30. Two geographic obstacles include mudslides and passing through a mountain range. Engineers had to build a dam, design and build locks, and remove huge amounts of earth and rock. A political obstacle was that the government of Colombia did not allow the U.S. to build the canal. The U.S. helped Panama revolt against Colombia, and Panama then gave the U.S. the permission it needed.

31. Acceptable challenges that students might list include overcrowding, homelessness, and unemployment. Possible solutions include creating more jobs, building more houses, schools, and hospitals; and providing public transportation and sanitation.

32. Acceptable causes that students might list include that Native Americans own little land, that the land they work is often of poor quality, and that they have little political power. To solve these problems, some native people are learning to read and write and organizing political movements.

33. Chapter 12, Section 2

34. Mexico

35. Chapter 10, Section 2

36. Chapter 11, Section 1

37. Chapter 10, Section 1

38. pages 41–43, 77–79

39. page 15

40. page 56

41. Yes, there is information about Columbus on pages 10 and 54, and it probably includes the dates he sailed to the Americas.

42. Yes, there are many pages devoted to the discussion of coffee.

A. KEY TERMS

Complete each sentence by writing the letter of the correct term in the blank. You will not use all the terms.

a. communist
b. citizen
c. exile
d. dictator
e. illiterate
f. dialect
g. Creole
h. commonwealth

1. _____ A Cuban who left Cuba because of political problems is called a(n) _____ .

2. _____ Today, many Haitians are supporting a return to their _____ roots, a mix of French and African cultures.

3. _____ A government that owns all large industries and most of its country's land and resources is a(n) _____ government.

4. _____ Someone who is unable to read or write is said to be _____ .

5. _____ Puerto Rico is a(n) _____ of the United States.

Match the descriptions with the terms. Write the correct letter in each blank. You will not use all the terms.

a. Creole
b. dictator
c. illiterate
d. lagoon
e. citizen
f. dialect
g. exile
h. commonwealth

6. _____ a ruler who has complete power

7. _____ a dialect spoken in Haiti which is partly based on French and African languages

8. _____ a person with certain rights and responsibilities under a particular government

9. _____ an independent political state with strong ties to a particular country

10. _____ a person who leaves his or her home country because of political problems

B. KEY CONCEPTS

Write the letter of the correct ending in the blank provided.

11. _____ In 1994, 35,000 Cubans tried to sail away from Cuba, hoping to
    a. return to Haiti.
    b. apply for entrance to the Soviet Union.
    c. leave the United States.
    d. apply for entrance to the United States.

12. _____ One of Cuba's most important agricultural resources is
    a. gold.   c. sugar.
    b. llamas.   d. wheat.

13. _____ In 1991, an event that drastically affected Cuba's economy was
    a. the breakup of the Soviet Union.
    b. a blockade imposed by the United States.
    c. thousands of Cubans leaving the island.
    d. an influx of tourists to Havana.

14. _____ Cuba was once a colony of
    a. the Soviet Union.   c. Great Britain.
    b. France.   d. Spain.

15. _____ Changes in the education system made by Fidel Castro in the 1960s and 1970s
    resulted in
    a. a higher literacy rate.
    b. a lower literacy rate.
    c. fewer students attending universities.
    d. students starting school at a later age.

16. _____ Jean-Bertrand Aristide of Haiti became the country's leader when he was
    a. crowned king.
    b. democratically elected president.
    c. a general in Haiti's military.
    d. elected to replace his father, Papa Doc.

17. _____ In 1790, slave revolts on Haiti that eventually led to independence were led by
    a. Toussaint L'Ouverture.   c. François Duvalier.
    b. Fidel Castro.   d. Jean-Claude Duvalier.

18. _____ Which of the following statements best describes the relationship between Puerto
    Rico and the United States?
    a. Puerto Rico is a state of the United States.
    b. Puerto Rico is an independent country.
    c. Puerto Rico is a colony of the United States.
    d. Puerto Rico is a commonwealth of the United States.

19. ____ Before the Spanish-American War of 1898, Puerto Rico was a colony of
    a. the United States.   c. France.
    b. Spain.   d. Cuba.

20. ____ After Cuba gained independence,
    a. it became the richest country in the Caribbean.
    b. it immediately became communist.
    c. it voted to re-join Spain.
    d. it isolated itself from the United States.

21. ____ The type of government in Cuba is
    a. democracy.   c. republic.
    b. communism.   d. parliamentarianism.

22. ____ Many Cuban immigrants to the United States settled in the state of
    a. California.   c. Texas.
    b. Florida.   d. Illinois.

23. ____ After the breakup of the Soviet Union, Cuba's economy
    a. improved.
    b. stayed about the same.
    c. suffered a decline.
    d. became linked with the United States.

24. ____ Before Haiti gained independence, it was a colony of
    a. France.   c. Cuba.
    b. the United States.   d. Germany.

25. ____ Francois Duvalier and Jean-Claude Duvalier were a father and son from Haiti who
    a. led the country to freedom.
    b. introduced economic and social reforms.
    c. ruled the country as dictators.
    d. won the confidence of the Haitian people.

26. ____ Most of the people of Haiti are
    a. factory workers.   c. politicians.
    b. miners.   d. farmers.

27. ____ Although Puerto Ricans are U.S. citizens, they cannot
    a. freely visit the United States.
    b. vote in U.S. presidential elections.
    c. have representation in the U.S. Congress.
    d. serve in the U.S. Army.

28. ____ In Puerto Rico, most people live in the
    a. country.   c. rain forest.
    b. cities.   d. highlands.

C. CRITICAL THINKING

Answer the following questions in the space provided, on the back of this paper or on a separate sheet of paper.

29. Making Comparisons: Compare and contrast the relationship of Cuba and Puerto Rico with that of the United States and Puerto Rico. How are they different? How are they similar?

30. Identifying Central Issues: How have political conditions in Haiti affected the economy of the country over the past 50 years? How are things in Haiti changing today?

31. Recognizing Cause and Effect: Give and explain at least two examples of how Cuba's location near the United States has affected events in Cuba.

32. Identifying Central Issues: What are Puerto Rico's three choices for the future?

D. SKILL: LOCATING INFORMATION

Read the assignment below. Use your ability to locate information to decide whether the sources listed below would help you to complete your assignment. In the space provided, state whether the source would be helpful or not and explain your answer.

   Assignment: Identify who is president of Haiti today.

33. A recent copy of the World Almanac. _____

_____

34. Encyclopedia article titled "Haiti" from Microsoft Encarta 95. _____

_____

35. An article from Time titled "The Once and Future President" by Amy Wilentz, dated September 26, 1994. _____

_____

36. A website on the Internet providing up-to-date information about Haiti. _____

_____

37. Encyclopedia article titled "Presidents" from 1990. _____

_____

Read the assignment below. Use your ability to locate information to decide whether the sources listed below would help you to complete your assignment. In the space provided, state why the source would be helpful or not and explain your answer.

Assignment: Find information about Fidel Castro's life.

38. Dictators of Latin America by Patricia Baum. _____

_____

39. Microfilm of issues of The New York Times for the year 1960. _____

_____

40. The Complete Atlas of the World by Keith Lye. _____

_____

41. An opportunity to interview Lydia Martin, a Cuban exile who left the country in 1970 when she was six years old. _____

_____

42. A website on the Internet providing up-to-date information on Cuba. _____

_____

ANSWER KEY

1. c	2. g	3. a	4. e	5. h
6. b	7. a	8. e	9. h	10. g
11. d	12. c	13. a	14. d	15. a
16. b	17. a	18. d	19. b	20. a
21. b	22. b	23. c	24. a	25. c
26. d	27. b	28. b		

29. Even though Cuba and Puerto Rico are both former Spanish colonies, they have much different relationships with the U.S. Puerto Rico is a commonwealth of the U.S. Puerto Ricans are U.S. citizens who can freely travel between Puerto Rico and the U.S. Cuba, on the other hand, is an independent country that has strained relations with the U.S. There are many restrictions on travel between the two countries.

30. For most of the past 50 years, corrupt dictators ruled Haiti. During this time, Haiti became the poorest country in the Western Hemisphere. Recently, a democratic government has been ruling Haiti. Hopefully, Haiti will become less poor as the government improves the economy.

31. Students should list two examples in their answer. After Cuba became independent of Spain, hotels were built for tourists from the U.S. After Cuba became a communist country, many Cubans fled the country and settled in nearby Florida.

32. The choices for Puerto Rico are that it can remain a U.S. commonwealth, become a U.S. state, or become an independent country.

33. Yes, almanacs generally contain this type of information.

34. No, if Haiti has elected a new president since 1995, the encyclopedia would not have the information.

35. No, the article is out of date.

36. Yes, the information would be up-to-date.

37. No, the article is out of date.

38. This source would probably be helpful because Castro is a dictator in Latin America.

39. Yes, because you might perhaps find articles during that year that feature Castro.

40. No, not relevant to the topic.

41. No, because Lydia Martin would have been too young when she left Cuba to provide any useful information about Castro's life.

42. Yes, recent events in Castro's life might be found here.

A. KEY TERMS

Complete each sentence by writing the letter of the correct term in the blank. You will not use all the terms.

      a. photosynthesis
      b. canopy
      c. altiplano
      d. maraca
      e. montana
      f. privatization
      g. pesticide
      h. tundra
      i. sierra

1. _____ The region of Peru that includes stretches of dense tropical forest is called the_____ .

2. _____ In the rain forest, the leaves of the highest trees form a dense roof-like cover called a(n) _____ .

3. _____ A frozen area of land is called a(n) _____ .

4. _____ When government-owned industries are sold to private owners, the process is called _____ .

5. _____ The process by which green plants and trees use water and sunlight to turn carbon dioxide into oxygen is called _____ .

Match the descriptions with the terms. Write the correct letter in each blank. You will not use all the terms.

      a. fiord
      b. altiplano
      c. photosynthesis
      d. tundra
      e. sierra
      f. privatization
      g. canopy
      h. montay
      i. boom

6. _____ the process of selling government-owned industries to private owners

7. _____ the dense roof-like cover that the leaves of the highest trees in the rain forest create

8. _____ a time of increased prosperity

9. _____ a process by which green plants and trees use water and sunlight to turn carbon dioxide into oxygen

CHAPTER 6

10. _____ the high plateau region in the Andes where a number of indigenous groups, including the Quechua, live

B. KEY CONCEPTS

Write the letter of the correct ending in the blank provided.

11. _____ Rain forests are important because they contribute to the Earth's supply of
   a. water.
   b. oxygen.
   c. food.
   d. harbors.

12. _____ The capital of Brazil was moved from the coast to the interior because the government wished to
   a. develop the interior by attracting people to it.
   b. provide services to people living in the rain forest.
   c. move from the flooding and heavy rains that plagued the coast.
   d. move the capital to where more people already lived.

13. _____ The three main geographic regions of Peru are the
   a. sierra, the rain forest, and the plateau.
   b. Pampas, the rain forest, and the montaeau.
   c. montas, the rain forest, and the monta
   d. sierra, the coastal plain, and the monta.

14. _____ Most Quechua people living in the altiplano make a living by
   a. trading goods with city people.
   b. farming and herding.
   c. mining gold.
   d. drilling for oil.

15. _____ Chile inspects all luggage brought into the country because
   a. the country tries to protect its agricultural products.
   b. maracas are illegal in Chile.
   c. most people try to avoid paying customs duties.
   d. it does not allow imports of gifts.

16. _____ Because Chile is located in the Southern Hemisphere, its seasons
   a. are much longer than those in the United States.
   b. are much shorter than those in the United States.
   c. occur at the same time as those in the United States.
   d. occur at the opposite time as those in the United States.

17. _____ Chile is the world's largest exporter of
   a. diamonds.
   b. potatoes.
   c. copper.
   d. oil.

18. _____ In the early 1980s, Venezuela was the richest country in Latin America because of
   a. a booming tourist industry.
   c. vast supplies of oil.
   b. abundant rain forest resources.
   d. thriving agricultural production.

19. _____ When oil prices fell in the mid-1980s, Venezuela's economy
   a. suffered a decline.
   c. stayed about the same.
   b. enjoyed an increase.
   d. began to show signs of recovery.

20. _____ Most of the people of Brazil live
   a. along the coasts.
   c. in the interior.
   b. in the rain forest.
   d. on the large plateau.

21. _____ Hundreds of years ago, much of Peru was controlled by the empire of the
   a. Mayas.
   c. Incas.
   b. Aztecs.
   d. Yanamamo.

22. _____ About a third of Brazil's farmland is
   a. unused.
   c. infertile.
   b. used to grow banana trees.
   d. owned by the government.

23. _____ In Chile, mestizos
   a. make up 75 percent of the population.
   b. are a small minority.
   c. are outnumbered by Native Americans.
   d. all share the same lifestyle.

24. _____ Chile has been protected from many agricultural pests and animal diseases by
   a. the protection of the Atacama Desert.
   b. its location on the coast of the Pacific Ocean.
   c. the shield created by the Andes Mountains.
   d. the composition of its soil.

25. _____ Chile's seasons are the reverse of those in the United States because Chile is
   a. located in the Southern Hemisphere.
   b. located in the Northern Hemisphere.
   c. shielded by the Andes Mountains.
   d. has a Pacific coastline.

26. _____ Santiago's pollution problem is caused in part by
   a. increased agricultural production.
   b. luxury trains that crisscross the country.
   c. the city's location in the Andes Mountains.
   d. winds from the Atacama Desert.

27. _____ Most of Venezuela's population lives
   a. in cities.
   c. on islands of floating reeds.
   b. in the countryside.
   d. in the rain forest.

CHAPTER 6

28. _____ After oil prices dropped in the mid-1980s, Venezuela's government decided to
   a. diversify its economy.
   b. pour more money into oil production.
   c. take over privately-owned businesses.
   d. invest in building subways and highways.

C. CRITICAL THINKING

Answer the following questions in the space provided, on the back of this paper or on a separate sheet of paper.

29. Making Comparisons: Compare the situation of the Yanamamo people of the rain forest with the Quechua people of the Andes. How do the environments of the two groups differ?

30. Identifying Central Issues: How have Brazil and Venezuela tried to use their natural resources to boost their economies?

31. Recognizing Cause and Effect: What are the causes of the influx of people to the rain forests of Brazil in recent years? What have been the effects of this movement?

32. Drawing Conclusions: How does Chile's economy compare with that of Venezuela? How has each country tried to diversify its economy?

CHAPTER 6

D. SKILL: USING ISOLINES TO SHOW ELEVATION

Use the map below to answer the following questions. Write your answers on the lines provided.

33. What is the highest elevation shown on the map? _____ _____ _____

34. As you head east from Lima, does the elevation increase or decrease? _____ _____ _____

35. Is the land flatter near Lima or 30 miles east of Lima? _____ _____

36. What mountain on the map is taller than Mt. Carhuachayo? _____ _____ _____

37. How can you tell that the land near Mt. Huayas is steep? _____ _____

Area in Peru: Contour Map

Mt. Huayas
16,030 ft
(4,886 m)

Mt. Carhuachayo
15,823 ft
(4,823 m)

Rimac River

12°S

Lima

PACIFIC OCEAN

0   5   10 mi

0   5   10 km

77°W

KEY
• City
Contour interval = 1,000 ft
Lambert Conformal Conic Projection

38. Is the land flatter near Lima or 30 miles east of Lima? _____ _____

39. As you head southwest toward Lima from Mt. Carhuachayo, does the elevation increase or decrease? _____ _____

40. What is the highest elevation shown on the map? _____ _____

41. What is the contour interval between each pair of isolines? _____ _____

42. How can you tell if the land near Lima is flatter than the land 30 miles east of Lima? _____ _____

CHAPTER 6

ANSWER KEY

1. e	2. b	3. h	4. f	5. a
6. f	7. g	8. i	9. c	10. e
11. b	12. a	13. d	14. b	15. a
16. d	17. c	18. c	19. a	20. a
21. c	22. a	23. a	24. c	25. a
26. c	27. a	28. a		

29. The Yanamamo live in a rain forest environment. There is a great variety of plants and animals. Most of the Quechua live in the cold, dry climate of the Andes. They grow crops and raise sheep.

30. For years, Brazil has produced large amounts of coffee and other farm goods. Recently, it has tried to use more of its rain forest resources. Venezuela's most important resource has been oil. But since the oil boom of the 1980s, Venezuela has been trying to diversify its economy to include products such as cocoa, coffee, and fruits.

31. People have moved to the rain forest to cut timber, mine, and build farms. This movement has helped to diversify Brazil's economy but has also led to the destruction of part of the rain forest.

32. Chile and Venezuela both have depended heavily on the export of one mineral—copper for Chile and oil for Venezuela. Both countries have produced more farming goods to diversify their economies.

33. Mt. Huayas

34. The elevation increases.

35. near Lima

36. Mt. Huayas

37. The isolines are close together.

38. near Lima

39. The elevation decreases.

40. Mt. Huayas

41. 1,000 feet

42. There is more space between isolines.

CHAPTER 6

Chapter 7 ▪ *Final Exam*

A. KEY TERMS

Complete each sentence by writing the correct term in the blank. You will not use all the terms.

a. mestizo
b. tributaries
c. pampas
d. dictator
e. rain forest
f. communists
g. plateau
h. privatization
i. altiplano
j. isthmus

1. _____ When a country sells government-owned industries to private owners, the process is called _____ .

2. _____ A person whose heritage is both Native American and Spanish is a(n) _____ .

3. _____ The Amazon River has many _____ , or smaller rivers that feed it.

4. _____ Central America is a(n) _____ , a narrow strip of land that has water on both sides and joins two larger bodies of land.

5. _____ Mexico's dominant physical feature is a large, mostly flat _____ area that lies between the country's two mountain ranges.

Match the descriptions with the terms. Write the correct letter in each blank. You will not use all the terms.

a. import
b. export
c. isthmus
d. commonwealth
e. lock
f. caudillos
g. privatization
h. emigrate

6. _____ independent political state with strong ties to a particular country

7. _____ a section of a waterway in which ships are raised or lowered by adjusting the water level

8. _____ to leave one's home country

CHAPTER 7

9. _____ to buy goods from other countries

10. _____ a narrow strip of land that has water on both sides and joins two larger bodies of land

B. KEY CONCEPTS

Write the letter of the correct ending in the blank provided.

11. _____ Latin America is divided into the following three regions
    a. South America, North America, and Central America.
    b. the Western Hemisphere, the Northern Hemisphere, and the Southern Hemisphere.
    c. Mexico, Canada, and Brazil.
    d. Mexico and Central America, the Caribbean, and South America.

12. _____ Climate in Latin America is affected by all of the following except
    a. elevation.   c. the Equator.
    b. natural resources.   d. wind patterns.

13. _____ Two world events that inspired many people of Latin America to fight for independence were
    a. the French Revolution and the American Revolution.
    b. World War I and World War II.
    c. the increase in oil prices during the 1970s.
    d. the Mexican-American War and the Spanish-American War.

14. _____ All over Latin America, more and more people are moving to
    a. rural areas.   c. cities.
    b. small towns.   d. the countryside.

15. _____ Many Mexican farmers who do not own their own land travel from one area to another working on large farms. They are called
    a. urban farmworkers.   c. squatters.
    b. migrant farmworkers.   d. immigrants.

16. _____ In Guatemala, most of the land is owned by
    a. ladinos.   c. Quechua.
    b. Spaniards.   d. Mayas.

17. _____ In 1959, Fidel Castro of Cuba established a government that is
    a. a democracy.   c. a monarchy.
    b. communist.   d. fascist.

18. _____ The Brazilian government has given permission for some people to clear rain forest lands because
   a. Yanamamo are moving to the cities in large numbers.
   b. airplanes make travel to the Amazonian forest possible.
   c. it needs to build a new capital city.
   d. farmers need the land to make a living.

19. _____ Both Chile and Venezuela are trying to change their economies by
   a. increasing the amount of oil they produce.
   b. decreasing the amount of copper exported.
   c. diversifying and developing new industries.
   d. building subways and railroads.

20. _____ What effect have high mountains and dense rain forests had on travel in Latin America?
   a. They have not had much impact.
   b. They have played a role in attracting European explorers to Latin America.
   c. They have made travel between the regions of Latin America difficult.
   d. They have made travel between the regions of Latin America easy.

21. _____ While the Incas did not have a written language, the Mayas and Aztecs wrote using
   a. hieroglyphics.   c. runners.
   b. quipus.   d. pyramids.

22. _____ The two European countries that came to dominate Latin America in the 1600s and 1700s were
   a. France and England.   c. Spain and England.
   b. Spain and Portugal.   d. Italy and Portugal.

23. _____ After European conquest, the population of many indigenous groups
   a. increased sharply.   c. stayed about the same.
   b. decreased sharply.   d. increased and then decreased.

24. _____ The Panama Canal is important because it
   a. is the only canal of its kind.
   b. is controlled by Colombia.
   c. allows ships to pass from the Indian Ocean to the Caribbean Sea.
   d. cuts shipping time between the Pacific and Atlantic oceans.

25. _____ Most of the people of Haiti make a living
   a. mining.   c. working for the government.
   b. farming.   d. importing and exporting goods.

26. _____ How is Puerto Rico related to the United States?
   a. It is a U.S. commonwealth.   c. It is independent.
   b. It is a U.S. state.   d. It is a protectorate.

27. _____ In Peru, the lives of the people of the altiplano are changing due in part to the
   a. changes in the climate.   c. destruction of the rain forest.
   b. movement of people to the cities. d. high altitude.

CHAPTER 7

28. _____ Volcanoes, plains, plateaus, and mountains are some examples of the _____ in Latin America.

    a. climates   c. landforms

    b. resources   d. ethnic groups

C. CRITICAL THINKING

Answer the following questions in the space provided, on the back of this paper or on a separate sheet of paper.

29. Recognizing Cause and Effect: Identify and explain how geography affects Latin America's culture and economy.

30. Identifying Central Issues: Explain why the use of the rain forest is an important issue in South America and around the world.

31. Making Comparisons: Compare the lives of Latin American people in the city and in the country. How does city life differ from life in the country?

32. Understanding Central Issues: Why are many Latin American nations trying to diversify their economies?

CHAPTER 7

D. SKILL: USING MAPS

Match the letters on the map with the places described below. Write your answers in the blanks provided.

33. _____ The Amazonian rain forest is located in this country.

34. _____ This country gained a great deal of wealth in the 1970s and 1980s due to oil production.

35. _____ This country borders the United States.

36. _____ Fidel Castro established communism in this country.

37. _____ The Panama Canal connects the Atlantic Ocean with this ocean.

38. _____ The Panama Canal connects the Atlantic Ocean with this ocean.

39. _____ This region is an isthmus.

40. _____ Many Quechua live in the altiplano of this country.

41. _____ This country was the first in Latin America to win independence.

42. _____ Some of the islands in this water are made of coral.

ANSWER KEY

1. h	2. a	3. b	4. j	5. g
6. d	7. e	8. h	9. a	10. c
11. d	12. b	13. a	14. c	15. b
16. a	17. b	18. d	19. c	20. c
21. a	22. b	23. b	24. d	25. b
26. a	27. b	28. c		

29. Students should give at least one example in which geography affects Latin America's culture and economy. One acceptable example would be that the Central Plateau in Mexico contains Mexico's best farmland, making this area the most heavily populated in the country.

30. Because the Amazon Basin rain forest produces much of the world's oxygen, the destruction of it for farms and other uses might have a worldwide impact.

31. In the country, most people are farmers. They know all or most of the people who live around them. People grow their own food and buy everything else in the town plaza. In the city, many people struggle to find work and live in crowded neighborhoods where they don't know everybody around them.

32. When a country's economy is based mostly on one product, such as copper, the entire economy can suffer when world prices for that one product fall. Many Latin American countries that have depended mostly on one product are trying to diversify their economies. When world prices for one of their products falls, the other products will keep the economy going strong.

33. I	34. G	35. C	36. E	37. A
38. A	39. D	30. H	41. F	42. B

World Explorer

THE ANCIENT WORLD

BOOK 2

A. KEY TERMS

Complete each sentence by writing the letter of the correct term in the blank. You will not use all the terms.

a. archaeologist
b. civilization
c. fertile
d. history
e. irrigation
f. oral tradition
g. prehistory
h. social class
i. surplus

1. _____ To find out about the past, you can study _____ , which is the recorded events of people.

2. _____ The period of time in the past before writing was invented is called _____ .

3. _____ People who pass stories by word of mouth from generation to generation have a(n) _____ .

4. _____ People in the ancient world sometimes used a(n) _____ system to water their crops during the dry summer months.

5. _____ Farmers prefer to grow crops in _____ soil, because it contains substances that plants need in order to grow well.

Match the definitions with the terms. Write the correct letter in each blank. You will not use all the terms.

a. archaeologist
b. artisan
c. domesticate
d. history
e. irrigation
f. nomad
g. oral tradition
h. prehistory
i. surplus

6. _____ to tame animals and raise them to be used by humans

7. _____ the written and other recorded events of people

8. _____ a worker who is especially skilled in making items such as baskets and leather goods

9. _____ a person who has no single, settled home

10. _____ supplying land with water from another place

B. KEY CONCEPTS

Write the letter of the correct answer in each blank.

11. _____ Scientists studied the Iceman's clothing, tools, and body to learn
    a. how people lived in Africa.   c. about the geography of the Alps.
    b. how early people learned to farm.   d. more about his life.

12. _____ The people in the Old Stone Age got their food by hunting animals
    a. and gathering roots and berries.   c. and farming the land.
    b. and domesticating them.   d. and selling the food they grew.

13. _____ In the New Stone Age, for the first time, people began to
    a. gather plants and seeds.   c. farm the land.
    b. search for new lands.   d. trade with other countries.

14. _____ During the period of prehistory, people developed the ability to
    a. write.   c. make tools from iron.
    b. use fire.   d. hunt alone.

15. _____ Which of the following resulted from having surplus food during the New Stone Age?
    a. rapid population growth   c. more hunting
    b. trade with other countries   d. fewer settlements

16. _____ Surplus food during the New Stone Age allowed more people to become
    a. farmers.   c. warriors.
    b. fishers.   d. artisans.

17. _____ During the New Stone Age, what did farming settlements need to develop into cities?
    a. a deposit of minerals   c. metal tools
    b. a dependable source of water   d. different kinds of cloth

18. _____ Which of the following characterizes a civilization of the ancient world?
    a. a system of writing   c. gatherers
    b. small, rural towns   d. one social class

19. _____ In the ancient world, who would have been most likely to help spread new ideas and tools from one civilization to another?
    a. a farmer   c. an irrigation specialist
    b. a trader   d. an artisan

20. ____ In the words prehistoric and prehistory, the word part pre- means
   a. toward.
   c. after.
   b. during.
   d. before.

21. ____ Scientists learned more about the Iceman's life by studying
   a. his clothing, tools, and body.
   c. his oral traditions.
   b. the written records of his people.
   d. the geography of Asia.

22. ____ The ancient Egyptian civilization began on the banks of the Nile River because
   a. Egyptians could not travel to the Euphrates River.
   b. Egyptians' oral traditions identified this location as their homeland.
   c. regular flooding resulted in rich soil for farming.
   d. fish in the Nile were easy to catch.

23. ____ Almost all of human prehistory took place during the
   a. Old Stone Age.
   c. Copper Age.
   b. New Stone Age.
   d. Bronze Age.

24. ____ The major difference between the Old Stone Age and the New Stone Age was
   a. the importance of oral stories.
   b. the exploration of the New World.
   c. the beginning of farming.
   d. hunting in groups.

25. ____ During the Old Stone Age, people got their food by
   a. storing surplus.
   c. herding animals.
   b. trading.
   d. hunting and gathering.

26. ____ How did farming change the way early people lived?
   a. They stopped eating meat.
   b. They built schools.
   c. They settled in one place.
   d. They moved from place to place.

27. ____ Having surplus food was a factor that led to
   a. the rise of nomadic life.
   c. the rise of smaller families.
   b. rapid population growth.
   d. the start of the Old Stone Age.

28. ____ Having a dependable source of water enabled some farming settlements to
   a. manufacture cloth.
   c. look for minerals.
   b. build defense systems.
   d. develop into cities.

C. CRITICAL THINKING

Answer the following questions in the space provided, on the back of this paper or on a separate sheet of paper.

29. Making Comparisons: Explain the similarities and differences in the ways people lived in the Old Stone Age and the New Stone Age.

30. Recognizing Cause and Effect: Explain how the presence of surplus food caused the growth of early cities. What was the effect of food supply on population growth? What was the effect of food supply on the size of the settlements and the variety of occupations?

31. Identifying Central Issues: What do we know about the ways people lived in the Old Stone Age and the New Stone Age?

32. Making Comparisons: How was life in the large cities of early civilizations different from life in the early farming villages?

D. SKILL: USING A TIME LINE

Use the time line below to answer the following questions. Write your answers on the lines provided.

7000 B.C.	6000 B.C.	5000 B.C.	4000 B.C.	3000 B.C.

7000 B.C.
Many people
have become
farmers.
Human
population of
the Earth is
about 66 million.

6600 B.C.
Beginning of the
Copper Age.

3500 B.C.
People in
Southwest Asia
and Africa develop
a writing system.
Some civilizations
develop the wheel
and axle.

3000 B.C.
Domesticated
animals are used
to carry heavy
loads.
Beginning of
the Bronze Age.

33. What was the Earth's human population around the year 7000 B.C.? _____

_____

34. What are two events that happened around 3500 B.C.? _____

_____

35. When did the Copper Age begin? _____

36. Which of these metals did people develop first: copper or bronze? _____

37. Which event occurred first: the development of the wheel and axle, or the use of domesticated animals to carry loads? _____

_____

Use the time line below to answer the following questions. Write your answers on the lines provided.

10,000 B.C.	9000 B.C.	8000 B.C.	7000 B.C.	6000 B.C.	5000 B.C.

10,000 B.C.
Humans have
reached Peru
in South
America.

9000 B.C.
People in
Southwest Asia
learn how to
plant grass seeds
for food. The New
Stone Age begins.

7000 B.C.
Human
population of the
Earth is about
66 million.

6600 B.C.
Beginning of the
Copper Age.

5000 B.C.
Chinese farmers
first begin
planting rice
and other crops.

38. When did the copper age begin? _____

39. When did farming begin in China? _____

40. When did humans reach Peru in South America? _____

41. About how many years before the beginning of the Copper Age did people start farming?

_____

42. When was the human population of the Earth about 66 million? _____

ANSWER KEY

1. d	2. g	3. f	4. e	5. c
6. c	7. d	8. b	9. f	10. e
11. d	12. a	13. c	14. b	15. a
16. d	17. b	18. a	19. b	20. d
21. a	22. c	23. a	24. c	25. d
26. c	27. b	28. d		

29. Answers will vary, but should include references to the following: Similarities: use of stone tools, weapons, and other materials; hunting of wild animals; cooperative behavior, such as hunting in groups in the Old Stone Age and trade between people in the New Stone Age. Differences: the development and spread of farming in the New Stone Age, which led to a settled rather than a nomadic life; an increase in the population; the development of villages and sometimes cities; the domestication of animals, such as cattle, camels, and horses; the development of social classes.

30. Answers will vary, but should include references to the link between surplus food and the ability of people to remain in one location all year; the rapid growth of the population; the growth of settlements into cities; the development of different occupations; the growth of trade between farmers and artisans.

31. Answers may vary, but should include the following: Old Stone Age—people were herders and gatherers and lived a nomadic existence; developed stone tools; learned to hunt in groups and make weapons. New Stone Age—people begin to farm and settle the land; a food surplus resulted in larger families; farming settlements developed into towns and sometimes cities.

32 Answers may vary, but should include the following: In large cities, people had several different types of jobs, becoming artisans, miners, and merchants. In early farming villages, most people were farmers. Cities developed large forms of government to maintain order; people created large public buildings; different social classes developed.

33. about 66 million

34. development of a writing system; development of the wheel

35. 6600 B.C.

36. copper

37. the development of the wheel and axle

38. 6600 B.C.

39. 5000 B.C.

40. 10,000 B.C.

41. 2,400 years

42. 7000 B.C.

A. KEY TERMS

Match the definitions with the terms. Write the correct letter in each blank. You will not use all the terms.

    a. caravan
    b. cuneiform
    c. empire
    d. exile
    e. famine
    f. monotheism
    g. myth
    h. polytheism
    i. scribe

1. _____ the belief in many gods

2. _____ a story about gods that explains people's beliefs

3. _____ a time when people starve because there is so little food

4. _____ many territories and people who are controlled by one government

5. _____ the belief in one god

Fill in the blanks with the terms. Write the correct letter in each blank. You will not use all the terms.

    a. alphabet
    b. caravan
    c. code
    d. covenant
    e. cuneiform
    f. empire
    g. exile
    h. famine
    i. myth

6. _____ A traditional story, or _____ , sometimes tells a legend that explains people's beliefs.

7. _____ In Mesopotamia, people eventually combined symbols into a script known as _____ .

8. _____ Often, many people starve during a period of _____ .

9. _____ A group of traders traveling together is called a(n) _____ .

10. _____ Symbols for writing that represent sounds are called a(n) _____ .

B. KEY CONCEPTS

Write the letter of the correct answer in each blank.

11. _____ Civilization developed in the Fertile Crescent because
    a. the Nile River made it a prosperous area.
    b. it was an important mining area.
    c. the area was difficult to defend.
    d. the rivers there created very rich farmland.

12. _____ Because the cities in Sumer were separated by long stretches of desert land,
    a. they united under one government.
    b. they developed into separate city-states.
    c. they were ruled by one King and Queen.
    d. they were frequently destroyed by floods.

13. _____ Babylon became an important center of trade because it was
    a. located between cities to the south and north.
    b. ruled by a powerful Queen.
    c. surrounded by massive walls.
    d. the site of a great library.

14. _____ In 612 B.C., the Medes and Chaldeans joined forces to
    a. build the city of Nineveh.
    b. found the overland trade route to Asia.
    c. destroy the Assyrian empire.
    d. conquer Mari.

15. _____ Hammurabi's Code was significant because
    a. it was part of the oral traditions of followed it.
    b. for the first time, laws were written down.
    c. everyone in the ancient world Babylonia.
    d. the laws applied equally to all citizens.

16. _____ The Phoenician alphabet made it easier for people in the ancient world to
    a. hire scribes.   c. teach cuneiform.
    b. learn to read and write.   d. learn cuneiform.

17. _____ One of the major events in the history of the Israelites was
    a. the discovery of cuneiform.   c. the conquest of Canaan.
    b. the conquest of Egypt.   d. the founding of Tyre.

18. _____ What were the Israelites known for that made them unique among ancient peoples?
    a. They worshiped one god.   c. They did not have a written Bible.
    b. They worshiped many gods.   d. They made purple dye from snails.

19. _____ Why did Phoenicia became a thriving and wealthy region?
   a. The warlike Phoenicians conquered their neighbors.
   b. Gold was discovered near the city of Tyre
   c. Phoenicia controlled access to the cities of Sumer.
   d. Phoenicians sold valuable wood and purple dye to neighboring peoples.

20. _____ Mesopotamia was located on land between
   a. the Nile and Tigris rivers.   c. the Tigris and Euphrates rivers.
   b. the Nile and Euphrates rivers.   d. the Red Sea and the Tigris River.

21. _____ Separate city-states developed in Sumer because the cities were
   a. separated by long distances.   c. united under one government.
   b. often destroyed by floods.   d. destroyed by Ur.

22. _____ Babylon was a crossroads of trade because of its location
   a. on the Nile River.   c. on the Mediterranean Sea.
   b. between cities to the south and north. d. near irrigation canals.

23 _____ In 612 B.C., the Assyrians were conquered by
   a. the Medes and the Sumerians.   c. the Medes and the Chaldeans.
   b. the Israelites and the Medes.   d. the Babylonians and the Chaldeans.

24. _____ Which of the following was the first written set of laws?
   a. the Epic of Gilgamesh   c. the Ten Commandments
   b. the ziggurat of Ur   d. Hammurabi's Code

25. _____ Where did writing first develop?
   a. Mesopotamia   c. Phoenicia
   b. Assyria   d. Canaan

26. _____ One important advantage of the Phoenician alphabet was
   a. it was only used by the scribes.
   b. it was simpler than cuneiform.
   c. it used only 100 symbols.
   d. all the people learned to read and write the symbols.

27. _____ The Phoenicians helped spread civilization throughout the Mediterranean area by
   a. using ships to trade goods with other peoples.
   b. telling tales of monsters that lived in the ocean.
   c. conquering all the lands west of the Persian Gulf.
   d. controlling the supply of a valuable purple dye.

28. _____ What did the Babylonians and Israelites have in common?
   a. They both looked for a trade route to the New World.
   b. They both destroyed the city of Tyre.
   c. They both conquered the Phoenicians.
   d. They both lived according to a code of laws.

C. CRITICAL THINKING

Answer the following questions in the space provided, on the back of this paper or on a separate sheet of paper.

29. Expressing Problems Clearly: What were three important contributions made by the ancient peoples living in the Fertile Crescent and the Mediterranean?

30. Drawing Conclusions: How did the people of Mesopotamia benefit from the physical geography of their region?

31. Distinguishing Fact From Opinion: Choose a civilization of the Fertile Crescent and write one fact about it. Then write one opinion about the same civilization.

32. Expressing Problems Clearly: How did Phoenicia's location near the Mediterranean Sea affect its development?

CHAPTER 2

D. SKILL: IDENTIFYING CENTRAL ISSUES

Read the passages below. Then answer the questions in the space provided.

1
The Tigris and Euphrates rivers were the source of life for the peoples of Mesopotamia. In the spring, melting snow picked up tons of topsoil as it rushed down from the mountains and flooded the land. The floods left this topsoil on the plain below. Farmers grew crops in this soil. The rivers also supplied fish; tall, strong reeds used to make boats; and clay for building.

2
The flood waters brought sorrows as well as gifts. The floods did not always happen at the same time each year. Racing down without warning, they sometimes swept away people, animals, and houses. Then, the survivors would slowly rebuild and pray that the next flood would not be so destructive.

33. Which sentence in the first passage identifies the central issue? _____

_____

34. Which sentence in the second passage identifies the central issue?_____

_____

35. What idea do the sentences in the passages have in common?_____

_____

36. How would you write the central issue in your own words? _____

_____

37. Why is identifying the central issue important? _____

Read the passages below. Then answer the questions in the space provided.

1
A stranger coming to a Sumerian city would first notice a giant stone building in the center of the city. This was the ziggurat, which contained the main temple to the gods of the city. Ziggurats were made of terraces, one on top of the other, linked by ramps and stairs. Some were more than seven stories high.

2
At the top of the ziggurat was a temple. The Sumerians believed that gods descended to the Earth using the ziggurat as a ladder.

38. Which sentence in the first passage identifies a central issue?_____

_____

39. Which sentence in the second passage identifies a central issue? _____

_____

40. What idea do the sentences in the passages have in common?_____

_____

41. How would you write the central issue in your own words? _____

_____

42. Why is identifying the central issue important? _____

_____

ANSWER KEY

1. h	2. g	3. e	4. c	5. f
6. i	7. e	8. h	9. b	10. a
11. d	12. b	13. a	14. c	15. b
16. b	17. c	18. a	19. d	20. c
21. a	22. b	23. c	24. d	25. a
26. b	27. a	28. d		

29. Answers may vary; however, students can refer to the following: the Babylonian King Hammurabi first set down a written code of laws for everyone in his empire to follow. The people of Sumer developed a system of writing called cuneiform. The Israelites contributed the Ten Commandments, which showed that the ruler was equal with his or her subjects before God.

30. Answers may vary; however, students can include references to the rich soil and life giving rivers or to the region's central location that attracted many traders, helping to make Sumer one of the most prosperous areas of the ancient world.

31. Answers may vary. Possible answers include: (fact) The Phoenicians traded valuable purple dye and wood to become the world's first trading empire; (opinion) Phoenicia was the best civilization of the Fertile Crescent because Phoenicians sailed all the way into the Atlantic Ocean.

32. Answers may vary, but should include references to the following: Phoenicia became a great sea power. Phoenician sailors and traders became very successful.

33. The Tigris and Euphrates rivers were the sources of life for the peoples of Mesopotamia.

34. The flood waters brought sorrows as well as gifts.

35. The Tigris and Euphrates rivers greatly affected the lives of the people of Mesopotamia.

36. Answers may vary. One possible response: The Tigris and Euphrates rivers brought both life and death to the people of Mesopotamia.

37. It helps you understand what you have read.

38. This was the ziggurat, the main temple to the gods of the city.

39. At the top of the ziggurat was a temple.

40. They all describe the ziggurat and its importance to the Sumerians.

41. Answers may vary. The ziggurat was an important building in any Sumerian city because of its religious significance.

42. It helps you understand what you read.

CHAPTER 2

A. KEY TERMS

Fill in the blanks with the terms. Write the correct letter in each blank. You will not use all the terms.

a. artisan
b. astronomer
c. cataract
d. dynasty
e. hieroglyph
f. papyrus
g. pharaoh
h. pyramid
i. regent
j. silt

1. _____ A rock-filled rapid in a river is called a(n) _____ .

2. _____ A powerful Egyptian ruler was called a(n) _____ .

3. _____ An Egyptian ruler was often buried in a triangular-shaped building called a(n) _____ .

4. _____ A family of rulers is called a(n) _____ .

5. _____ Egyptians used reedlike plants to make a type of paper called _____ .

Match the definitions with the terms. Write the correct letter in each blank. You will not use all the terms.

a. afterlife
b. artisan
c. astronomer
d. cataract
e. delta
f. dynasty
g. pharaoh
h. pyramid
i. regent
j. silt

6. _____ triangle-shaped area at the mouth of a river

7. _____ skilled worker

8. _____ rich, fertile soil deposited by the flooding of a river

9. _____ a scientist who studies the stars

10. _____ someone who rules for a child until the child is old enough to rule

B. KEY CONCEPTS

Write the letter of the correct answer in each blank.

11. _____ The Nile River affected ancient Egyptian life by creating
    a. hot winds that blew across the land.   c. rich farmland in the river valley.
    b. Lower and Upper Egypt.   d. a large desert.

12. _____ In about 4000 B.C., the earliest communities in the Nile River valley first developed
    a. in the delta of Lower Egypt.
    b. in the delta of Upper Egypt.
    c. in the deserts of Upper Egypt.
    d. between the Tigris and Euphrates rivers.

13. _____ The Egyptian pharaohs ruled with absolute power over
    a. all the people in Africa.   c. only slaves.
    b. only priests.   d. all Egyptians.

14. _____ Throughout the first six dynasties, Egypt became
    a. weak and divided.
    b. bigger and more prosperous.
    c. a target for conquering empires.
    d. the first civilization to be ruled by local governors.

15. _____ Religion played an important part in Egyptian life by
    a. encouraging Egypt to make peace with its neighbors.
    b. destroying the power of the pharaoh.
    c. explaining natural events to the people.
    d. supporting a democratic government.

16. _____ How did the ancient Egyptians demonstrate their belief in life after death?
    a. They believed in only one God.
    b. They preserved the bodies of their dead.
    c. They became famous warriors.
    d. They did not think the bodies of the dead should be preserved.

17. _____ In ancient Egypt, most of the people belonged to the social class of
    a. artisans.   c. kings and nobles.
    b. merchants.   d. workers and farmers.

18. _____ Ancient Egyptian astronomers studied the stars to
    a. predict the flooding of the Nile River.
    b. appoint the next pharaoh.
    c. create new medicines from plants.
    d. create a new writing system.

19. ____ What happened when Nubians took control of trade routes by using iron weapons?
   a. They made pyramids from metal instead of stone.
   b. Meroë became rich.
   c. They stopped spending time growing crops.
   d. Meroë controlled an empire that extended into Europe.

20. ____ Because ancient Egyptian civilization was located on the banks of the Nile River, Egypt had
   a. rich farmland.   c. no farmland.
   b. poor farmland.   d. hardly any farmland.

21. ____ Around 4000 B.C., which of the following appeared in the Nile River delta?
   a. traders from other countries
   b. Nubian soldiers
   c. the first communities in the Nile River valley
   d. the first Egyptian artisans and miners

22. ____ The greatest achievement of the pharaoh Menes was
   a. conquering the Nubians.
   b. uniting Upper and Lower Egypt.
   c. building a pyramid.
   d. ruling the empire from Abu Simbel.

23. ____ Egyptian rulers governed their empire
   a. by establishing a democracy.
   b. by maintaining absolute power over the people.
   c. by establishing dynasties that were unstable.
   d. with the help of governors elected by the citizens.

24. ____ In ancient Egypt, a very important religious practice was to
   a. worship the pharaoh's children.
   b. travel to the west bank of the Nile each night.
   c. prepare the dead for the afterlife.
   d. worship one God.

25. ____ The first pharaohs of the New Dynasty expanded Egypt's
   a. universities.   c. religion.
   b. power.   d. farmland.

26. ____ The lives of the Egyptian peasants were greatly influenced by
   a. their ability to read and write.
   b. the study of astronomy.
   c. the planting seasons.
   d. their contact with merchants from other countries.

27. ____ To keep track of the kingdom's growing wealth, ancient Egyptians began to
   a. use hieroglyphics.
   b. tax the farmers.
   c. use cuneiform.
   d. publish a list of the pharaoh's possessions each year.

28. _____ Because of Nubia's location between Egypt and Central Africa, it was
    a. destroyed by the people of Kush.   c. never very prosperous.
    b. a center for trade.   d. the first sea empire.

C. CRITICAL THINKING

Answer the following questions in the space provided, on the back of this paper or on a separate sheet of paper.

29. Drawing Conclusions: How did the physical geography of ancient Egypt shape the development of its civilization?

30. Identifying Central Issues: How did religion affect the lives of the ancient Egyptians?

31. Drawing Conclusions: Why was the Egyptian empire able to be controlled at times by rulers from Nubia?

32. Identifying Central Issues: Why was the Nile River so important to the lives of the ancient Egyptians?

D. SKILL: READING ROUTE MAPS

Study the map and map key. Use the information in the map below to answer the following questions. Write your answers on the lines provided.

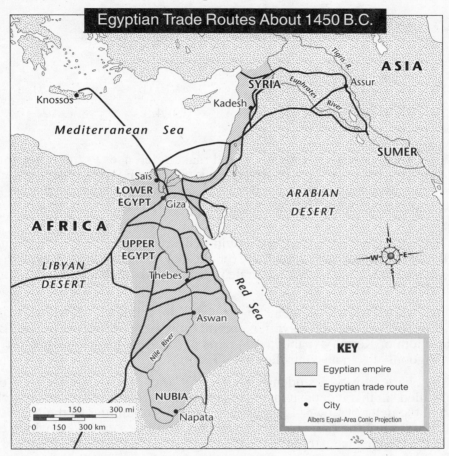

Egyptian Trade Routes About 1450 B.C.

KEY
Egyptian empire
Egyptian trade route
• City
Albers Equal-Area Conic Projection

33. What would be a good title for this map? _____

34. What is the main purpose of this map? _____

35. How are Egyptian trade routes shown on the map? _____

36. What are the names of two Egyptian towns or trading centers? _____

37. Would a Egyptian trade ship that sailed north toward Britain stay close to land, or would it sail far out into the ocean? _____

38. What major bodies of water does this map show? _____

39. What does the map key indicate? _____

40. How are trade routes shown on this map? _____

41. What island did Egyptians travel to in the Mediterranean Sea? _____

42. Which direction would an Egyptian trader travel to get from Saïs to Heliopolis? _____
_____

ANSWER KEY

1. c	2. g	3. h	4. d	5. f
6. e	7. b	8. j	9. c	10. i
11. c	12. a	13. d	14. b	15. c
16. b	17. d	18. a	19. b	20. a
21. c	22. b	23. b	24. c	25. b
26. c	27. a	28. b		

29. Answers may vary; however, students should make references to the following: The rich farmland along the banks of the Nile River was vital to the Egyptian economy and life. The earliest communities were built in the delta of Lower Egypt. Also, the market towns used the Nile as a trade highway. The desert beyond the fertile Nile riverbank protected Egypt from attack.

30. Answers may vary; however, students should make references to the following: Religion explained the workings of nature, such as drought, sickness, and death. Egyptians preserved the bodies of their dead and staged elaborate funerals for their pharaohs, who were buried in huge pyramids.

31. Answers may vary; however, students may refer to the following: Egypt was controlled at times by Nubians because the Egyptian empire grew weak. Students might also mention that the kingdom of Kerma expanded into parts of southern Egypt by 1600 b.c. In the late 700s, the kingdom of Napata controlled all of Egypt.

32. Answers may vary; however, students should refer to the following: the river carried rich fertile soil called silt that it deposited on the land when it flooded. As a result, rich farmland developed in the delta of Lower Egypt. The earliest communities in the Nile River valley developed here. Also, the rich land produced crop surpluses each year which encouraged community development and trade.

33. Answers may vary. Possible answers: Egyptian Trade Routes, Egyptian Trade in the Mediterranean Sea and Atlantic Ocean

34. to show the Egyptian trade routes and trading centers

35. with lines

36. Answers may vary. Possible answers: Thebes and Giza

37. It would sail far out into the ocean.

38. The Mediterranean Sea and the Red Sea. Students may also include rivers.

39. Egyptian trade routes and Egypt

40. with lines

41. Knossos

42. south or southeast

A. KEY TERMS

Match the definitions with the terms. Write the correct letter in each blank. You will not use all the terms.

a. ahimsa
b. caste
c. citadel
d. dharma
e. meditate
f. missionary
g. monsoon
h. nirvana
i. reincarnation
j. subcontinent

1. _____ strong seasonal wind that blows across a region at certain times of year

2. _____ to think deeply

3. _____ a lasting peace that Buddhists seek

4. _____ a large landmass that juts out from a continent

5. _____ a person who spreads his or her religious beliefs to others

Match the definitions with the terms. Write the correct letter in each blank. You will not use all the terms.

a. ahimsa
b. caste
c. citadel
d. dharma
e. meditate
f. migrate
g. missionary
h. monsoon
i. nirvana
j. reincarnation

6. _____ in Hinduism, the idea of being nonviolent

7. _____ in Hinduism, the religious and moral duties of each person

8. _____ a social class of people

9. _____ in Buddhism, the lasting peace achieved by giving up selfish desires

10. _____ a fortress in a city

B. KEY CONCEPTS

Write the letter of the correct ending in each blank.

11. _____ India's mountains and surrounding water influenced its development by
   a. providing contact with Asian lands.
   b. encouraging invasions by other countries to the east and west.
   c. limiting contact between the subcontinent and the rest of the world.
   d. providing unlimited contact with civilizations.

12. _____ The people of India depend on the summer monsoon to
   a. carry melting snow to the dry lands.
   b. create natural passages in the Himalaya Mountains.
   c. bring cold air to the subcontinent.
   d. carry moisture that provides seasonal rains.

13. _____ Archaeologists know that Mohenjo-Daro was carefully planned because
   a. the fertile soil eventually turned into desert.
   b. the streets were laid out in a grid.
   c. the city was built on a flat plain.d.
   d. the city was used for farming instead of trade.

14. _____ One way in which Hinduism differs from the other major religions is
   a. it has no single founder.   c. it has developed fairly recently.
   b. believers rely on a single sacred book. d. it has not attracted many followers.

15. _____ When the Aryan and Indian cultures blended, what religion resulted?
   a. Vedic   c. Hinduism
   b. Buddhism   d. Christianity

16. _____ According to the Hindu belief of reincarnation, faithful followers of Hinduism
   a. cannot escape from the cycle of death and rebirth.
   b. will be rewarded in the next life.
   c. will be reborn as animals.
   d. will not be rewarded in the next life.

17. _____ Buddha taught that the cure for human suffering was to
   a. worship many gods.   c. give up selfish desires.
   b. exercise and eat healthy food.   d. gain wealth through hard work.

18. _____ Like the Egyptian pharaohs, the Indian emperor Chandragupta believed in
   a. sharing his power with governors of city-states.
   b. maintaining a small army.
   c. the democratic principles of government.
   d. the absolute power of the ruler.

19. _____ Why is Asoka considered one of India's greatest leaders?
    a. Under his rule, the Maurya empire extended across China.
    b. He was a kind ruler who thought of his people as his children.
    c. He used his wealth to build huge, splendid palaces.
    d. He invented astronomy to predict when the Indus River would flood.

20. _____ Because of its geography, India was
    a. open to trade only with African peoples.
    b. a world trading power.
    c. limited in contact with the rest of the world.
    d. limited to trade with Asian lands.

21. _____ Monsoons are important to India because they carry
    a. rich soils that enable farmers to grow crops.
    b. rains that enable farmers to grow crops.
    c. dry air to farming regions.
    d. snow to the dry lands.

22. _____ What are two important rivers that start in the Himalaya Mountains?
    a. the Indus and the Arabian   c. the Tigris and the Euphrates
    b. the Nile and the Tigris   d. the Indus and the Ganges

23. _____ One important result of the Aryan invasion of India was
    a. the introduction of bronze weapons.
    b. the introduction of a strict caste system.
    c. the founding of Mohenjo-Daro.
    d. the introduction of powerful rulers called Brahmans.

24. _____ When the Aryan culture mixed with the culture of the people they conquered,
    a. a new form of writing developed.
    b. Hinduism developed.
    c. several religions flourished.
    d. the Vedas were no longer important to the people.

25. _____ At the center of Hinduism is the belief in
    a. ziggurats.   c. reincarnation.
    b. monotheism.   d. the Middle Way.

26. _____ One important achievement of the Maurya empire in India was
    a. the end of the caste system.
    b. the creation of a democratic government.
    c. the growth of foreign trade.
    d. the rise of Christianity.

27. _____ The Maurya ruler Asoka thought of his people as his
    a. children.   c. possible poisoners.
    b. slaves.   d. parents.

28. _____ After Asoka's death, the Maurya empire
    a. united all its territories.   c. increased its wealth.
    b. conquered all of Asia.   d. was destroyed.

C. CRITICAL THINKING

Answer the following questions in the space provided, on the back of this paper or on a separate sheet of paper.

29. Recognizing Cause and Effect: How was India influenced by its physical geography?

30. Making Comparisons: How were the reigns of Chandragupta and his grandson Asoka similar? How were they different?

31. Drawing Conclusions: How do you think the mountains and waters of India influenced the development of its civilization?

32. Identifying Central Issues: Do you think the Maurya empire should be called "India's Golden Age"? Support your opinion with facts. In your answer, identify three achievements of this empire.

D. SKILL: READING TABLES

Study the table below. Then answer the following questions. Write your answers on the lines provided.

Religion	When Founded	Where Founded
Buddhism	c. 525 B.C.	India
Christianity	c. A.D. 30	Southwest Asia
Hinduism	c. 1500 B.C.	India
Islam	c. A.D. 622	Southwest Asia
Judaism	c. 1800 B.C.	Southwest Asia

33. What would be a good title for this table? _____

34. When and where was Islam founded? _____

35. According to the table, what do Christianity and Judaism have in common? _____

36. How many years passed between the founding of Hinduism and Judaism? _____

37. Which two religions were founded in India? _____

Study the table below. Then answer the following questions. Write your answers on the lines provided.

Time Spans of Ancient Civilizations

Ancient Civilization	
Egypt and Nubia	c. 3100 B.C.–A.D. 350
India	c. 2500 B.C.–185 B.C.
China	c. 2000 B.C.–A.D. 1911
Greece	c. 2000 B.C.–146 B.C.
Rome	c. 900 B.C.–A.D. 476

38. What can you learn by reading this table? _____

39. What would be a good heading for the second column of this table? _____

40. Which two civilizations started around the same time? _____

41. According to the table, which civilization started first? _____

42. According to the table, which civilization lasted the longest? _____

ANSWER KEY

1. g	2. e	3. h	4. j	5. f
6. a	7. d	8. b	9. i	10. c
11. c	12. d	13. b	14. a	15. c
16. b	17. c	18. d	19. b	20. c
21. b	22. d	23. b	24. b	25. c
26. c	27. a	28. d		

29. Answers may vary; however, students might include the following points: 1) The Himalaya Mountains cut off India from the rest of the ancient world. However, invaders entered India through the steep passes of the mountains to conquer and settle the land. Three great river systems cut through these mountains and carried melting snow to the plains. 2) The Indian Ocean and the Arabian Sea limited contact with lands to the east and west. 3) Monsoons dominate the climate and bring rains that create fertile farmland. 4) The Indus River Valley contained fertile soil for farming. In ancient times, well-planned cities flourished here.

30. Answers may vary. Students should touch on the following points: 1) The reigns were similar in that both rulers were strong, bringing order and peace to their people. Also, during the early years of his rule, Asoka was warlike just like his grandfather. 2) The reigns were different because Asoka embraced Buddhism and encouraged his people to behave with tolerance and truthfulness. Chandragupta, on the other hand, feared for his own life, and thought that poisoners were everywhere.

31. Answers may vary; however, students should refer to the following: 1) The Himalaya Mountains separated India from Asia; however, invaders were able to enter India through the steep mountain passes. Also, the great river systems in the mountains made farming possible in the river valleys. 2) The Indian Ocean and the Arabian Sea limited contact with other lands to the east and west. However, the Indus River provided rich soil that enabled early farmers to harvest crops. Settlements grew into cities in this valley.

32. Answers may vary; however, students might refer to the following three important achievements: the development of foreign trade during the reign of the first emperor, Chandragupta; the use of the emperor's wealth to improve the empire by clearing forests, creating a network of roads and producing more food; and his son, Asoka's, concern with the welfare of the people, which led to the construction of hospitals and his religious toleration.

33. Answers may vary; possible answer, the Major Religions of the World

34. A.D. 622; Southwest Asia

35. both were founded in Southwest Asia

36. about 300 years

37. Buddhism and Hinduism

38. time spans of ancient civilizations

39. Time Span

40. China and Greece

41. Egypt and Nubia

42. China

Chapter 5 ■ *Ancient China*

A. KEY TERMS

Fill in the blanks with the terms. Write the correct letter in each blank. You will not use all the terms.

a. dike
b. civil service
c. loess
d. silk
e. extended family
f. philosophy
g. warlords
h. currency

1. _____ In ancient China, many aspects of life were ruled by the _____ of Confucius.

2. _____ The Huang He is muddy because it carries _____ , a yellow-brown soil.

3. _____ A valuable cloth made only in China, called _____ , was highly prized in Europe.

4. _____ To protect their lands from the effects of flooding, the people in an early Chinese village might build a(n) _____ .

5. _____ The teachings of Confucius were used as the basic training for the _____ , the people who carried out the work of government.

Match the definitions with the terms. Write the correct letter in each blank. You will not use all the terms.

a. civil service
b. silk
c. dike
d. currency
e. philosophy
f. loess
g. warlord
h. extended family

6. _____ leader of an armed local band

7. _____ the kind of money used by a group or nation

8. _____ a valuable cloth once made only in China

9. _____ closely related people, including parents, grandparents, brothers, sisters, aunts, uncles, and cousins

10. _____ a system of beliefs and values

B. KEY CONCEPTS

Write the letter of the correct answer in each blank.

11. _____ The physical geography around China affected Chinese civilization by
    a. making trade with Egypt easy.
    b. creating barriers to the outside world.
    c. making it easy for Babylonians to invade China.
    d. making it easy for Nubians to invade China.

12. _____ The first farming settlements in China developed
    a. near the highlands.
    b. near the mountains.
    c. on the level plains.
    d. along the rivers.

13. _____ The center of early Chinese society was
    a. the family.
    b. the individual.
    c. the state.
    d. the governor.

14. _____ Confucius believed that if people showed loyalty and respect within the family,
    a. China would become a world leader.
    b. a new king would be chosen.
    c. they would not obey their rulers.
    d. the same values would spread to society at large.

15. _____ Because of the government examinations based on Confucius's teachings, government jobs
    a. were held by anyone who wanted one.
    b. could be held by poor young men.
    c. were not highly prized.
    d. were held only by the sons of important people.

16. _____ Which of the following actions did Shi Huangdi take in order to control Chinese thought?
    a. He outlawed the ideas of Confucius and others.
    b. He built the only library in the empire.
    c. He trained all the scholars himself.
    d. He wrote the philosophy books read by the people.

17. _____ The main interest of the Chinese emperor Wudi was
    a. encouraging all Chinese people to read and write.
    b. improving Chinese society.
    c. expanding the Chinese empire by conquering other lands.
    d. building up the power of warlords.

18. _____ An important accomplishment of the Chinese during the Han dynasty was the
    a. invention of paper.
    b. production of bronze tools.
    c. construction of the Great Wall.
    d. building of royal tombs.

19. _____ During the Han dynasty, the influence of Confucianism grew because
    a. Confucius believed rulers did not have to set a good example.
    b. Confucius became an advisor to the emperor.
    c. all the people could read and write.
    d. the rulers wanted to bring back respect for tradition.

20. _____ China's physical geography influenced the growth of its civilization by
    a. creating trade routes with Sumer.
    b. creating trade routes with Egypt.
    c. allowing contact with other empires.
    d. creating barriers to the outside world.

21. _____ The ancient civilizations of China, Mesopotamia, and Egypt all developed
    a. because rivers deposited rich soil suitable for farming.
    b. because they were all surrounded by mountains.
    c. as a result of serious drought.
    d. because of vast deserts that attracted settlers.

22. _____ In contrast to the southern half of China, the northern part is
    a. cool and wet.   c. cool and dry.
    b. without rivers.   d. rainy and warm.

23. _____ The most important element in early Chinese life was the
    a. army.   c. central government.
    b. family.   d. local warlords.

24. _____ Confucian philosophy was important because the teaching
    a. influenced the civilization of India.
    b. ruled many aspects of Chinese life.
    c. stressed the need to educate only the rich.
    d. urged rulers to extend China's empire.

25. _____ One of the central ideas of Confucianism was
    a. to support religious intolerance.
    b. to ignore the Warring States.
    c. to question the power of rulers.
    d. to show loyalty and respect within the family.

26. _____ Confucius believed that people in authority should
    a. treat others harshly.
    b. set a good example by behaving well.
    c. train members of the civil service.
    d. honor important people.

27. _____ One of Shi Huangdi's greatest achievements was
    a. the construction of the Great Wall.
    b. the overthrow of the Han dynasty.
    c. establishing trade with Egypt.
    d. encouraging freedom of thought.

CHAPTER 5

28. ____ The Silk Road was important because
   a. it was the route followed by Confucius as he spread his philosophy.
   b. it enabled silk made in the West to be brought to China.
   c. it was a military route followed by Chinese armies.
   d. it was a trade route that connected China with the West.

C. CRITICAL THINKING

Answer the following questions in the space provided, on the back of this paper or on a separate sheet of paper.

29. Identifying Central Issues: How did China's physical geography affect the development of its early civilization?

30. Drawing Conclusions: Why do you think that people in China today call themselves "the children of Han"? In your answer, consider at least three important accomplishments of the Han dynasty.

31. Identifying Central Issues: How did the physical geography of China's river valleys affect the development of its civilization?

32. Drawing Conclusions: Why did Confucian philosophy have such a great impact on life in ancient China?

D. SKILL: TAKING NOTES

Use the paragraph below to answer the following questions. Write your answers on the lines provided. Use key words and phrases, rather than complete sentences.

The Chinese people also call the Huang He "China's Sorrow." The river was unpredictable and sometimes dangerous. It brought life to the land. But it also frequently took life away. Destructive floods could come without warning, sometimes as often as every two years. Sometimes a flood drowned thousands of people. At times, the river flooded with such force that the water cut an entirely new path over the land. The course of the river could change by hundreds of miles.

33. What is the main idea of this paragraph? Write the main idea as a heading. _____

_____

34. What is one detail that supports the main idea of the paragraph?_____

_____

35. Give a second detail that supports the main idea. _____

_____

36. What is a third detail supporting the main idea? _____

_____

37. Write a short paragraph about the Huang He in your own words, using only your answers to the above questions. _____

_____

Use the paragraph below to answer the following questions. Write your answer on the lines provided. Use key words and phrases, rather than complete sentences.

Traditional Chinese ideas flourished during the Han dynasty. Han rulers realized that during troubled times in the past, people had lost respect for tradition. To bring back this respect, rulers encouraged people to return to the teachings of Confucius. That was why the first Han emperor, Liu Bang, appointed Confucian scholars as his advisors. Rulers during the Han and later dynasties required members of the civil service to be educated in Confucian teachings.

38. What is the main idea of this paragraph? Write the main idea as a heading. _____

_____

39. What is one detail that supports the main idea of the paragraph?_____

_____

40. What is a second detail that supports the main idea of the paragraph?_____

_____

41. What is a third detail that supports the main idea of the paragraph? _____

_____

42. Write a short paragraph in your own words using only your answers to the above questions.

_____

CHAPTER 5

ANSWER KEY

1. f	2. c	3. d	4. a	5. b
6. g	7. d	8. b	9. h	10. c
11. b	12. d	13. a	14. d	15. b
16. a	17. c	18. a	19. d	20. d
21. a	22. c	23. b	24. b	25. d
26. b	27. a	28. d		

29. Answers may vary; however, students should refer to the following: the natural barriers created by the Himalaya Mountains and the deserts and high plateaus, which prevented the ancient Chinese from learning about other civilizations; the rivers that provided fertile topsoil for farming and enabled early Chinese to give up their nomadic existence and establish settlements.

30. Answers may vary; however, students should refer to some of the following: the establishment of a civil service system that employed men educated in Confucian teachings; advancements in the arts, scholarship, and history; technological advancements, including the development of iron farming tools and irrigation systems; numerous inventions, including paper, the compass, and herbal medicines. Because of the lasting impact of many of these accomplishments, modern Chinese might consider themselves to be "the children of Han."

31. Answers may vary; however, students should include the following: the Huang He, the greatest river in China, deposited fertile topsoil that was necessary for farming. As a result, the people gave up their nomadic life and began farming. Early farm settlements developed into villages. Fixed settlements resulted in a more orderly government, which led to a written language. However, the Huang He also caused loss of life by flooding. The flooding sometimes changed the course of the river.

32. Answers may vary; however, students should refer to the following points: Confucius lived in a period of political instability; the Chinese looked to Confucian teachings because of his emphasis on showing respect, which recalled life in an earlier, more peaceful period. Also, Confucianism emphasized order in relationships, beginning with the family and spreading to society at large. Confucius's teachings also had an impact on Chinese government, since they were used as the basis of civil service examinations.

33. The Huang He: China's Sorrow

34. was unpredictable and sometimes dangerous

35. no warnings of destructive floods, sometimes every two years

36. could drown thousands or could cause river to cut another path and change course.

37. Answers will vary, depending on the details chosen. A possible paragraph follows: The Huang He is a river that is called China's Sorrow. Its floods can be unpredictable and dangerous, sometimes coming every two years. These floods can drown thousands of people.

38. Return to Tradition Under the Han Dynasty

39. to teach respect, a return to teachings of Confucius

40. appointment of Confucian scholars as advisors

41. requirement that members of civil service know Confucian teachings

42. Answers will vary, depending on the details chosen. A possible paragraph for the answers above follows: During the Han dynasty, there was a return to tradition. To learn respect, people studied Confucianism. Han rulers appointed Confucian scholars as advisers and made members of the civil service learn Confucian teachings.

A. KEY TERMS

Match the definitions with the terms. Write the correct letter in each blank. You will not use all the terms.

a. peninsula
b. agora
c. barbarian
d. city-state
e. democracy
f. assassinate
g. acropolis
h. Hellenistic
i. plague

1. _____ a high place near rocky hills where settlers would be safe from attack

2. _____ a public market and meeting place in ancient Greece

3. _____ a form of government in which people govern themselves

4. _____ a piece of land surrounded by water on three sides

5. _____ a widespread sickness

Complete each sentence by writing the correct term in the blank. You will not use all the terms.

a. acropolis
b. city-state
c. philosopher
d. tribute
e. Hellenistic
f. peninsula
g. blockade
h. aristocrat
i. democracy

6. _____ After Alexander's death, his empire broke up into three _____ kingdoms.

7. _____ In ancient Greece, a(n) _____ was a person who used reason to understand natural events.

8. _____ Ships may surround and close, or _____ , a harbor in order to defeat an enemy.

9. _____ A member of a rich and powerful ruling family is called a(n) _____ .

10. _____ In ancient Greece, villages often joined to form a small, independent nation, or _____ .

B. KEY CONCEPTS

Write the letter of the correct answer in each blank.

11. _____ Because of the geography of ancient Greece, the Greek communities developed
    a. separate customs and beliefs.
    b. close ties with each other.
    c. new ways of hunting and gathering.
    d. one central government.

12. _____ One important event that took place during the Dark Ages of Greece was
    a. the destruction of all farmland.
    b. an increase in foreign trade.
    c. the disappearance of writing.
    d. the disappearance of oral traditions.

13. _____ The laws introduced by the Athenian leader Solon helped the city become
    a. a free city with no slaves.
    b. a leading democracy.
    c. an empire that extended to Egypt.
    d. an empire that extended to China.

14. _____ The goal of Greek art was
    a. to destroy the art of other peoples.
    b. to present fantastic images of people and events.
    c. to present images of human perfection in an orderly way.
    d. to teach the principles of Greek philosophy.

15. _____ Most Greeks believed their gods were
    a. immortal.
    b. moral beings.
    c. the source of everything.
    d. weak and ineffective.

16. _____ During the Golden Age of Greece, Athenians made great achievements in
    a. flood control.
    b. tomb building.
    c. farming technology.
    d. the arts.

17. _____ Some scholars believe that in ancient Athens, one third of all people were
    a. children.
    b. slaves.
    c. teachers.
    d. artists.

18. _____ Unlike Athens, in ancient Sparta the government concentrated all its resources on creating
    a. famous artisans.
    b. successful merchants.
    c. a pleasurable lifestyle.
    d. brave and skillful warriors.

19. _____ During the Hellenistic period, there were important achievements in
    a. tragedy and comedy.
    b. mathematics and science.
    c. writing and printing.
    d. warfare and government.

20. _____ The geography of ancient Greece made it hard for communities
    a. to worship different gods.
    b. to fight with each other.
    c. to speak different languages.
    d. to unify.

21. ____ The Greek myths were important because these stories explained
    a. the coming of the Dark Ages to Greece.
    b. the creation of the universe and the features of nature.
    c. the adventures of real people.
    d. the growth of the Egyptian empire.

22. ____ The collapse of the Greek civilization during the Dark Ages increased
    a. farming.   c. poverty.
    b. foreign trading.   d. income levels.

23. ____ Citizens of Athens during the Greek Golden Age saw
    a. the arts decline.   c. buildings destroyed.
    b. democracy flourish.   d. many rebellions.

24. ____ Unlike most early Greeks, philosophers believed that the gods were
    a. the source of everything.
    b. not the source of everything.
    c. in control of natural events.
    d. the key to understanding natural events.

25. ____ While the Acropolis was the center of Athens's religious life, the agora was the center of
    a. public life.   c. military life.
    b. private life.   d. government.

26. ____ Which phrase best describes Greece's geography?
    a. extensive farmlands   c. without islands
    b. few coasts   d. peninsulas and mountains

27. ____ After the end of the war between Athens and Sparta, Athens was
    a. never again a leader in the Greek world.
    b. a place where the arts again flourished.
    c. faced with a plague that killed many citizens.
    d. able to control Sparta's harbor.

28. ____ Under the leadership of Alexander the Great, Greece
    a. formed three main kingdoms.   c. expanded its empire.
    b. was conquered by Persia.   d. destroyed Alexandria.

CHAPTER 6

C. CRITICAL THINKING

Answer the following questions in the space provided, on the back of this paper or on a separate sheet of paper.

29. Identifying Central Issues: How did the physical geography of ancient Greece affect the development of its civilization? In your answer, consider the relationship between Greek communities and the relationship between Greece and other empires.

30. Making Comparisons: Compare life in Greece during the Dark Ages with that during the Golden Age.

31. Expressing Problems Clearly: Many people believe that Athens was a model of freedom and democracy. How is this belief true? How is it untrue? Support your answer with facts from your reading.

32. Making Comparisons: Compare and contrast the roles of women in Athens and Sparta. How do you think Sparta's focus on war affected the role played by women there?

D. SKILL: DRAWING CONCLUSIONS

To answer the questions below, draw conclusions based on what you already know and the information provided. Write your answer in the space provided.

33. Why would ancient people be safe from attack if they lived near hills?_____

_____

34. Why might people who controlled an area's good land be rich? _____

_____

35. What conclusion could you draw from this sentence?

Pericles had a great desire to glorify Athens with new buildings.

_____

_____

36. What is one thing you could conclude from this sentence?

Athenian men liked to gather and talk to their friends in the agora.

_____

_____

37. What could you conclude from the fact that young Alexander's hero was the great warrior Achilles?_____

_____

38. What conclusion could you draw about freedom in Athens from this sentence?

Greek comedies made fun of well-known citizens and politicians.

_____

_____

39. What can you conclude from the fact that Greek sculptures display order and balance?_____

_____

_____

40. What conclusion can you draw about Socrates from this statement?

Other philosophers were interested in the natural world; Socrates asked questions about justice and courage.

_____

_____

41. What are two things you might conclude from the statement that Alexander's soldiers grumbled at his orders, but obeyed him?_____

_____

42. What can you conclude from the fact that Alexander named cities he founded after himself?

_____

_____

CHAPTER 6

ANSWER KEY

1. g	2. b	3. e	4. a	5. i
6. c	7. c	8. g	9. h	10. b
11. a	12. c	13. b	14. c	15. c
16. d	17. b	18. d	19. b	20. d
21. b	22. c	23. b	24. b	25. a
26. d	27 a	28. c		

29. Answers may vary; however, students should mention the following points: since only small areas of the land could be farmed, Greeks used their access to the sea to become traders and sailors. The mountainous geography of Greece also resulted in a lack of contact between the communities there. As a result, throughout its history, Greek city-states fought one another rather than uniting in recognition of their common heritage.

30. Answers may vary; however, students should mention the following points: during the Dark Ages, civilization collapsed. The people were poor and didn't trade for food or goods. Writing disappeared. Families settled on farms near rocky hills where they would be safe from attack. These settlements eventually became city-states. During the Golden Age, after the defeat of the Persians, the people had more money. Democracy had developed in Athens and some other cities. The Athenians had the resources to improve their city and focus on the arts. There were advancements in math, philosophy, and science.

31. Answers will vary; however, students can refer to the following points: for citizens—males 18 or older who were not slaves or foreigners—Athens was a model. They had a direct say in government, could hold office, and were equal before the law. But freedom and democracy didn't extend to women, slaves, and foreigners, who had no part in the democracy and whose freedom was limited to different degrees. In their relations with the states in their fifth century empire, the Athenians behaved like tyrants.

32. Answers may vary, but students should include these points: Athenian women spent most of their time at home, where they ran the household and raised the children. They didn't participate in public life, engage in business, or own property. In Sparta, girls underwent physical training—so they would bear strong children who would grow up to be warriors. As women they were freer: they owned land and took some part in business. Students may conclude that the reason was that men were too busy being warriors to have much time for business.

33. Answers may vary, but students should understand that people would be safe because they could climb to the top of the hills, where it would be easier to fight off attackers.

34. Answers may vary, but students should conclude that people who control good land can grow the most crops. They can become rich by selling the surplus.

35. Answers will vary. Students might say that Pericles was proud of his city or loved it.

36. Answers will vary. Possible responses: They were friendly and sociable people; or women led a different sort of life from men.

37. Answers will vary. Possible responses: that Alexander had ambitions to be a great warrior himself.

38. There was freedom of speech in Athens.

39. The Greeks valued order and balance.

40. that Socrates was more interested in people than in nature

41. Answers will vary. Some possibilities: His orders were hard on his men. They were loyal or they loved him or feared what would happen to them if they disobeyed.

42. Answers will vary. Some possibilities: He had a very high opinion of himself. He wanted everyone to remember him.

Chapter 7 ■ Ancient Rome

A. KEY TERMS

Complete each sentence by writing the letter of the correct term in the blank. You will not use all the terms.

> a. aqueduct
> b. consul
> c. dictator
> d. disciple
> e. inflation
> f. mercenary
> g. patrician
> h. plebeian
> i. province
> j. republic

1. _____ In ancient Rome, a wealthy, upper-class person was called a(n) _____ .

2. _____ A follower of a person or belief is called a(n) _____ .

3. _____ Ancient Rome had a form of government, called a(n) _____ , in which citizens vote for their leader.

4. _____ In ancient Rome, a Roman governor ruled each _____ of the empire.

5. _____ A structure that carries water over long distances is called a(n) _____ .

Match the definitions with the terms. Write the correct letter in each blank. You will not use all the terms.

> a. aqueduct
> b. consul
> c. dictator
> d. disciple
> e. inflation
> f. mercenary
> g. patrician
> h. plebeian
> i. province
> j. veto

6. _____ the Latin word for "forbid"

7. _____ a foreign soldier who serves only for pay

8. _____ an ordinary citizen in the ancient Roman Republic

9. _____ a member of a wealthy, upper-class family in the ancient Roman Republic

10. _____ an economic situation in which there is more money, but it has less value

B. KEY CONCEPTS

Write the letter of the correct ending in each blank.

11. _____ Because the Roman government was led by two men, power was
   a. in the hands of the plebeians. c. given to local governors.
   b. divided equally between them. d. in the hands of the senate.

12. _____ Julius Caesar was able to gain control of Rome after he was
   a. elected governor by the citizens. c. victorious in the conquest of Gaul.
   b. able to conquer the Persians. d. appointed by Octavian.

13. _____ The Roman senate gave Augustus all the power he wanted because
   a. he made himself dictator.
   b. he threatened to destroy the republic.
   c. they were grateful for Rome's peace and prosperity.
   d. the conquered people threatened to revolt.

14. _____ Unlike the Greeks, who were interested in ideas, the Romans were more interested in
   a. focusing on trade instead of education.
   b. copying the Egyptians' approach to learning.
   c. spreading democracy throughout their empire.
   d. using knowledge to build things.

15. _____ Roman law was based on the idea of
   a. revenge. c. fairness.
   b. inequality. d. absolute rule.

16. _____ The majority of Roman citizens were
   a. unemployed. c. farmers.
   b. wealthy. d. merchants.

17. _____ The Roman emperors gave free grain to the poor
   a. whenever they had a surplus.
   b. whenever they were unemployed.
   c. to prevent riots when the harvest was poor.
   d. because the law required it.

18. _____ Romans were tolerant of other religions throughout their empire as long as the conquered people
   a. agreed to join the Roman army.
   b. agreed to give up their religion after a period of time.
   c. agreed to become slaves.
   d. were peaceful and paid taxes.

19. ____ Two reasons for Rome's serious economic problems were
    a. unemployment and inflation.
    b. low taxes and drought.
    c. the cost of maintaining a large army and low taxes.
    d. a severe plague and drought.

20. ____ Rome's geographic setting was important because
    a. strong winds brought heavy spring rains to the land.
    b. its position was central to Italy and the known Western world.
    c. it was surrounded by deserts and mountains, which insured its safety from invasions.
    d. farmers depended on yearly flooding to plant crops.

21. ____ If two Roman consuls disagreed on how to handle an emergency, Roman law provided for
    a. the appointment of a dictator.   c. the crowning of an emperor.
    b. the election of a king.   d. the appointment of a general.

22. ____ The two kinds of citizens in the Roman Republic were
    a. consuls and emperors
    b. patricians and consuls
    c. plebeians and patricians
    d. plebeians and slaves

23. ____ As long as the conquered people lived peacefully, they were
    a. strictly ruled by Roman generals.
    b. left alone by Roman governors.
    c. not allowed to follow their religion.
    d. exempt from paying taxes to Rome.

24. ____ Roman law is important to us today because
    a. it shows why the empire finally fell apart.
    b. it was extremely harsh and unfair to conquered peoples.
    c. it did not protect the rights of people accused of crimes.
    d. it developed ideas of justice that are the basis of our legal system.

25. ____ In ancient Rome, most people lived
    a. in tents.   c. in poor housing.
    b. in villas.   d. on small farms.

26. ____ Most of all, ancient Romans placed great emphasis on
    a. family life.   c. religious intolerance.
    b. military achievements.   d. freedom for their slaves.

27. ____ Under Constantine's rule, the Roman Empire
    a. was intolerant of all religions.
    b. collapsed.
    c. gained Christianity as its official religion.
    d. was divided into two parts.

CHAPTER 7

28. _____ One reason why the Roman Empire lost its power was
   a. the spread of inflation.   c. a series of droughts.
   b. the low price of food.   d. the increase in foreign trade.

C. CRITICAL THINKING

Answer the following questions in the space provided, on the back of this paper or on a separate sheet of paper.

29. Recognizing Cause and Effect: How do you think Rome's geographic setting affected the growth of its empire?

30. Expressing Problems Clearly: Do you think that the Romans treated the peoples they conquered fairly? Use facts from the chapter to support your opinion.

31. Making Comparisons: How would you compare the Romans' reaction to Christianity with their reaction to the religions of the people they conquered?

32. Identifying Central Issues: Why did the Roman Empire begin to decline with the rule of Commodus in A.D. 180?

D. SKILL: READING ACTIVELY

Read the following selection below. Then answer the following questions. Write your answers on the lines provided.

Then the captured weapons passed. There were bronze helmets, shields, . . . and glittering steel swords piled on wagons. Then followed 3,000 men carrying 750 trays heaped with silver coins. . . . Next came the king's small children, now slaves, and the king himself in a dark robe. Some in the crowd wept for the children, but not for the king. Suddenly our great consul himself appeared, in a golden chariot. . . . The crowd broke into a roar. . . . It was he who brought all this wealth and glory to Rome.

33. What question might you ask yourself after reading only the first sentence of this paragraph? _____

_____

34. Which two senses does this passage appeal to? _____

_____

35. Select one of the senses. Which words or phrases appeal to this sense? _____

_____

36. Select another one of the senses. Which words or phrases appeal to this other sense?_____

_____

37. What is another question raised in your mind by this passage? _____

_____

Read the following selection below. Then answer the following questions. Write your answer on the lines provided.

Few Romans could afford to eat like an emperor. Still, the wealthy were known for their feasts. Often they served game, perhaps partridge or wild boar. For very special occasions, they might also serve exotic dishes such as flamingo or ostrich. A special treat was dormouse cooked in honey. Roman feasts often had entertainment, including musicians, dancers, and performers reciting poems.

38. Which senses does this passage appeal to? _____

_____

39. Select one of the senses. Which words or phrases appeal to this sense? _____

_____

40. Select another one of the senses. Which words or phrases appeal to this sense? _____

_____

41.-42. What are two questions raised in your mind by this passage? _____

_____

_____

ANSWER KEY

1. g	2. d	3. j	4. i	5. a
6. j	7. f	8. h	9. g	10. e
11. b	12. c	13. c	14. d	15. c
16. a	17. c	18. d	19. a	20. b
21. a	22. c	23. b	24. d	25. c
26. a	27. c	28. a		

29. Answers may vary; however, students should refer to the following points: Rome was founded on seven hills that probably offered protection to the early settlements and helped the people to defend themselves against attack. Also, Rome's location was at the center of the Italian peninsula. This peninsula was at the center of the Mediterranean Sea, which was the center of the known Western world. After extending its control across Italy, Roman armies then had easy access to other empires. Their armies destroyed Carthage; seized control of Spain; and conquered Greece and Gaul.

30. Answers may vary; however, students should refer to the following: the Romans did treat the conquered peoples with some mercy. Although they took some slaves, they allowed most of the people they conquered to remain free. They governed them by appointing a Roman governor to rule each province; this governor was supported by a military force. Also, Romans did not force conquered peoples to live as the Romans did. They could follow their own religions. Most of all, Romans wanted to maintain peace in the provinces, so their governors kept out of the lives of the conquered peoples.

31. Answers may vary; however, students should refer to the following: the Roman conquerors were tolerant of the religions of the conquered peoples. As long as the conquered peoples lived peacefully, the Roman governors didn't interfere in their lives. However, the new religion, Christianity, alarmed the government because Christians refused to worship the Roman gods or the emperor. Roman officials considered the Christians a threat to the political stability of the empire, so they persecuted them.

32. Answers may vary; however, students should refer to the following: 1) Beginning with Commodus, who was a savage ruler, the emperors were almost always generals. Instead of governing fairly, they stole money from the treasury and used it to enrich themselves and pay their soldiers. 2) The army was filled with mercenaries rather than with citizen soldiers who loved their land. 3) Another serious problem was Rome's economic decline, including heavy taxes and severe unemployment.

33. Possible answers: Who captured the weapons? What did they pass?

34. sight and sound

35. sight: gleaming bronze helmets; robe of purple woven with gold

36. sound: crowd wept for the children; crowd broke into a roar

37. Answers may vary. Possible answers: What happened to the captive next? What happened to the consul?

38. Possible answers: sight, sound, and taste.

39. Answers may vary. For taste: exotic dishes such as flamingo or ostrich.

40. Answers may vary. For sound: musicians; performers reciting poems.

41-42. Answers may vary. Possible answers: What was the entertainment like? How long did the feast last?

A. KEY TERMS

Fill in the blanks with the terms. Write the correct letter in each blank. You will not use all the terms.

    a. aqueduct
    b. cuneiform
    c. diaspora
    d. domesticate
    e. hieroglyph
    f. inflation
    g. peninsula
    h. reincarnation
    i. silk
    j. subcontinent

1. _____ In ancient Mesopotamia, a type of writing called _____ was formed from groups of wedges and lines.

2. _____ During the Han dynasty, China traded a valuable cloth called _____ with other lands.

3. _____ During the New Stone Age, early humans learned to tame, or _____ , animals such as sheep and cows.

4. _____ An economic situation in which there is more money, but the money has less value, is called _____ .

5. _____ No area in Greece is far from the sea because the mainland is a(n) _____ .

Match the definitions with the terms. Write the correct letter in each blank. You will not use all the terms.

    a. artisan
    b. caste
    c. loess
    d. mercenary
    e. monotheism
    f. peninsula
    g. polytheism
    h. republic
    i. silt
    j. warlord

6. _____ a foreign soldier who serves in an army only for pay

7. _____ the belief in many gods

8. _____ a skilled worker

9. _____   a leader of an armed local band

10. _____   yellow-brown soil

B. KEY CONCEPTS

Write the letter of the correct answer in each blank.

11. _____   In ancient times, many cities first developed because people were able to
    a. make stone weapons to protect themselves from attack.
    b. make metals, such as copper and bronze.
    c. farm the fertile land near riverbeds.
    d. sell their goods in the marketplace.

12. _____   After early people had a steady supply of food all year long, they were able to
    a. travel to other lands in search of different food to gather.
    b. stay in one place.
    c. learn to hunt in order to feed themselves.
    d. start living in the period known as prehistory.

13. _____   As a result of Babylon's location on the southern Euphrates, it was
    a. destroyed by a great flood.   c. too far from other cities for traders.
    b. an important trade center.   d. unable to store a food supply.

14. _____   One of the most important achievements of the ancient Egyptians was
    a. merchants making silk cloth.
    b. scribes creating cuneiform writing.
    c. astronomers developing a calendar year that lasted 365 days.
    d. builders constructing the great Parthenon.

15. _____   Religion was important to the ancient Egyptians, because it explained
    a. the belief in one God.
    b. the natural world.
    c. the belief in death after life.
    d. the importance of burying the dead at sea.

16. _____   India's mountains and water affected its development by
    a. limiting contact with the rest of the world.
    b. keeping dangerous storms from destroying cities.
    c. limiting farming in the land.
    d. encouraging contact with the rest of the known world.

17. _____   Because of ancient China's mountains, deserts, and high plateaus, its people knew
    a. little about establishing early settlements.
    b. how to build the first cities in the "empty lands."
    c. how to establish contact with people in Egypt and Rome fairly early.
    d. nothing about other civilizations for a long time.

18. _____ The geography of ancient Greece affected its development by encouraging
    a. Greek settlements to establish close ties.
    b. Greek communities to think of themselves as separate.
    c. Greek citizens to speak different languages.
    d. Greek citizens to refuse to fight one another.

19. _____ Romans persecuted the early Christians in their empire because
    a. they encouraged people in the provinces to revolt.
    b. they plotted to kill Nero.
    c. they refused to worship the Roman gods or the emperor.
    d. they believed in a strict caste system.

20. _____ What happened when people learned to stay in one place and farm?
    a. Trade routes immediately developed.   c. The New Stone Age began.
    b. The Old Stone Age began.   d. Human prehistory started.

21. _____ What happened when early peoples had surplus food?
    a. Rapid population growth resulted.   c. Periods of famine resulted.
    b. Smaller families developed.   d. Settlements grew smaller.

22. _____ One of King Hammurabi's greatest achievements was
    a. the building of concrete aqueducts.   c. the development of stone weapons.
    b. the destruction of Babylon.   d. the first written code of laws.

23. _____ Ancient Egyptians depended on the Nile River because
    a. few Egyptian boats could sail the length of the river.
    b. it protected the country from attack.
    c. its floods created fertile land for farming.
    d. it enabled them to invade other lands.

24. _____ Because long-distance boat travel was impossible in Nubia, people there developed
    a. small farms and did not become traders.
    b. large farms and did not become traders.
    c. a system of canals for trading by boat.
    d. valuable overland trade routes.

25. _____ Because of King Asoka's concern for the welfare of his people, at the time of his death India was
    a. intolerant of Buddhist teachings.   c. united.
    b. divided.   d. opposed to Hindu worship.

26. _____ To encourage people to respect their traditions, the Han rulers
    a. led a return to Confucian teaching.   c. spread the teachings of Buddha.
    b. made people enter military service.   d. developed cuneiform script.

27. _____ Greek religion played an important part in the people's lives by explaining
    a. how democracy worked.   c. the creation of the universe.
    b. the importance of monotheism.   d. how to worship mortal gods.

CHAPTER 8

28. _____ After revolting and driving out the last Etruscan king from the throne, ancient Romans established a
   a. dictatorship.   c. citizen-king.
   b. republic.   d. democracy.

C. CRITICAL THINKING

Answer the following questions in the space provided, on the back of this paper or on a separate sheet of paper.

29. Expressing Problems Clearly: Do you agree or disagree with the following statement: "Rivers have often been the source of civilization"? In your answer, refer to three of the ancient civilizations you have studied.

30. Making Comparisons: How were the accomplishments of the ancient Egyptians similar to the accomplishments of the ancient Chinese? In your answer, give at least two examples.

31. Recognizing Cause and Effect: Identify and explain how geographic setting influenced the development of one of the following ancient civilizations: Egypt, India, or China. In your answer, refer to specific geographic features such as mountains, rivers, and deserts. How did they affect early settlements? Trade?

32. Making Comparisons: Compare the development of writing in ancient Phoenicia and Egypt. In your answer, describe the writing systems developed in these empires and how they were used.

CHAPTER 8

D. SKILL: DRAWING CONCLUSIONS

Read the following selection below. Then answer the following questions. Write your answer on the lines provided.

The world of the poor was a far cry from the feasts of the wealthy. In Rome, most people lived in poor housing. Many lived in tall apartment houses with no running water, toilets, or kitchens. All food and drink had to be carried up the stairs. Rubbish and human waste had to be carried down, or—as frequently happened—dumped out the window. Because most houses were made of wood, fires were frequent and often fatal. The worst, in A.D. 64, destroyed most of the city.

33. What were housing conditions like for the poor in ancient Rome? _____

_____

34. Why were fires a frequent problem for the poor in ancient Rome? _____

_____

35. How did most people in ancient Rome get rid of rubbish? _____

_____

36. What do you already know about the problems faced by people who live in unsanitary conditions? _____

37. What can you conclude about the health of the Roman poor in ancient times? _____

_____

Read the following selection below. Then answer the following questions. Write your answer on the lines provided.

A household in ancient China might contain as many as five generations living together. This meant that small children lived with their great-great-grandparents as well as their parents, uncles and aunts, cousins, brothers and sisters, and so on. These closely related people are called an extended family. In rich families, the members might live together in one big home. But most of China's people were poor. In farming villages, members of the extended family might live in separate one-room cottages. The cottages were within easy walking distance from one another.

38. What was an ancient Chinese household like? _____

_____

39. How many generations could live together? _____

40. Did most of the people in ancient China live with their extended family in one large house, or in separate, nearby cottages? _____

41. What do you know about how people learn about the customs and beliefs of their ancestors?

_____

42. What can you conclude about the relationship between the Chinese extended family and the preservation of ancient tradition? _____

Chapter 8 ■ *Final Exam*

ANSWER KEY

1. b	2. i	3. d	4. f	5. g
6. d	7. g	8. a	9. j	10. c
11. c	12. b	13. b	14. c	15. b
16. a	17. d	18. b	19. c	20. c
21. a	22. d	23. c	24. d	25. c
26. a	27. c	28. b		

29. Answers may vary; however, students should include the following: I agree with the statement because almost all ancient civilizations first developed in fertile river valleys where rich land enabled people to give up their nomadic existence and begin farming. For example, Mesopotamia developed around the Tigris and Euphrates rivers; Egypt developed along the banks of the Nile; and in China, the first settlements were founded along the Huang He.

30. Answers may vary. Possible answers: The ancient Egyptians and the ancient Chinese both invented similar writing surfaces. The Egyptians used papyrus and the Chinese used paper. Both civilizations built large tombs for their rulers. The Egyptians built the pyramids, and the Chinese built a tomb for the first emperor, which was guarded by an army of clay soldiers. Both civilizations built large empires and developed in river valleys.

31. Answers may vary; however, students should include some of the following. Egypt: The Nile River flooded regularly each year and deposited rich soil that enabled Egyptians to farm the land along the river. The earliest communities were founded in the delta of Lower Egypt. Crop surpluses enabled communities to develop crafts and trade, using the river as a highway. Beyond the Nile lay a vast desert, which was useless for farming. However, the deserts protected ancient Egypt from attack. India: A wall of mountains cut off India from the rest of the ancient world. In addition, the Indian Ocean and the Arabian Sea limited contact with lands to the east and west. The Himalaya Mountains also provided openings for invaders. The Indus River Valley provided fertile land for farming. Early communities that grew into cities developed there. China: In China the Himalaya Mountains and a region of vast deserts and plateaus prevented contact with the outside world. China's rivers were a source of life, bringing fertile soil to the land as a result of floods. The first farming settlements developed in the Huang He Valley. These settlements grew into a larger settled area and became the basis for Chinese civilization.

32. Answers may vary; however, students should include some of the following: the Phoenicians developed a simplified system with twenty-two letters. This less-complicated writing system was necessary because the Phoenicians had so much trade. Egyptian writing, called hieroglyphics, used pictures to stand for ideas and things. They developed hieroglyphics to keep track of the pharaoh's growing wealth. As the empires grew, they created more pictures to represent more complicated ideas.

33. Housing was poor, with no running water, toilets, or kitchens. Rubbish and human waste were dumped out the windows.

34. Their houses were made of wood.

35. They either carried it down the stairs or dumped it out the window.

36. Answers may vary. Students may note that their health suffers.

37. Answers may vary. However, students should note that they probably suffered from malnutrition and other illnesses.

38. An extended family lived in one home, or in separate cottages within easy walking distance.

39. as many as five

40. separate, nearby cottages

41. Answers may vary. Possible answer: They can read about them or they can be passed down by oral tradition.

42. Answers may vary. Possible answer: In extended families, the traditions were passed down from one generation to another, probably in the form of stories.

CHAPTER 8

World Explorer

GEOGRAPHY TOOLS AND CONCEPTS

BOOK 3

A. KEY TERMS

Fill in the blanks by writing the letter of the correct term. You will not use all the terms.

    a. cardinal direction
    b. degree
    c. Equator
    d. geography
    e. globe
    f. latitude
    g. meridian
    h. projection

1. _____ Geographers identify imaginary east-west circles, or _____ lines around the globe.

2. _____ Halfway between the North and the South poles, the _____ circles the globe.

3. _____ The study of the Earth is called _____ .

4. _____ The unit of measure used to determine an absolute location on a map or a globe is a(n) _____ .

5. _____ A representation of the Earth's rounded surface on a flat piece of paper is called a(n) _____ .

Match the definitions with the terms. Write the correct letter in each blank. You will not use all the terms.

    a. compass rose
    b. distortion
    c. Equator
    d. geography
    e. key
    f. longitude
    g. parallel
    h. projection

6. _____ the study of the Earth

7. _____ a type of imaginary line that circles the globe from north to south

8. _____ a change in the accuracy of shapes and distances

9. _____ a map feature that shows the four cardinal directions

10. _____ the section of a map that explains symbols for the map features

B. KEY CONCEPTS

Write the letter of the correct answer in each blank.

11. _____ Through their study of the Earth, geographers learn how the Earth and its people affect
   a. human health.   c. each other.
   b. the solar system.   d. political systems.

12. _____ To learn more about the Earth, geographers organize information according to what themes?
   a. region, population, and place
   b. latitude, longitude, and movement
   c. location, population, and longitude
   d. location, place, human-environment interaction, movement, and regions

13. _____ Which pair of basic questions guides geographers in their work?
   a. Where are things located? Why are they there?
   b. What is the climate? Why has it changed?
   c. When did the Earth form? What is it made from?
   d. Who lived where? When did they move?

14. _____ What do geographers learn by studying the theme of human-environment interaction?
   a. how people move from one region to another
   b. how cultural features define a location
   c. how people and the environment affect each other
   d. how regions differ from each other

15. _____ Latitude and longitude lines help geographers identify
   a. absolute location.   c. the Earth's distance from the sun.
   b. the depths of oceans.   d. the heights of mountains.

16. _____ The most accurate way to show the Earth's continents and bodies of water is with a
   a. Mercator projection.   c. Robinson projection.
   b. globe.   d. conformal map.

17. _____ Which of the following statements explains why there are always distortions in a map?
   a. Maps are flat and the Earth is round.
   b. Small towns are hard to represent on a map.
   c. Mountains or plains don't show up on a map.
   d. Maps are too small to hold enough information.

18. _____ A distorted map may change the shape of
   a. a globe.   c. the Prime Meridian.
   b. the Equator.   d. some land masses.

19. _____ The gaps in an interrupted projection map make it hard to
    a. carry in a back pack.
    b. determine the size of land masses correctly.
    c. figure distances correctly.
    d. read borders clearly.

20. _____ Which of the following things would geographers be most likely to study?
    a. the moon
    b. the planets
    c. landforms and their locations
    d. chemicals and chemical reactions

21. _____ Geographers study how people
    a. and the Earth affect each other.
    b. interact with each other.
    c. and animals communicate.
    d. learn.

22. _____ What themes do geographers use to organize information?
    a. population and size of cities
    b. location, place, human-environment interaction, movement, and regions
    c. population and transportation
    d. climate and occupation

23. _____ Geographers are able to pinpoint the location of a place from east to west by using
    a. latitude lines.
    b. the Equator.
    c. longitude lines.
    d. parallel lines.

24. _____ Geographers study regions so that they can
    a. get people to move there.
    b. change the cultures.
    c. understand folk music.
    d. make comparisons between areas.

25. _____ A globe is more accurate than a map because a globe can show
    a. the true shapes of continents and oceans.
    b. city streets.
    c. a distorted view of the Earth.
    d. a particular region in great detail.

26. _____ Flat maps were invented because it was impossible to make a globe that was
    a. pretty enough for people to want.
    b. big enough to fit the oceans on.
    c. complete enough to use and convenient enough to carry.
    d. strong enough to last.

27. _____ Why do flat maps distort shapes of land masses?
    a. No one is sure where the Equator really is.
    b. The Earth is round, not flat.
    c. The paper shrinks with time.
    d. Land masses are always shifting.

28. _____ What is the best way to find out the subject of a map?
    a. Find the map key.
    b. Study the scale.
    c. Study the compass rose.
    d. Read the title.

C. CRITICAL THINKING

Answer the following questions in the space provided, on the back of this paper or on a separate sheet of paper.

29. Understanding Central Issues: How do geographers use the theme of regions to organize information about the Earth?

30. Making Comparisons: What are some of the advantages and disadvantages of using only a map or only a globe to present information about the Earth?

31. Understanding Central Issues: Explain how the theme of movement helps geographers learn more about the Earth and its people.

32. Drawing Conclusions: If you were planning a two-day car trip to a different state, would you take a map or a globe to guide you? Explain your decision.

D. SKILL: EXPRESSING PROBLEMS CLEARLY

The paragraph below discusses some of the problems with a Mercator projection. Read the paragraph and think about the problems. Then answer the questions on the lines provided.

When Mercator made his map, he had to make some decisions. He made sure that the shapes of the land masses and ocean areas were similar to the shapes on a globe. But he had to stretch the spaces between the longitudes. This distorted the sizes of some of the land masses on his map. Land near the Equator was about right, but land near the poles became much larger than it should be.

33. Would you be able to determine the true shape of land masses and oceans by reading a Mercator projection? Why or why not?_____

_____

34. Would you be able to use a Mercator projection to determine the true size of a landmass near the Equator? Why or why not? _____

_____

35. Would you be able to use a Mercator projection to determine the true size of a landmass near the North Pole? Why or why not? _____

_____

36. Would you be able to use a Mercator projection to compare the sizes of different land masses?_____

_____

37. Write a sentence that expresses the problem with a Mercator projection. _____

_____

The paragraphs below discuss some of the problems with flat maps. Read the paragraphs and think about the problems. Then answer the questions on the lines provided.

Geographers call a Mercator projection a conformal map. It shows correct shapes but not true distances or sizes. Other mapmakers have used other techniques to try to draw an accurate map. For instance, an equal-area map shows the correct sizes of land masses but their shapes are altered. The Peters projection is an equal-area map.

Mapmakers have tried other techniques. The interrupted projection is like the ripped peel of an orange. By creating gaps in the picture of the world, mapmakers have shown the size and shape of land accurately. But the gaps make it impossible to figure distances correctly. You could not use this projection to chart a course across an ocean.

38. What types of map show the correct shapes of land masses?_____

_____

39. What types of map show the correct sizes of land masses? _____

_____

40. What type of map does not show correct distances? _____

_____

41. What type of map shows correct sizes, shapes, and distances? _____

_____

42. Write a sentence that expresses the problem with each type of map described in the paragraphs above. _____

_____

ANSWER KEY

1. f	2. c	3. d	4. b	5. h
6. d	7. f	8. b	9. a	10. e
11. c	12. d	13. a	14. c	15. a
16. b	17. a	18. d	19. c	20. c
21. a	22. b	23. c	24. d	25. a
26. c	27. b	28. d		

29. Answers may vary. Possible answer: The theme of regions allows comparisons to be made between areas that share certain similarities in things such as land and climate.

30. Answers may vary. Possible answer: Because a globe is round, like the Earth, it shows the continents and oceans much as they really are, although to scale. However, it's impossible to make a globe complete enough for people to use and small enough to be convenient, which is why maps are sometimes more useful. Maps, however, show land with some distortion.

31. Answers may vary. Possible answer: Movement concerns the relationships among different places, including how movement changes the cultural environment.

32. Answers may vary. Possible answer: I would take a map. Maps are easy to carry and can give the kind of detailed information, such as highway exits and road signs, that would be useful in a car trip. Globes are more difficult to travel with and do not provide detailed information.

33. yes, because the shapes of land masses and ocean areas are similar to those on a globe

34. yes, because land near the Equator is not very distorted on this map

35. no, because the size of land near the poles is very distorted

36. no, because while land near the Equator is shown accurately, the land masses near the poles are shown as much larger than they really are

37. Answers may vary. One possible response: Although a Mercator map can be used to determine the shapes of oceans and land masses and the sizes of areas close to the Equator, it distorts the sizes of areas near the poles.

38. conformal (or Mercator projection) maps and interrupted projection maps

39. equal-area (or Peters projection) maps and interrupted projection maps

40. interrupted projection maps

41. none of them

42. Answers may vary. Possible answer: Neither conformal maps, equal-area maps, nor interrupted projection maps can show the correct sizes and shapes of, and distances between, the Earth's land masses.

Chapter 2 ■ Earth's Physical Geography

A. KEY TERMS

Match the definitions with the terms. Write the correct letter in each blank. You will not use all the terms.

a. atmosphere
b. plateau
c. plate
d. precipitation
e. revolution
f. temperature
g. vegetation
h. vertical climate

1. _____ the degree of hotness or coldness

2. _____ a thick blanket of gases that surrounds the Earth

3. _____ a huge piece of the outer skin of the Earth's crust

4. _____ plants that grow in an area naturally

5. _____ one trip of the Earth around the sun

Complete each sentence by writing the letter of the correct term in the blank. You will not use all the terms.

a. atmosphere
b. axis
c. orbit
d. plains
e. temperature
f. tundra
g. vegetation
h. weather

6. _____ Wide, flat areas near the coast are called lowlands, or_____ .

7. _____ The Earth moves around the sun on a path called a(n) _____ .

8. _____ The day-to-day changes in the air are called _____ .

9. _____ Life on the Earth is made possible because of the _____ , or surrounding blanket of gases.

10. _____ When scientists know information about a climate, they can predict what plants, or _____ , will grow there.

B. KEY CONCEPTS

Write the letter of the correct answer in each blank.

11. _____ Why is the sun important to the planets in the solar system?
     a. It provides heat and light to the planets.
     b. It creates the gases that make up the planets.
     c. It orbits the planets.
     d. It is close to the planets.

12. _____ One result of the Earth's tilt is that the Earth has
     a. winds.   c. seasons.
     b. weather.   d. daylight.

13. _____ Most of the Earth's surface is covered by
     a. mountains.   c. land.
     b. plateaus.   d. water.

14. _____ As the huge pieces of the Earth's crust move, the Earth's surfaces
     a. collapse.   c. melt.
     b. change.   d. shrink.

15. _____ The Earth's climate is affected by latitude, landforms, and a combination of
     a. ice and sand.   c. ocean depth and sea life.
     b. wind and water.   d. volcanoes and earthquakes.

16. _____ The vegetation in a humid continental climate includes primarily
     a. forests and grasslands.   c. lichens and mosses.
     b. ice and snow.   d. different kinds of cacti.

17. _____ There is a great deal of vegetation in a rain forest because there is
     a. a long winter.   c. a lot of sunlight and water.
     b. a cool, dry climate.   d. a vast tundra.

18. _____ Where are moderate climates generally found?
     a. high in the mountains   c. in middle latitudes
     b. in low latitudes   d. near the Earth's poles

19. _____ Without wind and water working together, the Earth would
     a. freeze.   c. overheat.
     b. stand still.   d. rotate.

20. _____ The Earth travels completely around the sun every
     a. month.   c. year.
     b. day.   d. two weeks.

21. _____ The amount of heat that the Northern and Southern hemispheres receive during the year depends on
   a. the position of the moon.
   b. the Earth's tilt.
   c. the number of planets in the solar system.
   d. the Equator.

22. _____ Mountains, plateaus, and plains are types of
   a. plate tectonics.   c. magma.
   b. landforms.   d. ridges.

23. _____ The causes of weathering are
   a. erosion and plate movement.   c. night and day.
   b. volcanoes and earthquakes.   d. wind, rain, and ice.

24. _____ What is one factor that influences the climate of an area?
   a. the positions of the planets   c. the size
   b. the day of the week   d. the latitude

25. _____ One reason the Earth doesn't overheat is because of
   a. the movement of air.   c. the heights of mountains.
   b. the position of the moon.   d. the flatness of plains.

26. _____ What are the major climate regions on Earth?
   a. hot and dry
   b. wet and cold
   c. mountainous and flat
   d. tropical, dry, moderate, continental, and polar

27. _____ Thousands of kinds of plants grow in the rain forest because there is a good supply of
   a. heat, light, and water.   c. cool air currents.
   b. farmers to plant crops.   d. fertile soil.

28. _____ Desert vegetation adapts to the hot environment by
   a. releasing a great deal of moisture.
   b. producing dense forests.
   c. producing flowers when the sun shines.
   d. releasing little moisture.

C. CRITICAL THINKING

Answer the following questions in the space provided, on the back of this paper or on a separate sheet of paper.

29. Recognizing Cause and Effect: How do the Earth's tilt and orbit cause the seasons to change?

30. Distinguishing Fact From Opinion: Identify the kind of climate that you live in. Then write two facts and two opinions about that climate.

31. Identifying Central Issues: What are two major forces that shape and reshape the Earth? Describe how each force works.

32. Recognizing Cause and Effect: How have plants in continental and dry climates adapted to their environment?

D. SKILL: USING GEOGRAPHY GRAPHS

Use the graph below to answer the following questions. Write your answers on the lines provided.

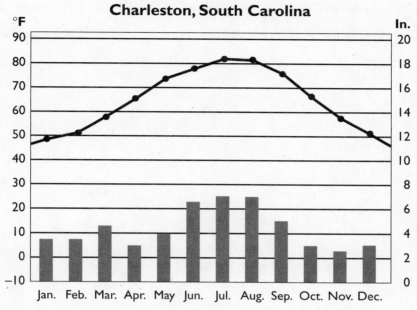

Charleston, South Carolina

Curved line shows temperatures in Fahrenheit degrees. **Bars** show precipitation in inches.

33. What is the coldest month of the year in Charleston? What is the hottest? _____
_____

34. Which months have the most precipitation in Charleston? Which month has the least? _____
_____

35. What appears to be the relationship between temperature and precipitation in Charleston? _
_____

36. Between which months does the greatest increase in precipitation occur? _____
_____

37. According to this graph, how would you describe Charleston's climate—as moderate or polar? _____

38. Which months have the same amount of precipitation? _____
_____

39. How much warmer is it in July than in April? _____
_____
_____

40. How much does the temperature change between August and September? _____

_____

41. Is Charleston's climate moderate or tropical? _____

_____

42. Which season is the wettest in Charleston? _____

_____

ANSWER KEY

1. f	2. a	3. c	4. g	5. e
6. d	7. c	8. h	9. a	10. g
11. a	12. c	13. d	14. b	15. b
16. a	17. c	18. c	19. c	20. c
21. b	22. b	23. d	24. d	25. a
26. d	27. a	28. d		

29. Answers may vary. Possible answer: The Earth's tilt and orbit affect the way temperatures change during seasons. The amount of heat that a part of the planet receives depends on the planet's tilt. When the North Pole tilts toward the sun, the Northern Hemisphere receives more direct sunlight, so it is summer. At the same time, the Southern Hemisphere receives less direct sunlight, so it's cooler and the season is winter.

30. Answers will vary. Possible answer: Facts—Moderate climates have a wide variety of vegetation. They are found in middle latitudes. Opinions—Moderate climates are the best climates. People in moderate climates are happier than people in polar climates.

31. Answers will vary. Possible answer: Plate tectonics shape the Earth because as the Earth's plates move, the shape of the Earth's surface is altered. Volcanoes shape the Earth because when the molten rock that explodes out of them cools, it creates new land.

32. Answers may vary. Possible answer: In the humid continental climate, summer temperatures are moderate, and winters can be cold. Vegetation grows during warmer parts of the year. Vegetation in deserts and other dry places have adaptations that prevent loss of water.

33. The coldest month is January. The hottest month is July.

34. July and August have the most precipitation. October has the least.

35. The hottest months have the most precipitation.

36. The greatest increase occurs between May and June.

37. Charleston has a moderate climate.

38. January and February; April, October, and December.

39. It is about 15° warmer in July than it is in April.

40. The temperature drops 5 degrees between August and September.

41. Charleston has a moderate climate.

42. Summer.

A. KEY TERMS

Complete each sentence by writing the letter of the correct term in the blank. You will not use all the terms.

a. birthrate
b. demographer
c. immigrant
d. life expectancy
e. migration
f. population
g. "push-pull" theory
h. rural area

1. _____ In a country with a high _____ , or total number of people, schools and public transportation can become overcrowded.

2. _____ A scientist who studies the people who live in certain areas is called a(n) _____ .

3. _____ A person who moves to a new country in order to settle there is called a(n) _____ .

4. _____ The number of live births each year per 1,000 people, or the _____ , varies from one country to another.

5. _____ When job opportunities appear in one region and disappear in another, a _____ , or mass movement of people may occur.

Match the definitions with the terms. Write the correct letter in each blank. You will not use all the terms.

a. death rate
b. Green Revolution
c. life expectancy
d. population density
e. population distribution
f. "push-pull" theory
g. rural area
h. urbanization

6. _____ the way people are spread out over an area

7. _____ the movement of people to cities and the growth of cities

8. _____ the average number of years a person is expected to live

9. _____ a place where few people live

10. _____ the average number of people who live in a square mile of land

B. KEY CONCEPTS

Write the letter of the correct answer in each blank.

11. _____ People tend to settle near places that have
    a. high mountains.
    b. extremely cold or hot climates.
    c. waterways that can be used for trade and travel.
    d. few natural resources.

12. _____ Why does the large continent of Australia have a relatively small population?
    a. Most of the country is covered by desert or dry grassland.
    b. Half of it is under water.
    c. There is too much swampy land.
    d. It is nearly covered in ice.

13. _____ Population density is the number of people that live in a region divided by
    a. the number of roads.
    b. the number of waterways.
    c. the number of square miles in the region.
    d. the number of people who used to live there.

14. _____ How do demographers figure out population growth?
    a. by studying the level of a water supply
    b. by comparing birthrates and death rates
    c. by counting all the new buildings
    d. by asking people how many children they have

15. _____ The world's population is rapidly increasing due to
    a. better health care.   c. global warming.
    b. public transportation.   d. the water supply.

16. _____ One serious problem caused by the growing population is
    a. a higher death rate.   c. too much energy production.
    b. fewer available jobs.   d. fewer medical advancements.

17. _____ The "push-pull" theory is used by scientists to explain
    a. how people fight.   c. immigration.
    b. mountains.   d. farming methods.

18. _____ Why did many people leave Ireland for the United States in the 1800s?
    a. They wanted to visit American cities.
    b. Ireland was experiencing a famine.
    c. They were escaping from religious persecution.
    d. There were too few schools in their native land.

19. _____ Large numbers of people have moved from rural areas to urban areas because they want to
a. learn many languages.
b. give their children more opportunities.
c. live life at a slower pace.
d. raise animals.

20. _____ What is one reason why more than 81 percent of the Earth's population lives in Asia, Europe, and North America?
a. These continents are covered by rain forests.
b. These continents have little rainfall.
c. These continents have sources of fresh water.
d. These continents have large deserts.

21. _____ Population distribution is uneven because people want to live in areas that have
a. thick rain forests.   c. dry grasslands.
b. extreme climates.   d. rich resources.

22. _____ A country that has a high population density has
a. few people under 65 years old.   c. some crowded areas.
b. a lot of land per person.   d. few urban areas.

23. _____ By comparing birthrates and death rates, demographers figure out
a. population density.   c. population growth.
b. where people are likely to move.   d. why people migrate.

24. _____ Because of an increase in food supply and better medical care, the world's population recently has
a. remained the same.   c. made educational gains.
b. slowly decreased.   d. rapidly increased.

25. _____ One problem faced by the world's population today is
a. too many jobs.
b. not enough schools.
c. a decline in foreign trade.
d. a decrease in the use of natural resources.

26. _____ To explain the reasons for immigration, demographers use
a. life expectancies.   c. the "push-pull" theory.
b. birthrates and death rates.   d. compasses.

27. _____ Why did many people leave Vietnam for the United States?
a. They knew that they spoke the same language.
b. They didn't want to live under the new government.
c. The cities in their country were too small.
d. They preferred the warmer weather in the United States.

28. _____ Many people leave the country for the city because they want
a. to improve their health.   c. to find jobs.
b. to increase food production.   d. to own land.

C. CRITICAL THINKING

Answer the following questions in the space provided, on the back of this paper or on a separate sheet of paper.

29. Identifying Central Issues: On what continents do most of the world's people live? In your answer, list what factors cause people to settle in a particular place.

30. Comparing and Contrasting: How does the growth of the world's population today compare with its growth 100 years ago?

31. Drawing Conclusions: What problems might result from the world's rapidly increasing population? Use facts from the chapter to support your conclusions.

32. Identifying Central Issues: How does the "push-pull" theory explain immigration? In your answer, tell what the theory is.

D. SKILL: USING DISTRIBUTION MAPS

Use the map below to answer the following questions. Write your answers in the blanks provided.

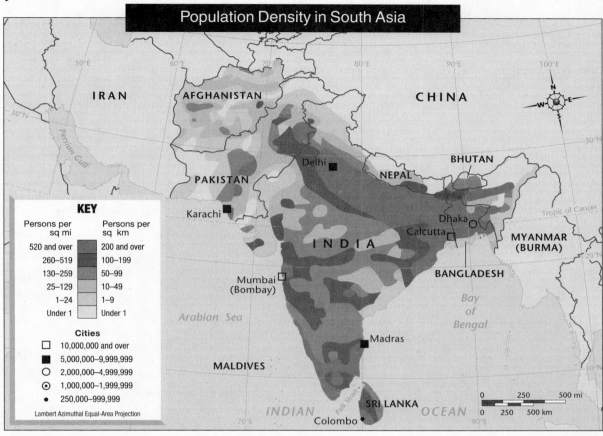

Population Density in South Asia

33. How is population represented on this map?_____

34. In general, how would you compare the population density of India with the population density of Afghanistan? _____

35. Is the population higher in Mumbai (Bombay) or Hyderabad? _____

36. What three countries have the highest population densities? _____

_____

37. What is the average population density in Sri Lanka?_____

38. How does the key help you understand the information on the map? _____

_____

39. Name two countries that have areas with population densities of under one person per square mile._____

40. In general, how would you compare the population density of Sri Lanka with the population density of Pakistan? _____

_____

41. What two cities have more than 10,000,000 people?_____

_____

42. What is the population density of Hyderabad? _____

_____

ANSWER KEY

1. f	2. b	3. c	4. a	5. e
6. e	7. h	8. c	9. g	10. d
11. c	12. a	13. c	14. b	15. a
16. b	17. c	18. b	19. b	20. c
21. d	22. c	23. c	24. d	25. b
26. c	27. b	28. c		

29. Answers may vary. Possible answer: Most of the world's population lives in Asia, Europe, and North America. People tend to settle where there are natural resources, waterways, and climates that are neither too hot nor too cold.

30. Answers may vary. Possible answer: One hundred years ago, the world's population was growing more slowly than it is today. One hundred years ago, farmers worked without modern machinery, and food supplies were scarce; more people died of diseases because fewer medicines were available; and the death rate was higher than the birthrate. Today, the world's population is soaring, largely because scientific methods have increased the world's food supply, and medical advances have increased the number of babies who live at birth and the number of years people live.

31. Answers may vary. Possible answer: The rapid growth in the world's population has led to serious problems for many poorer nations. These problems have arisen because in some parts of the world, there isn't enough food or water; there isn't enough money to import goods; people can't find jobs; there are too few schools; adequate housing is scarce and expensive; and transportation and sanitation are inadequate.

32. Answers may vary. Possible answer: The "push-pull" theory is used to explain why people leave their homes and move to another country. According to this theory, people migrate because certain things, such as economic or political reasons, "push" them to leave. Similarly, people can be "pulled" to migrate to another country because of factors such as better living conditions or a culture, climate, and vegetation similar to those found in their native lands.

33. Different shades of gray

34. India is an area of high population density; fewer people live in Afghanistan.

35. Mumbai (Bombay)

36. India, Sri Lanka, and Bangladesh

37. 260–519 people per square mile

38. It explains how patterns on the map relate to the area's population density.

39. Afghanistan, Pakistan, India, Nepal, or Bhutan

40. Sri Lanka has more areas with high population densities than Pakistan does.

41. Mumbai (Bombay) and Calcutta

42. 25–129 people per square mile

CHAPTER 3

A. KEY TERMS

Match the definitions with the terms. Write the correct letter in each blank. You will not use all the terms.

    a. agriculture
    b. capitalism
    c. cultural diffusion
    d. direct democracy
    e. ethics
    f. extended family
    g. social structure
    h. technology

1. ____ several generations of relatives living together

2. ____ the tools people use to change their natural resources

3. ____ a form of government in which people participate directly in decision making

4. ____ the way people in a culture are organized into smaller groups

5. ____ the movement of customs and ideas from one place to another

Complete each sentence by writing the letter of the correct term in the blank. You will not use all the terms.

    a. acculturation
    b. cultural landscape
    c. culture
    d. economy
    e. extended family
    f. monarchy
    g. nuclear family
    h. representative democracy
    i. technology

6. ____ When one country accepts, borrows, or exchanges ideas with another, ____ takes place.

7. ____ People can change their environment by using the ____ that is available to them.

8. ____ A system for producing, distributing, and consuming wealth is called a(n) ____ .

9. ____ In many industrial nations, such as the United States, parents and their children live in a(n) ____ .

10. ____ Citizens elect certain people to make laws in a(n) ____ .

B. KEY CONCEPTS

Write the letter of the correct answer in each blank.

11. _____ People's occupations, their behavior, and their beliefs are a part of their
    - a. government.
    - b. climate.
    - c. technology.
    - d. culture.

12. _____ When geographers study the theme of interaction, they learn
    - a. how schools are run.
    - b. how people and their environment affect each other.
    - c. how agriculture develops.
    - d. how the climate changes.

13. _____ The social unit most responsible for teaching the customs and traditions of a culture is
    - a. the family.
    - b. the government.
    - c. the army.
    - d. the capitalists.

14. _____ Three important features of a culture are
    - a. weather, technology, and writing.
    - b. language, values, and religious beliefs.
    - c. economy, population growth, and climate.
    - d. natural resources, landforms, and climate.

15. _____ Communism, socialism, and capitalism are examples of
    - a. political systems.
    - b. economic systems.
    - c. educational methods.
    - d. technological achievements.

16. _____ Three examples of forms of government are
    - a. constitutional monarchy, dictatorship, and literature.
    - b. democracy, capitalism, and constitutional monarchy.
    - c. monarchy, extended family, and population.
    - d. monarchy, democracy, and dictatorship.

17. _____ Which of the following changes as a result of discoveries and inventions, shifts in the natural environment, and new ideas?
    - a. culture
    - b. landforms
    - c. climate
    - d. atmosphere

18. _____ Communication around the world takes place quickly and easily because we live in a
    - a. nuclear family.
    - b. cultural landscape.
    - c. global village.
    - d. social structure.

19. ____ The rapid exchange of ideas in the computer age has increased
    a. the growth of communism.
    b. the number of patriarchal families.
    c. the rate of cultural change.
    d. the number of constitutional monarchies.

20. ____ The development of culture went through what stages?
    a. early, middle, and late
    b. the invention of tools, the discovery of fire, the growth of farming, and the use of writing
    c. war and peace
    d. the invention of the wheel, the beginning of dance, and the use of telescopes

21. ____ What was it called when people went from hunting and gathering their foods to relying on farming and herding?
    a. the age of discovery
    b. the global village
    c. the start of world history
    d. the agricultural revolution

22. ____ The most basic social unit of any culture is
    a. the family.
    b. the university.
    c. the businesses.
    d. the government.

23. ____ Cultures in which women have the most authority in the family are called
    a. matriarchal.
    b. democratic.
    c. patriarchal.
    d. communist.

24. ____ Three nations that have representative democracies are
    a. Sweden, Denmark, and Great Britain.
    b. Cuba, China, and North Korea.
    c. Russia, Canada, and China.
    d. The United States, Canada, and Israel.

25. ____ What are the main economic systems in the world today?
    a. communism, capitalism, and democracy
    b. democracy, socialism, and constitutional monarchy
    c. communism, monarchy, and democracy
    d. communism, socialism, and capitalism

26. ____ Democracy, monarchy, and dictatorship are examples of
    a. economic systems.
    b. kinds of social classes.
    c. forms of governments.
    d. kinds of families.

27. ____ Changes in our natural environment, technological discoveries and inventions, and the spread of new ideas all cause
    a. population density changes.
    b. an economic depression.
    c. an economic inflation.
    d. cultural changes.

CHAPTER 4

28. ____ In a global village, people from all over the world can
    a. communicate quickly and easily.
    b. remain culturally isolated.
    c. limit cultural diffusion.
    d. influence government decision making.

C. CRITICAL THINKING

Answer the following questions in the space provided, on the back of this paper or on a separate sheet of paper.

29. Comparing and Contrasting: What are the similarities and the differences between a constitutional monarchy and rule by a dictator?

30. Recognizing Cause and Effect: Explain how technology can affect culture. Use an example in your explanation.

31. Comparing and Contrasting: What are the similarities and the differences between a direct democracy and a representative democracy?

32. Recognizing Cause and Effect: Explain how a change in the environment can affect culture. Use an example in your explanation.

D. SKILL: LOCATING INFORMATION

Imagine you are writing a report about Hong Kong. Refer to the pyramid of knowledge below to answer the following questions on the lines provided.

Pyramid of Information About a Culture

Specific Information
travel books, articles by visitors, interviews with visitors or members of the culture

Somewhat Specific Information
books about the culture, magazine articles about the culture

General Information
encyclopedias, almanacs, atlases

33. What kind of information should be found at the base of the pyramid? _____

_____

34. At what level of the pyramid would you put articles written by people who have visited Hong Kong and interviews with people who live there? Why? _____

_____

35. What sources would you use for the middle of the pyramid? _____

_____

36. When preparing your report, which level of the pyramid would you use first? Why? _____

_____

37. In general, how do you think the pyramid of knowledge can help you with your schoolwork? _____

_____

38. Where on the pyramid would you put general information that you found in almanacs, encyclopedias, and atlases? _____

_____

39. Where would you put information you got from people who had lived in or visited Senegal? Why? _____

_____

40. From what kinds of sources would you get information to put in the middle level of the pyramid?_____

_____

41. Which level of the pyramid would provide the information you would use in the final stages of preparing your report? Why? _____

_____

42. Which level of the pyramid is most likely to provide quotes you could use in your report?___

_____

ANSWER KEY

1. f	2. h	3. d	4. g	5. c
6. a	7. i	8. d	9. g	10. h
11. d	12. b	13. a	14. b	15. b
16. d	17. a	18. c	19. c	20. b
21. d	22. a	23. a	24. d	25. d
26. c	27. d	28. a		

29. Answers will vary. Possible answer: In both forms of government, a single person is the most important person in the government. However, in a constitutional monarchy, the king or queen is often only a symbol of the country. Their actual power is limited by a constitution. A constitution sets laws and determines the government's power. In a country ruled by a dictator, there is no constitution to limit the dictator. The dictator has total power over the country.

30. Answers will vary. Possible answer: Technology affects culture by causing cultural change. For example, computers change how and where people work.

31. Answers will vary. Possible answer: In both kinds of democracy, people have a voice in how things are run. In a direct democracy, everyone participates in running the country's affairs. In a representative democracy, citizens elect people to run the country's affairs.

32. Answers will vary. Possible answer: A change in environment can affect the way people work, eat, and dress. For example, if the climate becomes much colder, people may start to wear heavier, warmer clothing.

33. general information

34. I would put this information at the top level because this is very specific material.

35. I would use sources that give somewhat specific information, such as books and magazine articles about the culture.

36. I would use the bottom level first, because I would want to start with general information.

37. It can be used with an assignment that requires research about a specific topic.

38. This information would go in the bottom level of the pyramid.

39. I would put this at the top of the pyramid because it is the most specific information.

40. Books and magazine articles about the culture would provide the information for the middle level of the pyramid.

41. I would use the information in the top level last because that is the most specific information.

42. The top level.

A. KEY TERMS

Complete each sentence by writing the correct term in the blank. You will not use all the terms.

a. commercial farming
b. developed nation
c. developing nation
d. foreign aid
e. plantation
f. recyclable resource
g. renewable resource
h. subsistence farming

1. _____ Workers grow a single crop on a specialized farm called a(n) _____ .

2. _____ A country with modern industries and a well-developed economy is called a(n) _____ .

3. _____ When farmers raise only enough food and animals for their own families, they are practicing _____ .

4. _____ Governments help one another by providing gifts and loans of money and military support called _____ .

5. _____ A resource that can be replaced is a(n) _____ .

Match the definitions with the terms. Write the correct letter in each blank. You will not use all the terms.

a. commercial farming
b. deforestation
c. developing nation
d. ecosystem
e. nonrenewable resource
f. ozone
g. recyclable resource
h. renewable resource

6. _____ a resource that can be replaced

7. _____ agricultural work done by companies that own huge farms

8. _____ a layer of gases in the upper part of our atmosphere

9. _____ a material in our environment that cannot be replaced

10. _____ a community of living things and their environment

B. KEY CONCEPTS

Write the letter of the correct answer in each blank.

11. _____ A natural resource is any useful material that humans
      a. can make.   c. can find in developed countries.
      b. cannot recycle.   d. can find in the environment.

12. _____ Minerals, coal, and natural gases are examples of
      a. renewable resources.   c. nonrenewable resources.
      b. second-level products.   d. synthetic materials.

13. _____ Resources that were created over millions of years from the remains of prehistoric plants and animals are called
      a. manufactured resources.   c. renewable resources.
      b. greenhouses gases.   d. fossil fuels.

14. _____ In the second stage of resource development, a person makes
      a. deliveries of products.
      b. products directly from natural resources.
      c. raw materials into things that people use.
      d. fossil fuels.

15. _____ Because commercial farms use modern technology, a small number of workers can
      a. feed only the farmers' families.
      b. raise enough food for an entire country.
      c. turn a developed nation into an undeveloped one.
      d. live without goods and services.

16. _____ What is one effect of the rapid population growth in developing countries?
      a. Food is being overproduced.
      b. Technological resources have expanded.
      c. Foreign aid is unnecessary.
      d. Resources are strained.

17. _____ In South America, rain forests are most threatened by
      a. relocation.   c. acid rain.
      b. drought.   d. deforestation.

18. _____ In order to reduce acid rain, Canada and the United States now have laws that require
      a. certain factories to reduce pollution.
      b. alternatives to ozone-destroying chemicals.
      c. the use of cheap energy sources.
      d. the protection of endangered species.

19. _____ What is one cause of global warming?
   a. the use of hydroelectric power
   b. the burning of fossil fuels
   c. the use of pesticides
   d. subsistence farming

20. _____ Soil, water, and minerals are examples of
   a. fossil fuels.
   b. vegetation.
   c. natural resources.
   d. synthetic resources.

21. _____ Two examples of nonrenewable resources are
   a. corn and wheat.
   b. coal and natural gas.
   c. pigs and goats.
   d. wind and water.

22. _____ Materials created over millions of years from the remains of prehistoric plants and animals are
   a. manufactured resources.
   b. synthetic resources.
   c. renewable resources.
   d. fossil fuels.

23. _____ What is the first stage of resource development?
   a. making raw materials into things that people use
   b. using the land and resources directly to make products
   c. distributing products to people who want them
   d. creating communications systems

24. _____ Countries with little industry are called
   a. industrialized nations.
   b. prehistoric nations.
   c. developed nations.
   d. developing nations.

25. _____ Subsistence farms raise enough food to
   a. feed only the farmers' families.
   b. feed an entire country.
   c. export food to other countries.
   d. turn a developing nation into a developed one.

26. _____ As a result of their rapid growth in population, many developing countries are
   a. decreasing foreign aid.
   b. using renewable resources.
   c. straining their resources.
   d. limiting their pollution.

27. _____ Examples of raw materials include
   a. fish and clothing.
   b. trees and cotton.
   c. bread and paper.
   d. steel and boards.

28. _____ Fertilizer, pesticides, and waste products are substances that
   a. produce acid rain.
   b. create greenhouse gases.
   c. encourage commercial farming.
   d. pollute the water.

C. CRITICAL THINKING

Answer the following questions in the space provided, on the back of this paper or on a separate sheet of paper.

29. Identifying Main Ideas: What are renewable resources? In your answer, give two examples of renewable resources.

30. Drawing Conclusions: Which of the three stages of resource development do you think subsistence farmers participate in? In your answer, explain each stage of resource development.

31. Identifying Main Ideas: What are nonrenewable resources? In your answer, give two examples of nonrenewable resources.

32. Drawing Conclusions: Which of the three stages of resource development do you think is most common in the United States? In your answer, explain each stage of resource development.

D. SKILL: WRITING FOR A PURPOSE

Imagine that you are going to write an essay trying to persuade others to share your opinion on the subject of using fossil fuels. Read the selection below. Then answer the questions on the lines provided.

The summer of 1995 in New England was unusually hot and dry. Temperatures stayed above 90 degrees for weeks. Heat and drought caused water shortages and killed crops. Some scientists feared this was the start of global warming, a slow increase in the Earth's temperature. Global warming may be caused by gases like carbon dioxide that are released into the air. They are called greenhouse gases. Developed countries produce about 75 percent of these gases. They are released when fossil fuels burn. These fuels produce most of the world's electricity. They also run the world's 550 million cars, buses, and trucks. Developing countries produce these gases when they burn forests to clear land and use wood for heating and cooking.

33. What is your opinion about the use of fossil fuels? _____
_____
_____

34. Who would you like to share your opinion with? Why? _____
_____
_____

35. What two reasons can you give to support your opinion? _____
_____
_____

36. What is one fact that can support the reasons for your opinion? _____
_____
_____

37. Write a sentence that would appeal to the emotions of your audience. _____
_____
_____

Imagine that you are going to write an essay trying to persuade others to share your opinion on the subject of endangered species. Read the selection below. Then answer the questions on the lines provided.

Extinction has many causes. People may build houses or businesses on land that is the habitat of particular animals or plants. The air, soil, or water may be too polluted for a species of plant or animal to survive. Sometimes, a species is hunted until it disappears. Usually, more than one thing endangers a species. The goal of the Endangered Species Act is to stop extinction. But people disagree about the law. Some think that humans should be allowed to use natural resources as they need them. Others think people should stop doing things that hurt other species.

38. What is your opinion about government efforts to protect endangered species? _____

_____

_____

39. Who would you like to share your opinion with? Why? _____

_____

_____

40. What two reasons can you give to support your opinion? _____

_____

_____

41. What is one fact that can support the reasons for your opinion? _____

_____

_____

42. Write a sentence that might appeal to the emotions of your audience._____

_____

_____

ANSWER KEY

1. e	2. b	3. h	4. d	5. g
6. h	7. a	8. f	9. e	10. d
11. c	12. c	13. d	14. c	15. b
16. d	17. d	18. a	19. b	20. c
21. b	22. d	23. b	24. d	25. a
26. c	27. b	28. d		

29. Answers may vary. Possible answer: A renewable resource is one that can be replaced, such as a tree, an animal, and other living things.

30. Answers may vary. Possible answer: In the first stage, people use land and resources directly to make products. In the second stage, people make raw materials into things they can use by manufacturing. In the third stage, people distribute the products they make to the consumers who need them. This involves the development of service industries, including transportation and communications. I think that subsistence farmers participate in the first stage of resource development. They use land to make food.

31. Answers may vary. Possible answer: A nonrenewable resource is one that cannot be replaced once it is used up. Oil and coal are two examples of nonrenewable resources.

32. Answers may vary. Possible answer: In the first stage, people use land and resources directly to make products. In the second stage, people make raw materials into things they can use by manufacturing. In the third stage, people distribute the products they make to the consumers who need them. This involves the development of service industries, including transportation and communications. The third stage of development is probably most common in the U.S.

33. Answers will vary. Possible answer: I think that the government should spend money to find more fossil fuels, not to get rid of them.

34. Answers will vary. Possible answer: I would like to share my opinion with my senator because she can vote on laws concerning fossil fuels.

35. Answers will vary. Possible answer: Fossil fuels are very important to the world's economy. Scientists aren't sure whether fossil fuels cause global warming.

36. Answers may vary. Possible answer: 550 million cars run on fossil fuels.

37. Answers may vary. Possible answer: Concern over a problem that may not even exist could endanger the American way of life.

38. Answers will vary. Possible answer: I think that the government is doing the right thing.

39. Answers will vary. Possible answer: I would like to share my opinion with my senator because she can vote on laws to protect endangered species.

40. Answers will vary. Possible answer: If these animals aren't protected they will die out, which may upset the ecosystem. Also, people should be discouraged from destroying the environment.

41. Answers may vary. Possible answer: The fact that pollution is one cause of extinction supports the fact that people will destroy the environment unless there are laws against it.

42. Answers may vary. Possible answer: As a young American, I am concerned about the way we treat the other species that share this country with us.

CHAPTER 5

Chapter 6 ■ Final Exam

A. KEY TERMS

Match the definitions the terms. Write the correct letter in each blank. You will not use all the terms.

      a. culture
      b. demographer
      c. developed nation
      d. developing nation
      e. natural resource
      f. orbit
      g. population density
      h. recyclable resource
      i. social structure

1. _____ the way of life of a group of people who share similar beliefs or customs

2. _____ a country with little industry

3. _____ the average number of people who live in a square mile of land

4. _____ any useful material found in the environment

5. _____ an oval-shaped path around the sun

Complete each sentence by writing the correct term in the blank. You will not use all the terms.

      a. acid rain
      b. cultural trait
      c. deforestation
      d. ecosystem
      e. extended family
      f. geography
      g. population distribution
      h. raw material
      i. rotation

6. _____ A community of living things and their environment is called a(n) _____ .

7. _____ In some cultures, several generations of relatives live together in a(n) _____ .

8. _____ A resource that has to be altered or changed before being used is called a(n) _____ .

9. _____ Every 24 hours the Earth completes one _____ on its axis.

10. _____ A characteristic behavior of a people, such as a language, skill, or custom passed from one generation to another, is called a(n) _____ .

CHAPTER 6

B. KEY CONCEPTS

Write the letter of the correct answer in each blank.

11. _____ What are three of the five themes that geographers use to study the Earth?
    a. meridians, geography, and culture   c. location, place, and movement
    b. regions, hemispheres, and latitude   d. parallels, longitude and latitude

12. _____ Why are flat maps sometimes used instead of globes?
    a. Globes are too inaccurate to show the Earth as it is.
    b. Globes are not detailed enough for all uses.
    c. Globes are not the same shape as the Earth.
    d. Globes are too difficult to manufacture.

13. _____ Seasons change because of the Earth's
    a. rotation.   c. atmosphere.
    b. continents and oceans.   d. tilt and orbit.

14. _____ What are the Earth's major climate regions?
    a. prairie, plateau, and dry
    b. summer, fall, winter, and spring
    c. tropical, dry, moderate, continental, and polar
    d. Equator, rain forest, and grassland

15. _____ Most of the Earth's population lives in
    a. Asia, Europe, and Africa.
    b. Australia, Europe, and North America.
    c. the Caribbean and Australia.
    d. South America.

16. _____ Demographers use the "push-pull" theory to explain
    a. where people farm.   c. why people migrate.
    b. how people live.   d. when people began to trade.

17. _____ Three important features of a culture are
    a. vegetation, climate, and seasonal change.
    b. language, values, and religious beliefs.
    c. population density, economy, and industry.
    d. industry, agriculture, and natural resources.

18. _____ Socialism, communism, and capitalism are the three major
    a. systems of government.   c. cultures.
    b. economic systems.   d. social structures.

19. _____ What is the first step that cultures take in working with resources?
    a. distributing products to people who want them
    b. processing raw materials into finished products
    c. using fossil fuels to heat homes
    d. using land and resources directly to make products

20. ____ Ocean currents have a major impact on
   a. culture and belief.
   b. vegetation.
   c. population density.
   d. Earth's climates.

21. ____ What special features help people understand the information on maps?
   a. projection and distortion
   b. compass rose, legend, and scale
   c. columns, rows, and diagonals
   d. rotation, distortion, and tilt

22. ____ When the North Pole tilts toward the sun, the Northern Hemisphere experiences
   a. more darkness.
   b. the same season as the Southern Hemisphere.
   c. autumn.
   d. summer.

23. ____ Millions of years ago Pangaea, a huge landmass, split into
   a. the seven seas.
   b. the Rocky Mountains.
   c. separate continents.
   d. separate ocean floors.

24. ____ Which three continents have a relatively small population?
   a. Asia, Europe, and North America
   b. South America, North America, and Australia
   c. Africa, Asia, and North America
   d. Australia, Africa, and South America

25. ____ The world's population is increasing because
   a. the Industrial Revolution took place.
   b. the Green Revolution took place.
   c. the food supply increased and medical care improved.
   d. the birthrate and death rate are now equal.

26. ____ The basic social unit in any culture is
   a. the family.
   b. the school.
   c. the government.
   d. the community.

27. ____ Minerals, oil, and coal are examples of
   a. nonrenewable resources.
   b. renewable resources.
   c. manufactured resources.
   d. technological resources.

28. ____ One result of the Industrial Revolution was that countries were split into
   a. North and South America.
   b. developed and developing nations.
   c. socialist and capitalist nations.
   d. democracies and dictatorships.

CHAPTER 6

C. CRITICAL THINKING

Answer the following questions in the space provided, on the back of this paper or on a separate sheet of paper.

29. Understanding Central Issues: Why do you think geographers are interested in the effect that the environment has on culture and the effect that people have on their environment? In your answer, define what culture is and explain its relationship to the surrounding environment.

30. Drawing Conclusions: Name and describe the five themes of geography.

31. Expressing Problems Clearly: What are three major problems caused by the tremendous increase in world population in recent years?

32. Recognizing Cause and Effect   Identify two environmental problems and describe their causes.

D. SKILL: LOCATING INFORMATION

Imagine that you are writing a report about how to live in the Andes Mountains in South America. You have the following sources of information available: encyclopedias, maps, interviews with local people, travel books about South America, books and magazines about the Andes Mountains. Think about the information you would need to complete the assignment. Then answer the following questions on the lines provided.

33. What are two sources of general information that you would use in your report? _____

_____

_____

34. What are two sources of very specific information you would use? _____

_____

_____

35. What are two sources of somewhat specific information you would use? _____

_____

_____

36. What information would you find first, second, and third? _____

_____

_____

37. If you were building a "pyramid of knowledge," what information would you put on the base level, the middle level, and the top level? _____

_____

_____

Imagine that you are writing a report about how people in the United States are protecting endangered species. You have the following information available: map of the United States, statistics on endangered species, article on laws passed to protect endangered species, Internet site that describes animal characteristics, biography of a woman who started a shelter to treat and release injured birds, and magazine and newspaper articles about environmental action groups. Think about the information you need to complete the assignment. Then answer the questions in the blanks provided.

38. What are two sources of general information that you would use in your report? _____

_____

_____

39. What are two sources of very specific information you would use? _____

_____

_____

40. What are two sources of somewhat specific information you would use? _____

_____

_____

41. What information would you find first, second, and third? _____

_____

_____

42. If you were building a "pyramid of knowledge," what information would you put on the base level, the middle level, and the top level? _____

_____

_____

ANSWER KEY

1. a	2. d	3. g	4. e	5. f
6. d	7. e	8. h	9. i	10. b
11. c	12. b	13. d	14. c	15. a
16. c	17. b	18. b	19. d	20. d
21. b	22. d	23. c	24. d	25. c
26. a	27. a	28. b		

29. Answers may vary. A possible answer: Culture is the way of life of a group of people who share similar values and beliefs. Geographers want to know how the environment, including climate, vegetation, and available resources, affects culture. They're also interested in how people use technology to change their surroundings. This interaction between people and the environment is important because it affects everything that makes up the culture of a region, including the food people eat, the houses they live in, and the kinds of work they do.

30. Answers may vary. Possible answer: The five themes are location, which enables geographers to identify absolute and relative locations; place, which includes the natural and cultural features of a location; human-environment interaction, which shows how the environment and people affect one another; movement, which explains the relationship between places; and regions, which is used to make comparisons. These five themes are important because they enable geographers to organize the information they find about a particular place.

31. Answers may vary. Possible answer: One of the problems caused by the increase in the world's population is that more resources are being used, which leads to shortages of fresh water, energy, and food supplies. Also, there aren't enough jobs to support the growing population, and there aren't enough services, like education, transportation, and sanitation, to ensure everyone a decent standard of living.

32. Answers may vary. A possible answer: One environmental problem is acid rain, which has caused great damage to the forests of New York. Acid rain is produced when the chemicals released by cars and industries combine with water vapor in the air. Another environmental problem is river and sewage pollution, which can destroy living things in the water and endanger people. This pollution is caused people dumping waste into the waters and by fertilizers and pesticides that farmers use.

33. an encyclopedia article about South America; an atlas map of South America

34. travel books about the Andes region of South America; interviews with people who live in the area

35. a book about the culture of South America; magazine articles about the Andes Mountains

36. general information; somewhat specific information; very specific information

37. general information on the base level, somewhat specific information on the middle level, very specific information on the top level

38. an encyclopedia article about endangered species; an atlas map of the United States

39. an interview with a person who works with endangered species; an article by someone who has passed laws to protect species

40. a book about endangered species; a magazine article about efforts to protect animals

41. general information; somewhat specific information; very specific information

42. general information on the base level, somewhat specific information on the middle level, very specific information on the top level

World Explorer

AFRICA

BOOK 4

A. KEY TERMS

Complete each sentence by writing the correct term in the blank. You will not use all the terms.

a. cash crop
b. cataract
c. diversify
d. economy
e. escarpment
f. fertile
g. irrigate
h. plateau
i. tributary

1. _____ A large, raised area of mostly level land is called a(n) _____ .

2. _____ A larger river can be fed by a(n) _____ , which is a small river or stream that flows into it.

3. _____ Many plants can be grown in soil that is _____ .

4. _____ Sometimes farmers must _____ , or artificially water their crops.

5. _____ Many African countries want to _____ , or add variety to, their economies.

Match the definitions with the terms. Write the correct letter in each blank. You will not use all the terms.

a. cash crop
b. diversify
c. elevation
d. nomad
e. oasis
f. plateau
g. rift
h. silt
i. subsistence farming

6. _____ a deep trench

7. _____ a large, raised area of mostly level land

8. _____ add variety to an economy

9. _____ a person who moves from place to place to make a living

10. _____ bits of rock and dirt on river bottoms

B. KEY CONCEPTS

Write the letter of the correct answer in each blank.

11. _____ Because the land area of much of Africa is high, the continent is often called a
    a. coastal plain.   c. plateau.
    b. mountain.   d. river valley.

12. _____ The Nile, Congo, Zambezi, and Niger are the names of
    a. major mountains in Africa.   c. major coastal plains in Africa.
    b. major rivers in Africa.   d. major rift valleys in Africa.

13. _____ Why is it impossible for ships to sail from Africa's interior to the sea?
    a. Cataracts interrupt the rivers' flow.
    b. Escarpments interrupt the rivers' flow.
    c. Rift valleys interrupt the rivers' flow.
    d. Tributaries interrupt the rivers' flow.

14. _____ Africa's location near the Equator, its elevation, and its relationship to large bodies of water and landforms affect its
    a. language.   c. archaeology.
    b. government.   d. climate.

15. _____ What area of land supports tall grasses, thorny bushes, and scattered trees?
    a. coastal plain   c. rain forest
    b. desert   d. savanna

16. _____ How do many nomads make their living in the Sahara?
    a. They live in one place so they can care for their herds.
    b. They live in the cities where they can sell their goods.
    c. They travel to find water and food for their herds.
    d. They create large farms in the desert to grow food.

17. _____ Three fifths of Africa's farmland is used for
    a. harvesting trees.   c. commercial farming.
    b. cash crops.   d. subsistence farming.

18. _____ The major part of Africa's economy is
    a. trading.   c. farming.
    b. mining.   d. manufacturing.

19. _____ Why are African countries diversifying their economies?
    a. to protect the workers against economic hardships
    b. to focus on one important cash crop
    c. to produce only one major mineral each year
    d. to produce only goods that are made in factories

20. _____ The four geographic regions of Africa defined in this book are
    a. North, South, East, and West.
    b. Northeast, South, Central and South, and East.
    c. North, West, East, and Central and Southern.
    d. South, East, North, and Central and Eastern.

21. _____ Africa is often called the "plateau continent" because the elevation of much of the land is
    a. high.   c. uneven.
    b. low.   d. flat.

22. _____ Because of the cataracts found in Africa's major rivers, it is impossible for ships to
    a. control the flooding of the Nile.
    b. sail all the way from the interior to the sea.
    c. sail to other lands.
    d. carry much cargo.

23. _____ Because much of Africa is between the Tropic of Cancer and the Tropic of Capricorn, most of the country is located in a
    a. moderate climate region.   c. tropical climate region.
    b. subtropical climate region.   d. temperate climate region.

24. _____ What are the three factors that influence the climate of Africa?
    a. location near the Arctic, amount of rain, and large plateaus
    b. location near the Equator, elevation, and how close a place is to bodies of water and landforms
    c. elevation, large desert areas, and the distance from the South Pole
    d. flat grasslands, temperature, and the amount of rain

25. _____ The landform that extends across most of North Africa is
    a. the Sahara.   c. the Nile River.
    b. the Namib Desert.   d. Mount Kilimanjaro.

26. _____ Africa's most important natural resources are
    a. electricity, trade, and timber.   c. manufacturing, trade, and crops.
    b. crops, minerals, and timber.   d. solar energy, trade, and timber.

27. _____ Unlike farmers who raise cash crops, subsistence farmers raise crops to
    a. sell to Western countries.   c. support their families.
    b. support entire villages.   d. sell to other African countries.

28. _____ How does producing a variety of crops, raw materials, and manufactured goods affect African countries?
    a. They can afford to buy costly equipment for mining.
    b. They can protect their economies in an unstable world market.
    c. They cannot protect themselves if a major cash crop fails.
    d. They cannot survive a serious drought.

C. CRITICAL THINKING

Answer the following questions in the space provided, on the back of this paper or on a separate sheet of paper.

29. Identifying Central Issues: Explain how the Nile affects the lives of people in Africa. In your answer, briefly identify what the Nile is and where it is located.

30. Expressing Problems Clearly: Why do you think that Africa must balance crops, minerals, and industry to protect its economy in the modern world?

31. Making Comparisons: Compare and contrast the deserts and tropical savannas of Africa. In your answer, describe the climate, vegetation, and daily life of the people living in each place.

32. Drawing Conclusions: Based on what you know about Africa's landforms, rivers, climate, vegetation, and economy, where do you think most people in Africa live? Explain your answer.

D. SKILLS: INTERPRETING DIAGRAMS

Use the diagram below to answer the following questions. Write your answers on the lines provided.

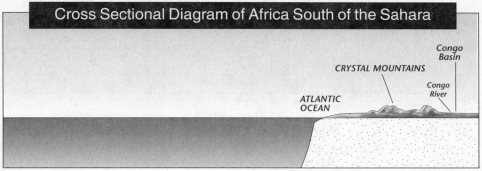

Cross Sectional Diagram of Africa South of the Sahara

33. In general, how would you describe the subject of the diagram?_____

_____

34. What major body of water is labeled on the diagram?_____

35. Name two landforms labeled on the diagram. _____

36. What is the name of the landform at the highest point on the diagram?_____

37. How can this diagram help you describe the physical geography of Africa?_____

_____

Use the diagram below to answer the following questions. Write your answers on the lines provided.

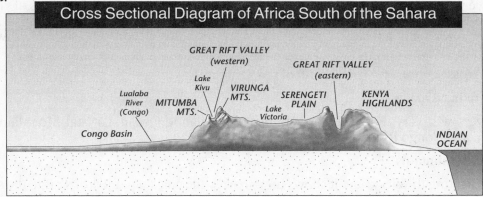

Cross Sectional Diagram of Africa South of the Sahara

38. What is shown on this diagram? _____

39. What are two landforms indicated on the diagram? _____

40. What major body of water is shown on the diagram? _____

41. Is the Great Rift Valley higher or lower in elevation than the surrounding land?_____

42. What are two facts about the geography of Africa that you can learn by studying this diagram?_____

ANSWER KEY

1. h	2. i	3. f	4. g	5. c
6. g	7. f	8. b	9. d	10. h
11. c	12. b	13. a	14. d	15. d
16. c	17. d	18. c	19. a	20. c
21. a	22. b	23. c	24. b	25. a
26. b	27. c	28. b		

29. Answers will vary. A possible answer: The Nile is a river that flows north from its two sources, the White Nile and the Blue Nile, into the Mediterranean Sea. It's the world's longest river, and it carries water from the mountains of Africa's plateaus to the sea. It's also useful for traveling. The land surrounding the Nile is fertile farmland. The Aswan High Dam created Lake Nasser, which waters desert crops and provides electricity.

30. Answers will vary. A possible answer: Most of Africa's workers are farmers, and three fifths of the farmland is used by subsistence farmers, who raise crops to support their families. As a result, the economy is sensitive to influences such as rainfall and the world price of crops. To protect itself economically, Africa must diversify by producing a variety of raw materials, crops, and manufactured goods that the rest of the world needs.

31. Answers may vary. A possible answer: Deserts have a hot, dry climate. It may not rain for years at a time. Very few things can grow here. The people who live in the desert are usually nomads and herders. They herd their livestock from one area to another in order to get enough food and water. In the savanna, there is also a dry season. During this time, trees lose their leaves and rivers dry up. However, there is a wet season also, when plants can grow. Tall grasses, thorny bushes, and some trees grow in the savanna. In the dry season, people trade, build houses, and visit friends. In the wet season, farmers plant their crops.

32. Answers may vary. A possible answer: I think most people live on the banks of rivers such as the Nile. Most people in Africa make their living from farming, and the Nile deposits fertile soil along its banks. Also, the river provides a constant source of water and transportation.

33. It's a cross section of Africa, south of the Sahara.

34. the Atlantic Ocean

35. Answers will vary. Possible answers include: Atlantic Ocean, Crystal Mountains, Congo Basin, and Congo River.

36. Crystal Mountains

37. By indicating the elevation, it shows how sharply the coastal plain drops off to the shoreline.

38. It's a cross section of half of Africa.

39. Answers may vary. Possible answers include: Congo Basin, Lualaba River, Mitumba Mountains, Lake Kiru, Great Rift Valley, Virunga Mountains, Lake Victoria, Serengeti Plain, Kenya Highlands, Indian Ocean.

40. the Indian Ocean

41. lower

42. Answers may vary. A possible answer: You can learn the length of the great plateau that makes up much of Africa. You can learn the length of the Congo Basin.

A. KEY TERMS

Match the definitions with the terms. Write the correct letter in each blank. You will not use all the terms.

    a. city-state
    b. civilization
    c. colonize
    d. democracy
    e. fertile
    f. literacy
    g. pilgrimage
    h. surplus

1. _____ a society with cities, government, and social classes

2. _____ a religious journey

3. _____ to settle an area and take over its government

4. _____ a form of government in which citizens help to make government decisions

5. _____ the ability to read and write

Complete each sentence by writing the letter of the correct term in each blank. You will not use all the terms.

    a. boycott
    b. colonize
    c. domesticate
    d. fertile
    e. literacy
    f. migrate
    g. nationalism
    h. pilgrimage

6. _____ To adapt plants and tame animals for human use is to _____ them.

7. _____ Many Muslims make a religious journey, or a _____ , to Mecca.

8. _____ Throughout Africa's history, European countries sought to _____ the continent, or settle the land and take over the government.

9. _____ In order to protest colonial rule, Africans would sometimes _____ , or refuse to use, a product or service.

10. _____ A feeling of pride in one's homeland is called _____ .

B. KEY CONCEPTS

Write the letter of the correct answer in each blank.

11. _____ The earliest humans in East Africa got their food by
    a. hunting and gathering.
    b. trading and hunting.
    c. domesticating and herding.
    d. farming and gathering.

12. _____ The earliest people in Egypt settled
    a. in the mountains.
    b. near the coast.
    c. along the banks of the Nile River.
    d. in the Sahara.

13. _____ The power of West African kingdoms was based on
    a. the herding of sheep and cows.
    b. the trade of salt and gold.
    c. the manufacture of clothing.
    d. the farming of oats and wheat.

14. _____ Which European country controlled the trade on East Africa's coast until well into the 1600s?
    a. England
    b. Spain
    c. France
    d. Portugal

15. _____ Why did Europeans build empires in Africa after the end of the African slave trade?
    a. for the natural resources found there
    c. to unite the African people
    b. to stop the spread of Islam
    d. because they were overcrowded in Europe

16. _____ In order to win independence from the colonial powers, African leaders encouraged the growth of
    a. religion.
    b. farming.
    c. nationalism.
    d. trade.

17. _____ How did World War II affect Africa?
    a. It inspired Africans to demand their independence.
    c. It decreased the growth of cash crops.
    b. It increased trade between Africa and the United States.
    d. It encouraged European countries to seize more African colonies.

18. _____ In order to depend less on one export, African countries are trying to
    a. decrease their exports.
    b. diversify their economies.
    c. increase their foreign debt.
    d. expand their farm communities.

19. _____ A serious environmental problem facing Africa today is a decrease in the
    a. crop harvests.
    b. size of the desert.
    c. amount of fertile land.
    d. number of trees that are planted.

20. ____ What is a civilization that arose on the Nile River about 5,000 years ago?
   a. South Africa
   b. Nigeria
   c. Egypt
   d. Senegal

21. ____ When Bantu-speaking peoples settled in Central and Southern Africa they introduced
   a. farming, herding, and iron tools.
   b. manufacturing, forestry, and farming.
   c. farming, mining, and forestry.
   d. trade, mining, and forestry.

22. ____ The kingdoms in West Africa were powerful because of
   a. the farming of wheat and corn.
   b. the trading of salt and gold.
   c. the manufacturing of cloth and tools.
   d. the herding of cows and sheep.

23. ____ Islam was spread from Mali into many other parts of Africa by
   a. British soldiers.
   b. Muslim traders.
   c. Arab farmers.
   d. Portuguese sailors.

24. ____ One important effect of trade on the culture of coastal East Africa was the development of
   a. Buddhism.
   b. Christianity.
   c. farming.
   d. Swahili.

25. ____ When the Portuguese realized how wealthy the East African city-states were, they wanted to
   a. establish schools in the area.
   b. seize the riches of the area.
   c. introduce English to the area.
   d. teach farmers new methods to grow crops.

26. ____ By the 1600s, Portuguese traders were trading
   a. gold for African salt.
   b. guns for enslaved Africans.
   c. clothing for African crops.
   d. salt for African guns.

27. ____ How did World War II affect European colonial powers like Great Britain?
   a. It weakened them economically.
   b. It strengthened them economically.
   c. It expanded their colonial holdings in Africa.
   d. It encouraged them to seek new colonies.

28. ____ In order to meet the challenges faced by African countries, African governments are working to increase the
   a. rate of land erosion.
   b. literacy rate.
   c. sale of only one food export.
   d. rate of foreign debt.

C. CRITICAL THINKING

Answer the following questions in the space provided, on the back of this paper or on a separate sheet of paper.

29. Drawing Conclusions: How was the Nile River important to the history of Egypt?

30. Identifying Central Issues: How did Europe's relationship with Africa change after 1500?

31. Recognizing Cause and Effect: How do you think Pan-Africanism helped African countries gain their independence?

32. Identifying Central Issues: What are two economic problems facing many African countries today, and how are the leaders trying to solve these problems?

D. SKILL: RECOGNIZING BIAS

The selection bellow describes literacy in Africa. Read the selection. Then answer the following questions by writing your answers in the blanks provided.

In African countries, the number of people who know how to read is growing. The growth in the literacy rates has come after the countries have gained independence. In Tanzania, 15 percent of people could write when the country became independent. Now the literacy rate is about 90 percent. These figures show that people need freedom so they can learn to read and write.

33. What is one opinion stated as a fact in this selection? _____

_____

34. What statements in the selection are facts? _____

_____

35. Are any facts in the selection used to support opinions? _____
   _____

36. What is the bias in this selection? _____
   _____

37. Write the last sentence of an unbiased paragraph about literacy in Africa. _____
   _____

The selection bellow describes life in East Africa. Read the selection. Then answer the following questions by writing your answers in the blanks provided.

Africa can be divided into four regions: (1) North, (2) West, (3) East, and (4) Central and Southern. The best place to live in Africa is East Africa. East Africa has beautiful mountains—the most beautiful in the world—and plateaus. The grasslands are nicer than the grasslands in any other part of Africa. Some countries in East Africa lie on the coast. Anyone who likes mountains, oceans, or grasslands would love to live in East Africa.

38. What is one opinion stated as a fact in this selection? _____
   _____

39. What phrase in the passage makes a biased comparison between East Africa and the other areas in Africa? _____
   _____

40. What kind of information could the writer add that would make the passage less biased? __
   _____

41. How would you describe the tone of the selection?_____
   _____

42. Revise the second sentence in the passage so it is not biased. _____
   _____

ANSWER KEY

1. b	2. g	3. c	4. d	5. f
6. c	7. h	8. b	9. a	10. g
11. a	12. c	13. b	14. d	15. a
16. c	17. a	18. b	19. c	20. c
21. a	22. b	23. b	24. d	25. b
26. b	27. a	28. b		

29. Answers may vary. A possible answer: The Nile River was very important because it was the place where the Egyptian and Nubian civilizations arose. People settled there because they could farm the land along the banks of the river. This land had been made fertile by the layer of silt left behind during the annual Nile flood.

30. Answers may vary. A possible answer: The relationship had begun as trade between equals. However, the Europeans wanted to control the African trade themselves and settle the continent. The slave trade forced the migration of millions of Africans from their homeland. After it ended, European countries colonized the continent to capture its resources and to establish empires there.

31. Answers may vary. A possible answer: The movement probably encouraged countries to seek their independence because it stressed unity and cooperation among all Africans. The Pan-African leaders tried to unify all Africans, whether they lived in Africa or not. Their slogan, "Africa for the Africans," encouraged people on the continent to free themselves from their European rulers.

32. Answers may vary. A possible answer: Because most African countries depend economically on exporting one or two products, they are sensitive to the rise and fall of world prices. To solve this problem, African countries are trying to diversify their economies. A second problem is how to feed their growing populations. To grow more food, governments are helping farmers develop hybrid plants.

33. Answers will vary. Possible response: People need freedom before they can learn to read and write.

34. Fifteen percent of people in Tanzania were literate when independence was gained. Today 90 percent of people are literate.

35. Answers will vary. Possible response: The growth in literacy rates has occurred after countries have gained independence.

36. The bias is that people must be free in order to read and write.

37. Answers will vary. Sample response: As countries have gained their independence, more people are learning to read and write.

38. Answers will vary. Possible response: The best place to live in Africa is East Africa.

39. Answers will vary. Possible response: The grasslands are nicer than the grasslands in any other part of Africa.

40. Answers will vary. Possible response: The writer could add information about other areas in Africa.

41. Answers will vary. Possible response: The tone is superior. Students may say the writer is bragging.

42. Answers will vary. Possible response: East Africa is a good place for people to live.

A. KEY TERMS

Complete each sentence by writing the letter of the correct term in the blank. You will not use all the terms.

 a. clan
 b. cultural diffusion
 c. griot
 d. kinship
 e. lineage
 f. plantation

1. _____ The movement of customs and ideas from one place to another is called _____ .

2. _____ An _____ is a group of lineages that share one ancestor .

3. _____ A West African storyteller is called a _____ .

4. _____ The people of West Africa value the bond of _____ , or family relationship.

5. _____ When the British ruled East Africa, people would work on a _____ , a large farm where cash crops are grown.

Match the definitions with the terms. Write the correct letter in each blank. You will not use all the terms.

 a. clan
 b. cultural diffusion
 c. culture
 d. lineage
 e. migrant worker
 f. nuclear family
 g. plantation

6. _____ groups of people who trace their roots to an early ancestor

7. _____ family that includes parents and children

8. _____ the spread of customs and ideas

9. _____ the way of life of a group of people who share similar beliefs and customs

10. _____ a person who moves from place to place to work

B. KEY CONCEPTS

Write the letter of the correct answer in each blank.

11. _____ Why is Islam so important in North Africa?
    a. People must practice Islam in order to trade here.
    b. It divides the people who live in rural and urban areas.
    c. It forms a common bond of culture among the people.
    d. Only the wealthiest people practice Islam.

12. _____ The mixing of cultures in North Africa occurred because of
    a. geographic isolation and trade.   c. language and trade.
    b. trade and conquest.   d. disease and conquest.

13. _____ The countries that form North Africa are
    a. Kenya, Algeria, Ethiopia, Mali, and Egypt.
    b. Egypt, Libya, Tunisia, Algeria, and Morocco.
    c. Ethiopia, Nigeria, Mali, Algeria, and Egypt.
    d. Niger, Congo (Zaire), Mali, Nigeria, and Algeria.

14. _____ Why does West Africa have a wide variety of cultures?
    a. There are many ethnic groups living here.
    b. There are five main languages in the area.
    c. There is only one religion uniting all the people.
    d. There is only one way of making a living.

15. _____ One important change affecting family life in West Africa is that people are moving
    a. from one village to another.   c. from cities to villages.
    b. within their clan.   d. from villages to cities.

16. _____ Why does East Africa have great cultural diversity?
    a. It is along the Indian Ocean.
    b. It is on the Atlantic Ocean.
    c. It is on the Mediterranean Sea.
    d. It has many rivers running through it.

17. _____ The Swahili language is important in East Africa because it is used
    a. only in schools.   c. by educated people in the cities.
    b. for business and communication.   d. in the home.

18. _____ South Africa influenced nearby countries by inspiring people
    a. to struggle for majority rule.
    b. to establish monarchies.
    c. not to take part in their governments.
    d. to form political parties abroad.

19. ____ What is one way in which the country of South Africa has affected the region of Southern Africa economically?
   a. by borrowing money from every country in the region
   b. by mining minerals from nearby countries
   c. by buying most of its manufactured goods from other countries
   d. by using workers from all over the area in its mines

20. ____ The different peoples of North Africa are unified by
   a. the French language and Islam.
   b. a common heritage and Confucianism.
   c. Islam and the Arabic language.
   d. a family relationship and Buddhism.

21. ____ The idea of privately owned land was introduced to East Africa when
   a. East Africans became farmers.
   b. Swahili culture spread.
   c. Europeans set up plantations.
   d. urbanization began.

22. ____ Because West Africa has hundreds of different ethnic groups, it has
   a. one central government.   c. two common languages.
   b. a variety of cultures.   d. two religions.

23. ____ How has urbanization affected life in West Africa?
   a. People are moving from cities to villages.
   b. Schools are being built in cities.
   c. People are moving from villages to cities.
   d. Highways are being built linking one village to another.

24. ____ One important method of preserving West African traditions is
   a. through sign language.   c. by living on plantations.
   b. by speaking a common language.   d. storytelling by griots.

25. ____ East Africa's cultural diversity results from its
   a. government.   c. trade.
   b. location.   d. politics.

26. ____ What culture do Africans who have African and Arab ancestry belong to?
   a. Berber   c. Tuareg
   b. Swahili   d. Congolese (Zairian)

27. ____ The economic needs of the country of South Africa have affected the whole region of Southern Africa because they create a great demand for
   a. labor.   c. imported food.
   b. manufactured goods.   d. water.

28. ____ What was one important result of the formation of the National Union of Mineworkers in South Africa?
   a. The workers' union was illegal.
   b. The workers led a movement for equal rights.
   c. The workers gained great economic power.
   d. The workers' interest in education led to school reform.

C. CRITICAL THINKING

Answer the following questions in the space provided, on the back of this paper or on a separate sheet of paper.

29. **Making Comparisons:** Compare the relationship among ethnic groups in North Africa to that among groups in West Africa.

30. **Recognizing Cause and Effect:** How has location affected the development of East African and North African cultures?

31. **Recognizing Cause and Effect:** What effect does Islam have on the culture of North Africa?

32. **Identifying Central Issues:** Explain this statement "South Africa is just one country in Southern Africa, but it has had the greatest impact on the region."

D. SKILL: ASSESSING YOUR UNDERSTANDING

Read the following passage. Then answer the questions. Write your answers on the lines provided.

There are several reasons why ancient Egyptian civilization developed close to the Nile River. The soil near the banks of the Nile was fertile, so farmers grew most of their crops here. The regular flooding of the river left deposits that kept the soil rich year after year. During the time of flooding, when farmers couldn't plant and take care of crops, many of them worked as builders. The Nile also provided a way to travel. Egyptians built boats with huge sails that they used to sail from city to city.

33. What is this passage about?_____

_____

34. How does this passage relate to what you already know about Egypt? _____

_____

35. What most interested you in this passage? _____

_____

36. What does this passage tell you about the importance of the Nile River in the history of Egypt? _____

_____

37. How could the information in this passage help you in your future schoolwork? _____

_____

Read the following passage. Then answer the questions. Write your answers on the lines provided.

Ancient Egypt is one of the world's oldest civilizations. Its early history is divided into three periods: the Old Kingdom, the Middle Kingdom, and the New Kingdom. In between each period, there was a time of weak and unstable governments. During the Old Kingdom, the pyramids were built. During the Middle Kingdom, the capital was moved to Thebes. During the New Kingdom, Thebes and another city, Memphis, became important cultural and commercial centers in the world.

38. What is the main point of this passage? _____

_____

39. How does this passage relate to what you already know about Egypt? _____

_____

40. What topic in the reading do you want to learn more about? _____

_____

41. What does this passage tell you about ancient Egyptian history? _____

_____

42. How could you use the information in this passage in a school report? _____

_____

ANSWER KEY

1. b	2. e	3. c	4. d	5. f
6. d	7. f	8. b	9. a	10. e
11. c	12. b	13. b	14. a	15. d
16. a	17. b	18. a	19. d	20. c
21. c	22. b	23. c	24. d	25. b
26. b	27. a	28. b		

29. Answers will vary. A possible answer: In North Africa the different groups are united by Islam and the Arabic language. On the other hand, in West Africa, the hundreds of different ethnic groups practice different religions and speak different languages. The groups are not as united.

30. Answers may vary. A possible answer: Because North Africa is located on the Mediterranean Sea, it has always been a center of trade. As a result of this trade link and the conquest of other empires, a mixing of cultures in North Africa, occurred. Similarly, East Africa's cultural diversity has resulted from its location along the Indian Ocean. When Arab traders settled in the coastal villages of East Africa, their culture mixed with African cultures and resulted in Swahili.

31. Answers may vary. A possible answer: In North Africa, people are united across ethnic lines by their common belief in the Muslim religion. Islamic law affects every aspect of daily life.

32. Answers may vary. A possible answer: South Africa has had great political influence. The struggle of black South Africans for political rights inspired similar movements in nearby countries, especially in Namibia and Zimbabwe. South Africa has also had economic influence. Because it produces so many of the manufactured goods, minerals, and agricultural products of the continent, South Africa has had a tremendous need for labor. As a result, workers come to South Africa from other countries in the region.

33. life along the Nile River in ancient Egypt

34. Answers will vary. A possible answer: It tells about life in a North African country I read about in the chapter.

35. Answers may vary. A possible answer: I was interested in the idea that farmers worked on the pyramids during the yearly flood.

36. Egyptian civilization was founded along the banks of the Nile.

37. Answers may vary. A possible answer: I could use this information in a report about ancient Egypt.

38. to describe different periods of ancient Egyptian history

39. Answers will vary. Possible answer: I already knew about the pyramids. This selection tells me during what period they were built.

40. Answers may vary. Possible answer: I'd like to know more about Thebes and Memphis.

41. There are three periods of ancient Egyptian history, with periods of instability between them.

42. Answers may vary. A possible answer: I could use this information in a report about the pyramids.

A. KEY TERMS

Match the definitions with the terms. Write the correct letter in each blank. You will not use all the terms.

a. Arab
b. bazaar
c. Berber
d. Cairo
e. extended family
f. terrace
g. fellaheen
h. casbah

1. _____ a platform cut into the mountainside

2. _____ rural Egyptian farmers

3. _____ an old section of a city in Algeria

4. _____ an open-air market

5. _____ a household that includes more relatives than a mother, father, and their children

Complete each sentence by writing the letter of the correct term in the blank. You will not use all the terms.

a. Arab
b. bazaar
c. Berber
d. Cairo
e. extended family
f. fellaheen
g. casbah
h. terrace

6. _____ The rural farmers of Egypt are called _____ .

7. _____ The old section of an Algerian city is the _____ .

8. _____ In Cairo, people often shop in an open-air market called a(n) _____ .

9. _____ More relatives than a mother, father, and their children live together in a(n) _____ .

10. _____ In order to grow crops in a steep place, a Berber farmer creates a(n) _____ , which is a platform cut into the mountainside.

B. KEY CONCEPTS

Write the letter of the correct answer in each blank.

11. _____ The official religion of Egypt is
    a. Judaism.
    b. Christianity.
    c. Islam.
    d. Buddhism.

12. _____ Most fellaheen
    a. do not own land.
    b. live in Cairo.
    c. do not follow Islamic practices.
    d. make a living by fishing.

13. _____ Egyptian Muslims bring their religion into their daily life by
    a. obeying the words of Buddha.
    b. traveling to Cairo.
    c. following the teaching of the Quran.
    d. eating only during Ramadan.

14. _____ Many Egyptian people move to the cities from rural areas in order to
    a. live in large homes.
    b. expand their farms.
    c. practice their religion.
    d. find jobs and a better education.

15. _____ One way that Islam affects everyday life in Egypt is by requiring that men and women
    a. live in separate compounds.
    b. dress modestly.
    c. pray once a day.
    d. do not eat meat.

16. _____ Unlike the Berbers, the Arabs who conquered North Africa were
    a. navigators.
    b. nomads.
    c. sailors.
    d. artisans.

17. _____ The Berber village governments are based on
    a. the military.
    b. a dictatorship.
    c. the family.
    d. a monarchy.

18. _____ Most people living in Berber villages are
    a. teachers and craft persons.
    b. farmers and herders.
    c. traders and gatherers.
    d. sailors and farmers.

19. _____ What unites many of the Berbers and Arabs who live in Algeria's cities?
    a. They speak Spanish and are nomads.
    b. They all practice Christianity.
    c. They speak Arabic and practice Islam.
    d. They work in separate neighborhoods.

20. _____ The Quran is sacred to Muslims because they believe
    a. it is the word of God.
    c. it tells the story of Muhammad's life.
    b. it is an exciting book to read.
    d. it contains the story of Islam.

21. _____ How do Egyptian Muslims bring their religion into their daily lives?
    a. by praying once a day in a church
    b. by not reading the Sharia
    c. by praying and fasting
    d. by keeping Islamic law separate from Egyptian law

22. _____ Islamic law requires that all men and women
    a. eat during the day.
    b. pray once a day.
    c. face away from Mecca during prayer.
    d. dress modestly in public.

23. _____ Why do people move to Cairo from rural areas?
    a. to find jobs and a better education
    b. to live in places that are not crowded
    c. to avoid traffic jams and housing shortages
    d. to build large farms for their families

24. _____ One of the main sources of Sharia is
    a. the Bible.   c. Egyptian songs.
    b. the Quran.   d. village life.

25. _____ The Berbers and the Arabs are the two main ethnic groups of
    a. Egypt.   c. Cairo.
    b. Algeria.   d. Saudi Arabia.

26. _____ What was one key difference between the early Berbers and Arabs?
    a. The Arabs were farmers and the Berbers were nomads.
    b. The Arabs were craft persons, and the Berbers were nomads.
    c. The Berbers were farmers, and the Arabs were nomads.
    d. The Arabs were sailors, and the Berbers were nomads.

27. _____ Egyptian Muslims disagree about
    a. whether they should follow the Sharia.
    b. which mosque to go to.
    c. how many times a day they should pray.
    d. how to interpret Islamic law.

28. _____ After the Arabs conquered North Africa, the Berbers learned to
    a. accept Islam.
    b. fight their conquerors.
    c. destroy their own village governments.
    d. give up farming.

C. CRITICAL THINKING

Answer the following questions in the space provided, on the back of this paper or on a separate sheet of paper.

29. Drawing Conclusions: Why do you think the Berbers eventually learned to live peacefully with their Arab conquerors? In your answer, consider the importance of religion and customs to both peoples.

30. Making Comparisons: Compare how people live in Egyptian and Algerian cities and towns.

31. Recognizing Cause and Effect: What effects does the practice of Islam have on daily life in Egypt? In your answer, discuss at least three effects.

32. Making Comparisons: How are Arab and Berber traditions similar and different?

D. SKILL: USING REGIONAL MAPS

Use the map below to answer the following questions. Write your answers on the lines provided.

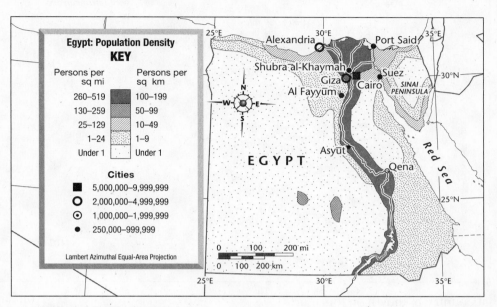

33. What region is shown on the map? _____

34. What basic information does the map provide about the region? _____

_____

_____

35. Name a city with a population density between 2,000,000 and 4,999,999. _____

_____

_____

36. What areas of the country have the largest population? The smallest? _____

_____

_____

37. How might a population distribution map be helpful in learning about the way of life of the people of a particular region? _____

_____

_____

Use the map below to answer the following questions. Write your answers on the lines provided.

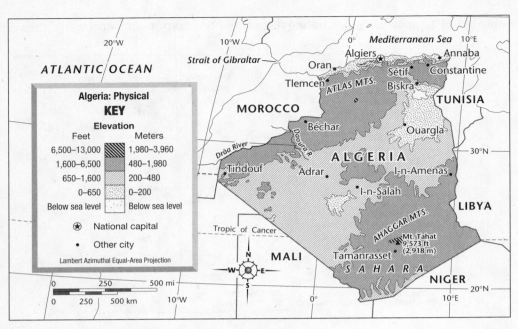

38. What country is shown on this map? _____

_____

_____

39. What basic information can this map give you? _____

_____

_____

40. What is the elevation of Adrar? _____

_____

_____

41. What is the capital of Algeria and what is its elevation? _____

_____

_____

42. What countries border Algeria? _____

_____

_____

Chapter 4 ■ Answer Key

ANSWER KEY

1. f	2. g	3. h	4. b	5. e
6. f	7. g	8. b	9. e	10. h
11. c	12. a	13. c	14. d	15. b
16. b	17. c	18. b	19. c	20. a
21. c	22. d	23. a	24. b	25. b
26. c	27. d	28. a		

29. Answers will vary. A possible answer: When most Berbers accepted Islam, the Arabs' religion, peace came to the region. Also, the traditions of both people are similar. They both live in extended families. To accommodate differences between the two traditions, the Berbers were willing to compromise. For example, they adapted to Arab rule by keeping their own village governments along with the Arab central government in Algeria.

30. Answers will vary. A possible answer: The life-styles in Egyptian and Algerian cities and towns are very similar. The cities in both countries are crowded, since about half of all Egyptians and Algerians live in these urban centers. In both countries, the cities blend the modern with the traditional; in Egypt there are bazaars, and in Algeria there are mosques and open-air markets. Most of the Egyptians in the rural areas are farmers who live in villages along the Nile River or the Suez Canal. In Algeria, the Berbers and Arabs who live in rural areas are farmers and nomads. Many of these villagers in both countries have retained a way of life that has remained unchanged since ancient times.

31. Answers will vary. A possible answer: Since the teachings of the Quran affect Egyptian law as well as the behavior of individual Muslims, Islam has many effects on daily life in Egypt. One effect is that men and women both dress modestly in public. Another effect is that five times a day, people face toward Mecca and pray. A third effect is that people try to follow the Quran's teachings about honesty, honor, and giving to others.

32. Answers may vary. A possible answer: Traditionally, both Arabs and Berbers live in extended families. However, Arabs are traditionally nomads while Berbers are traditionally farmers. Also, Berbers ruled themselves with family-based village governments while Arabs had larger governments.

33. Egypt

34. It tells where people live.

35. Possible answers: Alexandria and Giza.

36. Many people live along the Nile River and the Suez Canal. That is where the major cities are. Fewer people live in the Sahara.

37. Answers may vary. A possible answer: This map shows that although Egypt is a fairly large country, most of its population lives in the highly dense area around the waterways. For this reason, people in Egypt might have some problems with crowding.

38. Algeria

39. This map tells you Algeria's elevation, the locations of cities, and the location of the capital. It also shows major land forms and political boundaries.

40. 650–1,600 feet

41. Algiers, which has an elevation of 0–650 feet

42. Libya, Mali, Niger, Morocco, and Tunisia

A. KEY TERMS

Complete each sentence by writing the letter of the correct term in the blank. You will not use all the terms.

      a. census
      b. coup
      c. desertification
      d. drought
      e. erode
      f. multiethnic
      g. sovereignty

1. _____ By taking a count of all the people living in a country, or a(n) _____ , the government finds out how many citizens actually live here.

2. _____ Throughout history, many countries have fought for their _____ , or political independence.

3. _____ Grazing large herds of animals in one place can _____ , or slowly wear away, the soil there.

4. _____ When there is a long period with little or no rain, or a(n) _____ , many crops die.

5. _____ Because many ethnic groups live in West Africa, it is a(n) _____ region.

Match the definitions with the terms. Write the correct letter in each blank. You will not use all the terms.

      a. census
      b. coup
      c. desertification
      d. drought
      e. ethnic group
      f. multiethnic
      g. sovereignty

6. _____ a long period of little or no rain

7. _____ including many ethnic groups living within a country's borders

8. _____ political independence

9. _____ a takeover of a government

10. _____ a count of all the people living in a country

CHAPTER 5

B. KEY CONCEPTS

Write the letter of the correct answer in each blank.

11. _____ Tombouctou became an important trade center because
    a. the desert provided many raw materials.
    b. its location in the Sahel was a crossroads for travelers.
    c. it was close to important seaports.
    d. the Tuareg people have historically been traders.

12. _____ For hundreds of years, the Hausa-Fulani have been known as great
    a. artisans.   c. farmers.
    b. traders.   d. miners.

13. _____ How do most Yoruba who live in Nigeria make their living?
    a. by herding   c. by farming
    b. by manufacturing   d. by trading

14. _____ What was Great Britain's main goal when it ruled the Gold Coast?
    a. encouraging the growth of traditional religions
    b. controlling the country's economy
    c. expanding the growth of food crops
    d. encouraging the country's independence

15. _____ What was one important change that Kwame Nkrumah made after becoming president of Ghana?
    a. increasing world prices for the country's chief export, cocoa
    b. paying back the country's loans
    c. renaming the country
    d. solving the country's economic problems

16. _____ President Jerry Rawlings reformed Ghana's politics and economy by
    a. encouraging European traditions and values.
    b. building a dam on the Volta River.
    c. spending millions of dollars to build a conference center.
    d. stressing the traditional African value of hard work.

17. _____ Why is the Sahel so important to Mali?
    a. A small part of the country lies in this zone.
    b. A great percentage of the country lies in this zone.
    c. A large number of the citizens live beyond this zone.
    d. Many large factories are located here.

18. _____ What environmental change is threatening the way of life of the people of Mali?
    a. The desert is spreading south.
    b. The forests are spreading north.
    c. The savanna is getting too little rainfall.
    d. The Sahel is getting too much rainfall.

19. _____ Most people in Mali make their living by
    a. manufacturing, trading, and weaving.
    b. mining, forestry, and farming.
    c. trading, farming, and herding.
    d. manufacturing, mining, and herding.

20. _____ The three main ethnic groups in Nigeria are
    a. Yoruba, Fulani, and Hausa.   c. Hausa-Fulani, Muslim, and Tuareg.
    b. Ibo, Yoruba, and Hausa-Fulani.   d. Tuareg, Fulani, and Hausa.

21. _____ Where do most Ibo live?
    a. in large cities   c. on communes
    b. in city-states   d. in farming villages

22. _____ Why are the results of the census so important to the people of Nigeria?
    a. The three smallest ethnic groups will not vote in the election.
    b. The three largest ethnic groups will elect the president.
    c. The smallest ethnic group will receive extra government benefits.
    d. The largest ethnic group will have the most power in government.

23. _____ Why did Great Britain make the Gold Coast a colony?
    a. to improve the living conditions of the people
    b. to control the country's economy
    c. to establish a monarchy
    d. to encourage the people to become independent

24. _____ Kwame Nkrumah was thrown out of office because the people blamed him for the
    a. country's economic problems.
    b. growth of West African traditions.
    c. conflicts between ethnic groups.
    d. desertification of the Sahel.

25. _____ Ghana's economy depended on which crop?
    a. cocoa   c. tea
    b. coffee   d. cotton

26. _____ How is the Sahara a threat to the people of Mali?
    a. It is shrinking and will destroy the nomadic way of life.
    b. It is spreading south and will destroy the Sahel.
    c. It is attracting settlers who used to live in the Sahel.
    d. It is spreading to the east and will destroy the rain forest.

27. _____ The people in Mali who are most affected by desertification are the
    a. Tuareg.   c. Akan.
    b. Ibo.   d. Yoruba.

CHAPTER 5

28. ____ One possible cause of desertification is
    a. mining.   c. over planting.
    b. overgrazing.   d. planting.

C. CRITICAL THINKING

Answer the following questions in the space provided, on the back of this paper or on a separate sheet of paper.

29. Recognizing Cause and Effect: What effect is desertification having in Mali and other countries of the Sahel? In your answer, include a brief description of what desertification is.

30. Making Comparisons: How would you compare the contributions of Kwame Nkrumah and Jerry Rawlings to Ghana's economic development?

31. Identifying Central Issues: What are three ways in which Ghana has changed since its independence?

32. Expressing Problems Clearly: How is desertification affecting the way of life for people in parts of Mali? In your answer, explain what desertification is.

CHAPTER 5

D. SKILL: USING DISTRIBUTION MAPS

Use the distribution map below to answer the following questions. Write your answers on the lines provided.

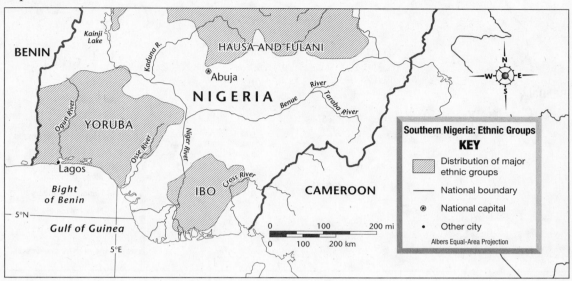

33. What does this map show the distribution of? _____

_____

_____

34. How is the distribution shown on this map? _____

_____

_____

35. What ethnic groups are shown? _____

_____

_____

36. What geographic features lie between the areas lived in by the Yoruba and Ibo ethnic groups? _____

_____

_____

37. What geographic features lie between the areas lived in by the Yoruba and the Hausa and Fulani ethnic groups? _____

_____

_____

Use the distribution map below to answer the following questions. Write your answers on the lines provided.

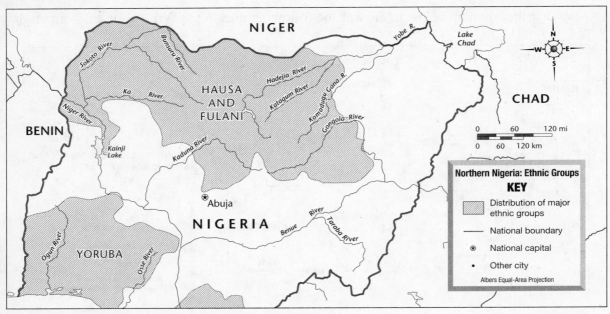

38. What does this map show the distribution of? _____

_____

_____

39. What does the shading mean on this map? _____

_____

_____

40. What two ethnic groups are labeled? _____

_____

_____

41. What ethnic group is in the majority in this part of Nigeria? _____

_____

_____

42. How do rivers appear to affect the distribution of ethnic groups? _____

_____

_____

ANSWER KEY

1. a	2. g	3. e	4. d	5. f
6. d	7. f	8. g	9. b	10. a
11. b	12. b	13. c	14. b	15. c
16. d	17. b	18. a	19. c	20. b
21. d	22. d	23. b	24. a	25. c
26. b	27. a	28. b		

29. Answers may vary. A possible answer: Desertification takes place when fertile lands are changed into lands that are too dry or damaged to support life. As the Sahara spreads south, countries of the Sahel, including Mali, are threatened by desertification. If the land becomes infertile, people will be unable to farm or graze their livestock here, as they have for hundreds of years.

30. Answers may vary. A possible answer: Under Nkrumah, Ghana developed serious economic problems. He borrowed millions of dollars to build expensive projects, such as a dam and a superhighway. However, when the world prices for cocoa fell, Ghana could not repay its loans. Under Rawlings, however, Ghana's economy has grown. As a result of this growth, the country has built better roads and irrigation systems.

31. Answers may vary. A possible answer: 1. Ghana has brought in more modern technology. 2. Nkrumah hurt the economy of the country by spending too much money. 3. Rawlings improved the economy by stressing traditional values of hard work and sacrifice. He built roads and irrigation systems.

32. Answers may vary. A possible answer: Desertification is the change of fertile land into land that is too dry or damaged to support life. For hundreds of years, the Tuareg have lived in the Sahel, which is now being threatened by desertification. The Tuareg are nomads who make their living by herding livestock from place to place. Desertification has threatened their food and water supplies, and many of their livestock have died during droughts. If the Sahel can't support the Tuareg and their herds, these people may have to settle permanently near towns or cities.

33. ethnic groups in southern Nigeria

34. Different shadings are used to show the different ethnic groups.

35. The Yoruba, the Ibo, and the Hausa and Fulani are shown.

36. the Niger and the Kaduna rivers

37. the Niger and the Osse rivers

38. ethnic groups in northern Nigeria

39. Shading is used to show the distribution of different ethnic groups.

40. the Yoruba and the Hausa and Fulani

41. The Hausa and Fulani are the majority group.

42. Both groups live near many rivers.

CHAPTER 5

Chapter 6 ■ *Exploring East Africa*

A. KEY TERMS

Match the definitions with the terms. Write the correct letter in each blank. You will not use all the terms.

  a. foreign debt
  b. harambee
  c. lingua franca
  d. multiparty system
  e. monastery
  f. shamba

1. _____ a place where priests and nuns live, work, and study

2. _____ money owed to foreign countries

3. _____ A language that many people speak as a second language is a _____ .

4. _____ a national campaign in Kenya that encouraged the people there to work together to improve their country

5. _____ A country that has more than two political parties has a _____ .

Complete each sentence by writing the letter of the correct term in the blank. You will not use all the terms.

  a. foreign debt
  b. harambee
  c. lingua franca
  d. monastery
  e. shamba
  f. multiparty system
  g. urban

6. _____ A monk is a priest who lives, works, and studies in a(n) _____ .

7. _____ The president of Kenya began a campaign called _____ , which encouraged all citizens to work together to improve their country.

8. _____ Many governments have elections using a _____ system.

9. _____ Often a poor nation will have a large _____ , which is money owed to a foreign country.

10. _____ People who speak different first languages can communicate in a common language called _____ .

B. KEY CONCEPTS

Write the letter of the correct answer in each blank.

11. _____ The religions practiced by most Ethiopians today are
   a. traditional African religions and Christianity.
   b. Coptic Christianity and Islam.
   c. Judaism and Christianity.
   d. Buddhism and Islam.

12. _____ Why did the Ethiopian Christian Church develop in a unique way?
   a. Ethiopian Christians were isolated from other Christians.
   b. Ethiopian Christians wanted to develop their own religion.
   c. Ethiopians encouraged Christians to convert to Judaism.
   d. Many Ethiopian Christians could not read English.

13. _____ The rural town of Lalibela is famous as a(n)
   a. manufacturing center.   c. educational center.
   b. political center.   d. religious center.

14. _____ Why did President Nyerere adopt a new national language for Tanzania?
   a. so the people would keep their traditions
   b. so the government wouldn't be controlled by one ethnic group
   c. so the government wouldn't be controlled by the military
   d. so the people would vote in every election

15. _____ President Nyerere believed that a one-party system would help to
   a. continue a dictatorship.   c. begin a civil war.
   b. avoid ethnic hatred.   d. overthrow the monarchy.

16. _____ One important change made by Tanzania's new leaders was
   a. ending the foreign debt.   c. ending ujamaa.
   b. adopting a new national language. d. raising fewer cash crops.

17. _____ Why do many Kenyan women remain in the countryside?
   a. They don't have to work as hard in the villages.
   b. They don't have to take care of children in their villages.
   c. There are few jobs in the cities.
   d. It's easier to support their families by farming.

18. _____ In Kenyan villages, the women solve community problems by
   a. asking the local government for help.   c. forming self-help groups.
   b. asking their extended families for help. d. attending schools.

19. _____ Because of Kenya's geography, most of the people there are
   a. miners.   c. artisans.
   b. farmers.   d. manufacturers.

20. _____ Most Ethiopians live
   a. in Lalibela.
   b. on the coast.
   c. in rural areas.
   d. in large cities.

21. _____ As Arabs took control of North and East Africa, some Ethiopians
   a. adopted Islam.
   b. adopted Christianity.
   c. resisted the Arabs.
   d. took control of West Africa.

22. _____ Why did the Christian Church in Ethiopia develop differently than it did in other countries?
   a. Few Ethiopians became Christians.
   b. Most Ethiopians practiced traditional African religions.
   c. Ethiopian Christians had little contact with other Christians.
   d. Ethiopian Christians maintained close ties with other Christians.

23. _____ What was one way President Nyerere kept peace among different ethnic groups in Tanzania?
   a. by encouraging ethnic groups to speak their own language
   b. by adopting a national language that reflected only Arab culture
   c. by encouraging people to speak only English
   d. by adopting a national language that mixed African and Arab cultures

24. _____ President Nyerere's ujamaa program failed because many people
   a. didn't have enough water.
   b. wanted to work their own land.
   c. refused to work on family homesteads.
   d. produced too many crops.

25. _____ One major success brought about by Nyerere was
   a. the ujamaa program.
   b. a multi-party system in politics.
   c. economic stability.
   d. a rise in literacy.

26. _____ Because of Kenya's geography and climate, the land there is suitable for
   a. manufacturing.
   b. mining.
   c. farming.
   d. forestry.

27. _____ What is one example of how harambee affects life in Kenya?
   a. People place little value on their family relationships.
   b. People work together in villages to build schools.
   c. People leave Kenya to live in other countries.
   d. People refuse to help other villagers farm their land.

28. _____ Which religions do mot Kenyans practice?
   a. Christianity and Islam.
   b. Coptic Christianity and Islam.
   c. Hinduism and Christianity.
   d. Judaism and Islam.

CHAPTER 6

C. CRITICAL THINKING

Answer the following questions in the space provided, on the back of this paper or on a separate sheet of paper.

29. Identifying Central Issues: What are two major changes leaders in Tanzania made after President Nyerere left office?

30. Making Comparisons: Explain the similarities and differences in the ways people live in Nairobi and in Addis Ababa.

31. Recognizing Cause and Effect: How did Ethiopia's location affect its early development? In your answer, consider the country's economy and its religion.

32. Drawing Conclusions: In Kenya, many people are moving from the country to the city. How does the principle of harambee affect the people who move as well as the people who stay? In your answer, tell what harambee is and give at least two examples of it.

D. SKILL: USING ISOLINES

Use your knowledge about isolines and the map below to answer the following questions. Write your answers on the lines provided.

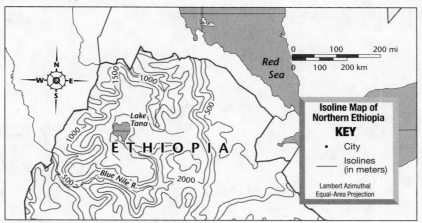

33. What is the difference in elevation, or interval, between each pair of isolines? _____

_____

_____

34. What is the lowest elevation shown on this map? _____

_____

_____

35. How does the land in the eastern part of this area differ from the land in the western part? ___

_____

_____

36. How can you tell whether an incline is steep or gradual by looking on this map? _____

_____

_____

37. If you were traveling to Lake Tana, why would you avoid traveling from the South? _____

_____

_____

CHAPTER 6

Use your knowledge about isolines and the map below to answer the following questions. Write your answers on the lines provided.

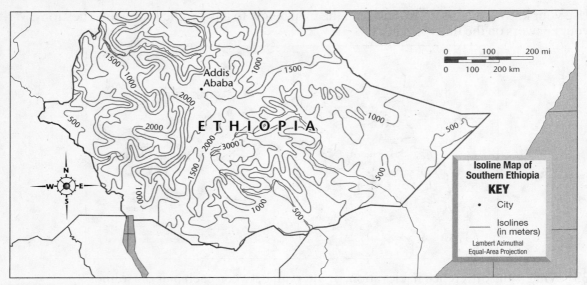

38. What is the difference in elevation, or interval, between each pair of isolines? _____
_____
_____

39. What is the highest elevation shown on this map?_____
_____
_____

40. What is the elevation of Addis Ababa? _____
_____
_____

41. How can you tell whether an incline is steep or gradual by looking at this map?_____
_____
_____

42. If you were traveling to Addis Ababa, from which direction would you come? _____
_____
_____

ANSWER KEY

1. e 2. a 3. c 4. b 5. d
6. d 7. b 8. f 9. a 10. c
11. b 12. a 13. d 14. b 15. b
16. c 17. d 18. c 19. b 20. c
21. a 22. c 23. d 24. b 25. d
26. c 27. b 28. a

29. Answers may vary. A possible answer: The new leaders ended ujamaa and decided that farms should produce more cash crops. They also changed the election system and allowed new political parties to form. As a result, Tanzania now has a multiparty system of government.

30. Answers will vary. A possible answer: Similarities: Addis Ababa is the capital of Ethiopia, and Nairobi is the capital of Kenya. Both are modern cities with all the amenities of city life. Differences: Addis Ababa has a traditional, rural side with some residents living in houses made of stone and mud. Only a small percentage of Ethiopia's people live here. However, the population of Nairobi continues to grow as more people arrive here from villages looking for work.

31. Answers will vary. A possible answer: Ancient Ethiopia bordered the Red Sea, and the main source of the Nile River was in its highlands. As a result, the country was a center of trade. People also learned about each other's religions by trading goods along the Nile River and the Red Sea, and Coptic Christianity slowly spread from Egypt to Ethiopia.

32. Answers will vary. A possible answer: Harambee is a Swahili word meaning to pull together. Independent Kenya's first president had a campaign called harambee. One example of harambee is that when men move to the city, members of their ethnic group will share rooms with them and help them out. Another example of harambee is that the women who have stayed at home have formed self-help groups to help each other earn money and solve problems.

33. 500 meters

34. 500 meters

35. The land in the eastern part is lower and more level than the land in the western part, which is higher.

36. The closer the isolines are, the steeper the incline is.

37. Traveling from the South would require going through rugged hills and crossing the Blue Nile River.

38. 500 meters

39. 3000 meters

40. 2000 meters

41. The closer the isolines are, the steeper the incline is.

42. Answers will vary. A possible answer: I would travel from the Northeast, where there are fewer steep hills.

CHAPTER 6

A. KEY TERMS

Complete each sentence by writing the letter of the correct term in the blank. You will not use all the terms.

      a. apartheid
      b. authoritarian
      c. discriminate
      d. homeland
      e. Mandela
      f. nationalize
      g. Shaba

1. _____ To take a foreign-owned company and put it under government control is to _____ it.

2. _____ A single leader or small group of leaders have all the power in a(n) _____ government.

3. _____ The South African system in which racial groups were kept separate is called _____ .

4. _____ When people treat a person unfairly because of his or her race, religion, or gender, they _____ against that person.

5. _____ An area of land on which South African blacks were forced to live is a(n) _____ .

Match the definitions with the terms. Write the correct letter in each blank. You will not use all the terms.

      a. apartheid
      b. authoritarian
      c. F. W. de Klerk
      d. discriminate
      e. homeland
      f. Mobutu
      g. nationalize

6. _____ to take under government control industries owned by foreign countries

7. _____ a kind of government in which a single leader or small group of leaders have all the power

8. _____ a South African system that legalized unfair treatment of blacks

9. _____ to treat people unfairly based on race, religion, or gender

10. _____ an area of South Africa where blacks were forced to live

CHAPTER 7

B. KEY CONCEPTS

Write the letter of the correct answer in each blank.

11. _____ Some of Congo's (Zaire's) most important natural resources include
    a. water, natural gas, and sugar.   c. sugar, wheat, and cocoa.
    b. copper, forests, and wildlife.   d. forests, fruits, and vegetables.

12. _____ The Belgian rulers of the Congo were mainly interested in the country's
    a. resources.   c. language.
    b. history.   d. culture.

13. _____ What is one change Mobutu made after assuming control of the Congo?
    a. He built many schools.
    b. He called for a general election.
    c. He nationalized foreign owned industries.
    d. He established a monarchy.

14. _____ What happened after Congo's (Zaire's) economy collapsed?
    a. The government raised taxes.
    b. The government spent less money on schools.
    c. The government spent more money on health services.
    d. The government gave food to the poor people of the country.

15. _____ Since independence, what has happened to the living conditions of most of the
    people in Congo (Zaire)?
    a. They have improved slightly.   c. They have declined.
    b. They have remained the same.   d. They have improved a great deal.

16. _____ After South Africa became independent, the white-led government passed laws
    that
    a. permitted black people to own good land.
    b. kept land and wealth in white hands.
    c. improved the living conditions of black citizens.
    d. punished the British, French, and German settlers.

17. _____ How did the apartheid laws affect South Africans?
    a. Everyone paid higher taxes.
    b. White and black workers were united.
    c. Racial discrimination became legal.
    d. All South Africans could vote.

18. _____ Who did South Africans elect as their new president after the end of apartheid?
    a. Mobutu Sese Seko   c. F. W. de Klerk
    b. Nelson Mandela   d. Monique de Preez

CHAPTER 7

19. _____ The new South African government passed laws that ended
   a. black ownership of some land.
   b. economic problems facing the country.
   c. higher taxes in many poor villages.
   d. legal discrimination on the basis of race.

20. _____ Most of Congo's (Zaire's) wealth is produced by
   a. farming.   c. mining.
   b. forestry.   d. manufacturing.

21. _____ Belgium ruled the Congo in order to control the country's
   a. manufacturing.   c. forestry and water.
   b. copper and diamonds. d. crops and wildlife.

22. _____ Why did foreign companies help Mobutu Sese Seko take control of the Congo?
   a. to protect their businesses
   b. to provide medical care for the people
   c. to educate the children
   d. to improve the transportation system

23. _____ What did Mobutu do after he assumed power in the Congo?
   a. improved the educational system
   b. held a general election
   c. nationalized foreign-owned industries
   d. established a multiparty political system

24. _____ Congo's (Zaire's) economy collapsed in the late 1970s because the price of copper
   a. went up and down.   c. stayed the same.
   b. increased.   d. dropped sharply.

25. _____ Why did the British battle the Afrikaners for control of the Transvaal?
   a. because diamonds and gold were discovered here
   b. because the government collapsed
   c. because black Africans asked the British for help
   d. because copper was discovered here

26. _____ The apartheid laws passed by the National Party made
   a. racial discrimination legal.   c. a one-party system permanent.
   b. state elections necessary.   d. a dictatorship possible.

27. _____ How did blacks in South Africa live under the apartheid system?
   a. They attended the same schools as whites.
   b. They made economic advancements.
   c. They had practically no rights at all.
   d. They moved to cities and villages throughout the country.

CHAPTER 7

28. ____ How did the election of Nelson Mandela change life in South Africa?
    a. All black citizens had to carry identification cards.
    b. White people were no longer able to own land.
    c. Legal discrimination on the basis of race ended.
    d. All farms became nationalized.

C. CRITICAL THINKING

Answer the following questions in the space provided, on the back of this paper or on a separate sheet of paper.

29. Identifying Central Issues: How would you describe life in Congo (Zaire) since independence? In your answer, discuss the social, political, and economic situations.

30. Drawing Conclusions: Why do you think the Africans living in the Congo Free State and South Africa fought for their independence from their white-led governments?

31. Identifying Central Issues: Comment briefly on the following statement: "Resources dominate the history of Congo (Zaire)." Refer to at least two facts from the chapter in your answer.

32. Recognizing Cause and Effect: How did South Africa's apartheid laws affect the lives of black people there?

D. SKILL: ORGANIZING YOUR TIME

Imagine that you have two weeks to write a three-page paper about life in South Africa today. Then answer the following questions about the plan you would make before you start the assignment. Write your answers on the lines provided.

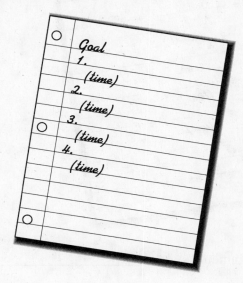

33. What goal would you write at the top of the page? _____
_____
_____

34. What would be the first step in your plan? _____
_____
_____

35. What would be the next three steps in your plan? _____
_____
_____

36. How much time would each step take? _____
_____
_____

37. After completing your plan, what is your final step in organizing your time? _____
_____
_____

CHAPTER 7

Imagine that you have three weeks to write a five-page paper about the history of Congo (Zaire). Then answer the following questions about the plan you would make before you start the assignment. Write your answers on the lines provided.

38. When would you start the assignment? _____
_____
_____

39. What would be the first step in your plan and how much time would it take? _____
_____
_____

40. What would be the second step in your plan and how much time would it take? _____
_____
_____

41. What would be the third step and how much time would it take? _____
_____
_____

42. How much time would you have left to complete the last step? _____
_____
_____

ANSWER KEY

1. f	2. b	3. a	4. c	5. d
6. g	7. b	8. a	9. d	10. e
11. b	12. a	13. c	14. b	15. c
16. b	17. c	18. b	19. d	20. c
21. b	22. a	23. c	24. d	25. a
26. a	27. c	28. c		

29. Answers may vary. A possible answer: Economically, socially, and politically, life has been very difficult for people in Congo (Zaire) since independence. Mobutu's economic plans failed, and the economy collapsed. Congolese (Zairians) today face economic problems and instability in government.

30. Answers will vary. A possible answer: Under their Belgian rulers, the Africans in the Congo Free State suffered and starved. The Belgians were only interested in mining the country's vast mineral resources. In South Africa, the white-led government enforced apartheid, which made discrimination legal and granted black South Africans practically no rights.

31. Answers will vary. A possible answer: The power of the early rulers of the Congo depended on their knowledge of ironworking. The first Europeans who came to the area were looking for gold. Later, the Belgians were interested in controlling the Congo's resources, especially its copper and diamonds.

32. Answers may vary. A possible answer: The apartheid laws divided South Africans into categories based on race that left blacks with practically no rights at all. Black South Africans lived in poverty in poor rural areas. They were denied citizenship rights, including the right to vote and were kept in low-paying jobs. They weren't allowed to enter white restaurants, schools, or hospitals.

33. Write a three-page paper about life in South Africa today.

34. researching life in South Africa today

35. review notes; write first draft of report; review the final copy

36. Answers may vary. A possible answer: Step 1: four days, Step 2: one day, Step 3: two days, Step 4: one day

37. transferring the information to a calendar, writing down which step of the chart I will work on each day.

38. today

39. Research the history of Congo (Zaire). This would take five days. [Time may vary.]

40. Review notes. This would take one day. [Time may vary.]

41. Write draft of assignment. This would take four days. [Time may vary.]

42. I would have four days to review and revise my final paper. [Time may vary.]

CHAPTER 7

A. KEY TERMS

Complete each sentence by writing the letter of the correct term in the blank. You will not use all the terms.

    a. coup
    b. drought
    c. escarpment
    d. cataract
    e. harambee
    f. nomad
    g. oasis
    h. Quran
    i. sovereignty

1. _____ A person who moves around to various places to make a living is called a(n) _____ .

2. _____ The holy book of the religion of Islam is called the _____ .

3. _____ A(n) _____ is a section of rocky rapids or a waterfall.

4. _____ Throughout Africa's history, countries fought for their _____ , or political independence from colonial rulers.

5. _____ After Kenya gained independence, the new president began a campaign called _____ , which encouraged people to work together.

Match the definitions with the terms. Write the correct letter in each blank. You will not use all the terms.

    a. authoritarian
    b. bazaar
    c. coup
    d. desertification
    e. drought
    f. fertile
    g. pilgrimage
    h. plateau
    i. Quran

6. _____ the holy book of the religion of Islam

7. _____ able to support many plants

8. _____ traditional open-air market

9. _____ kind of government controlled by one person or one small group

10. _____ the change of productive land into land that is too dry or damaged to support life

CHAPTER 8

B. KEY CONCEPTS

Write the letter of the correct answer in each blank.

11. _____ Why is Africa often called the "plateau continent"?
    a. The elevation of much of the land area is high.
    b. The elevation of much of the land area is low.
    c. The land covering much of the continent rises near the sea.
    d. The land covering much of the continent is very hilly.

12. _____ What was one important effect of World War II on the people of Africa?
    a. It decreased their economic dependence on farming.
    b. It increased their dependence on their European rulers.
    c. It inspired them to win their freedom.
    d. It encouraged them to decrease their foreign debt.

13. _____ Most of Africa's major lakes are located in or near
    a. the Great Rift Valley.
    b. Egypt.
    c. the grasslands of West Africa.
    d. South Africa.

14. _____ What is the major part of Africa's economy?
    a. mining
    b. forestry
    c. manufacturing
    d. farming

15. _____ What is one important difference between the peoples of North Africa and West Africa?
    a. North Africans have not been influenced by cultures of other countries.
    b. West Africans are not united by a single religion or common language.
    c. West Africans are members of one major ethnic group.
    d. North Africans are not united by a single religion.

16. _____ Egyptian Muslims have brought Islam into their daily lives by
    a. encouraging immodest dress.
    b. keeping their country's laws separate from the Sharia.
    c. praying and fasting.
    d. closing many mosques.

17. _____ How does desertification threaten the people of Mali?
    a. by ruining the forests in the savanna
    b. by making manufacturing in the cities impossible
    c. by destroying the fertile land of the Sahel
    d. by causing flooding of the major rivers

18. _____ The major religions of Ethiopia are
    a. Christianity and Judaism.
    b. Buddhism and Christianity.
    c. Islam and Judaism.
    d. Christianity and Islam.

19. _____ In South Africa, the system that legalized racial discrimination was called
    a. Swahili.   c. ujamaa.
    b. apartheid.   d. souq.

20. _____ Africa is called the "plateau continent" because the elevation of the land is generally
    a. low.   c. hilly.
    b. high.   d. mountainous.

21. _____ Most of North Africa is covered by
    a. the Kalahari Desert.   c. the Sahara.
    b. a tropical rain forest.   d. savanna.

22. _____ In the 1400s, the Portuguese began exploring the coast of West Africa in order to
    a. build cities along the Nile River.   c. buy African slaves.
    b. establish farms in the area.   d. trade directly for gold and ivory.

23. _____ As Muslim traders traveled to different parts of Africa, they spread their
    a. religion.   c. weapons.
    b. monarchy.   d. politics.

24 _____ What two factors contributed to the mixing of cultures in North Africa?
    a. farming and forestry   c. trade and conquest
    b. government and education   d. religion and history

25. _____ Most Muslims in Egypt agree that the laws of the country should be based on
    a. Buddhist teachings.   c. Confucian sayings.
    b. Islamic law.   d. Christian practices.

26. _____ Why was Nkrumah overthrown by a military coup in Ghana?
    a. Many people blamed him for the country's economic problems.
    b. Citizens didn't like the monarchy he started.
    c. People didn't want a return to traditional African values.
    d. Farmers were producing too many crops to sell to other countries.

27. _____ Why did the Ethiopian Christian Church develop its own unique form of Christianity?
    a. It fought continually with the Muslim Arabs.
    b. It had little contact with Christians in other countries.
    c. It wasn't founded until the middle of the 1900s.
    d. It was influenced by the Muslim Arabs.

28. _____ What was the name of the system that made racial discrimination legal in South Africa?
    a. apartheid   c. ujamaa
    b. harambee   d. desertification

C. CRITICAL THINKING

Answer the following questions in the space provided, on the back of this paper or on a separate sheet of paper.

29. **Making Comparisons:** Explain the similarities and differences between the ways of life in Cairo, Egypt, and an Egyptian village or between those in Nairobi, Kenya, and a Kenyan village.

30. **Identifying Central Issues:** Briefly describe one economic, one social, and one environmental issue facing African countries today. In your description, tell how African countries are trying to meet these challenges.

31. **Identifying Central Issues:** What is meant by the phrase "the scramble for Africa" when referring to the 1700s and 1800s? In your answer, explain why Great Britain wanted control of the Gold Coast and South Africa.

32. **Distinguishing Fact From Opinion:** Read the following statements. Then identify each as either a fact or an opinion. Give a reason for your choice. a. In 1990, South Africa's president, F. W. de Klerk, introduced laws that tore down the apartheid system. b. On the surface, things do not appear much different. But you know they are—you can feel it. The laws have changed, and that is a big deal.

D. SKILL: ORGANIZING YOUR TIME

Use the distribution map below to answer the following questions. Write your answers on the lines provided.

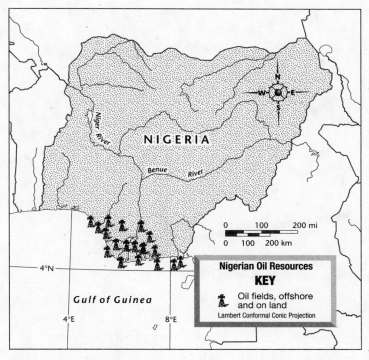

33. In general, what does this map show? _____
_____
_____

34. How is this resource indicated on the map key? _____
_____
_____

35. In general, what part of Nigeria has the most petroleum resources? _____
_____
_____

36. Are there more oil fields on land or offshore? How can you tell? _____
_____
_____

37. How could you use this map in writing a report about Nigeria? _____
_____
_____

Imagine that you have one week to write a two-page paper about the climate and vegetation in North Africa. Then answer the following questions about the plan you would make before you start the assignment. Write your answers on the lines provided.

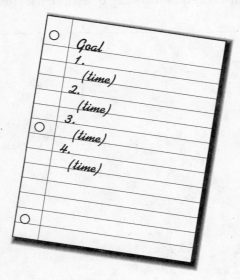

38. What goal would you write at the top of the page? _____
_____
_____

39. When would you start working on the assignment? _____
_____
_____

40. What would be the first step in your plan? How long would it take? _____
_____
_____

41. What would be the next three steps in your plan? How long would they take? _____
_____
_____

42. After completing the plan, what would be your final step to organize your time? _____
_____
_____

ANSWER KEY

1. f	2. h	3. d	4. i	5. e
6. i	7. f	8. b	9. a	10. d
11. a	12. c	13. a	14. d	15. b
16. c	17. c	18. d	19. b	20. b
21. c	22. d	23. a	24. c	25. b
26. a	27. b	28. a		

29. Answers will vary. Possible answer (1): Cairo is the largest city in Africa. While parts of the city look like a modern Western city, there are also traditional bazaars. Since many people move there from rural areas to find jobs and a better education, the city is crowded with traffic jams and housing shortages. Some people live on rowboats on the Nile. In Egyptian villages, traditions have changed little in 4,000 years. The farmers here live in homes built of mud bricks or stones and still use ancient farming techniques. In both the city and the villages, Islam is an important part of daily life. Possible answer (2): In Nairobi, the capital of Kenya, the population is always increasing. People arrive daily looking for work. Many of the newcomers walk to their jobs from the outskirts of the city, where they live. Men from the same ethnic group often live together and help each other. Women and children often stay behind in Kenyan villages when the men leave to seek work in the cities. In villages, the women grow cash crops in addition to the food they grow to feed their own families. They work together in self-help groups to solve common problems. In both the city and the villages, people practice harambee.

30. Answers may vary. A possible answer: Since about 75 percent of African countries have economies that depend on the export of one or two products, they are extremely sensitive to the rise and fall of world prices. To solve this problem, they are diversifying their economies. An important social issue is education. African children often work on family farms or sell products in the markets instead of attending school. Now countries are building more schools and working to increase the literacy rate. An environmental problem is soil erosion. When forests are cut down, the soil is washed away. To solve this problem, farmers in some countries now plant certain crops, such as yams, in long rows. Between the rows they plant trees to hold the soil in place.

31. Answers may vary. A possible answer: The "scramble for Africa" refers to the efforts by European countries to colonize Africa because of the vast mineral resources and opportunities to establish empires here. Great Britain made the Gold Coast into a colony because it wanted to control the economy of the country, particularly the cocoa, timber, and gold. Great Britain fought the Afrikaners for control of South Africa for the same reason— they wanted to control the land and wealth. For example, when diamonds and gold were discovered in the Transvaal, the British pushed the Afrikaners off their land.

32. Statement a is a fact because it can be proved to be true. Statement b is an opinion because it reflects a personal point of view.

33. petroleum resources in Nigeria

34. an oil derrig

35. The area along the southern coast has the most oil fields.

36. You can tell that there are more oil fields on land because there are more icons on land.

37. Answers may vary. A possible answer: I could use this map in writing a report about the resources of Nigeria.

38. Write a two-page paper about the climate and vegetation of North Africa in one week.

39. today

40. Research the climate and vegetation of North Africa in the library. I would take two days. [Times may vary.]

41. review notes (one day); write first draft of report (two days); review the final copy (one day) [Times may vary.]

42. It is to get a calendar and write down which step of the flowchart I will work on each day.

World Explorer

EUROPE AND RUSSIA

BOOK 5

A. KEY TERMS

Complete each sentence writing the letter of the correct term in the blank. You will not use all the terms.

    a. loess
    b. navigable
    c. peninsula
    d. polder
    e. prairie
    f. rain shadow
    g. reserves
    h. steppe
    i. tundra

1. _____ A patch of new land reclaimed from the sea is called a _____ .

2. _____ A treeless plain where grasses and mosses grow is a _____ .

3. _____ When a river is blocked by ice, it is not _____ , or clear enough for ships to travel.

4. _____ In Europe winds have deposited a type of rich, dustlike soil known as _____ .

5. _____ Many countries have a large available supply, or _____ , of natural resources, such as oil.

Match the definitions with the terms. Write the correct letter in each blank. You will not use all the terms.

    a. fossil fuel
    b. hydroelectric power
    c. peninsula
    d. plateau
    e. polder
    f. rain shadow
    g. steppe
    h. taiga
    i. tributary

6. _____ a body of land nearly surrounded by water

7. _____ a large, raised area of mostly level land

8. _____ an area on the dry, sheltered side of a mountain that receives little rainfall

9. _____ Russian grassland

10. _____ an energy source that developed from the remains of ancient plants and animals

B. KEY CONCEPTS

Write the letter of the correct answer in each blank.

11. _____ How do the population densities of Europe and Russia compare?
   a. Europe's population density is greater than most of the world's, and Russia's is lower.
   b. Europe and Russia have very low population densities.
   c. Russia's population density is greater than most of the world's, and Europe's is lower.
   d. Europe and Russia have very high population densities.

12. _____ More than half of Europe is covered by a landform called the
   a. Central Uplands.   c. North European Plain.
   b. Alpine Mountain System.   d. Northwestern Highlands.

13. _____ How does Siberia's harsh climate affect life in that region?
   a. Many people live here.   c. Few people live here.
   b. It is a major transportation center. d. Many major cities are located here.

14. _____ Western Europe's peninsulas and bays have enabled the countries here to become leaders in
   a. culture.   c. the mining industry.
   b. manufacturing.   d. the shipping industry.

15. _____ The North Atlantic Current affects northwestern Europe by
   a. carrying cold water and ice.   c. bringing warm water and winds.
   b. bringing stormy weather and snow.   d. carrying snow and ice.

16. _____ Areas of Europe that are west of the mountains receive
   a. no rainfall.   c. heavy rainfall.
   b. little sunlight.   d. mostly clouds.

17. _____ The three great vegetation zones of Russia are
   a. the rain forests, the prairies, and the grasslands.
   b. the tundra, the prairies, and the grasslands.
   c. the plains, the forests, and the grasslands.
   d. the plateaus, the prairies, and the grasslands.

18. _____ What are the most important natural resources of Europe?
   a. oil, natural gas, and coal
   b. fertile soil, water, and fuels
   c. forests, natural gas, and coal
   d. minerals, fossil fuels, and solar energy

19. _____ Because of Russia's size, harsh climate, and few rivers suitable for travel, the country has not developed its
   a. cultural resources.   c. natural resources.
   b. scientific resources.   d. communications resources.

CHAPTER 1

20. _____ Which statement best compares the sizes of Europe and Russia?
    a. Europe and Russia are approximately the same size.
    b. Europe is a small continent and Russia is the largest country in the world.
    c. Both Europe and Russia are large continents.
    d. Russia is a medium-sized continent and Europe is a small country.

21. _____ Which landform is shared by both Europe and Russia?
    a. the Alpine Mountain System   c. the North European Plain
    b. the Central Uplands   d. the West Siberian Plain

22. _____ Two important rivers on the continent of Europe are
    a. the Ural and the Rhine.   c. the Volga and the Rhine.
    b. the Siberian and the Volga.   d. the Nile and the Volga.

23. _____ Northwestern Europe receives warm water from the Gulf of Mexico that is carried by the
    a. Pacific Ocean.   c. South Atlantic Current.
    b. North Atlantic Current.   d. Volga River.

24. _____ In Europe, the areas that are west of mountains receive
    a. little sunlight.   c. heavy rainfall.
    b. heavy winds.   d. little rainfall.

25. _____ What separates Europe and Asia?
    a. the Atlantic Ocean   c. the Black Sea
    b. the Alps   d. the Ural Mountains

26. _____ Siberia is important to Russia because
    a. of its ski slopes.
    b. it has most of the nation's natural resources.
    c. it is the seat of government.
    d. it draws many tourists.

27. _____ Why is most of Russia's industry west of the Ural Mountains?
    a. The natural resources cannot be mined in western Russia.
    b. The Siberian rivers flow toward Russia's important cities.
    c. The country's fossil fuels are on the continent of Asia.
    d. The country's reserves of iron ore are on the continent of Europe.

28. _____ How do Russia's harsh climate, size, and few navigable rivers affect its economic development?
    a. Russia is the richest nation on the Earth.
    b. Russia's natural resources are difficult to use.
    c. Russia can easily transport manufactured goods to Asia.
    d. The land in Ukraine is hard to farm.

C. CRITICAL THINKING

Answer the following questions in the space provided, on the back of this paper or on a separate sheet of paper.

29. Making Comparisons: Compare how location and climate affect the shipping industry in both Europe and Russia. In your answer, consider the bodies of water located near each place.

30. Recognizing Cause and Effect: How has Russia's climate affected the settlement and economy of the country?

31. Making Comparisons: How do you think the climate and landforms of Europe and Russia have affected each places population density?

32. Drawing Conclusions: Think about the location of Europe and Russia on bodies of water. How do you think the location affected trade between Europe and Russia and the rest of the world throughout history?

D. SKILL: USING REGIONAL MAPS

Use the time zone map of Europe below to answer the following questions. Write your answers on the lines provided.

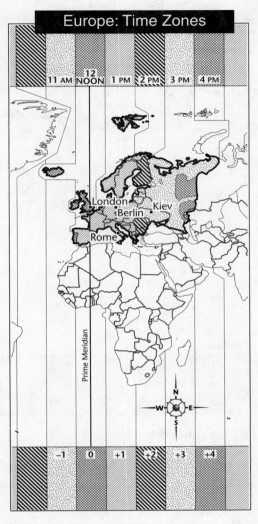

33. How many of the world's time zones does Europe include? _____

34. If you started out in London, in which direction would you have to travel to get to a time zone that is one hour earlier? _____

35. When it is 2 p.m. in London, what time is it in Kiev? _____

36. When it is 6 p.m. in Berlin, what time is it in Rome? _____

37. In Europe, how many hours' difference is there between the time zone farthest east and the time zone farthest west? _____

Use the time zone map of Russia to answer the following questions. Write your answers on the lines provided.

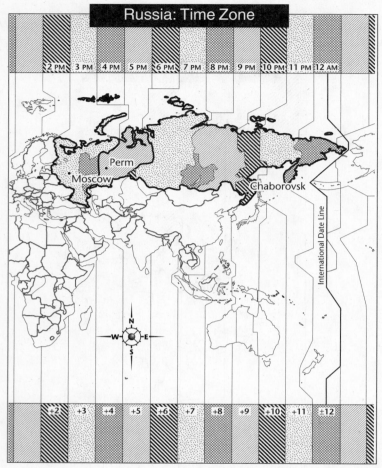

Russia: Time Zone

38. How many of the world's time zones does Russia include? _____

39. If you traveled west from Russia to Europe, would you be entering an earlier or later time zone? _____

40. When it is 2 p.m. in Moscow, what time is it in Perm? _____

41. When it is 6 p.m. in Perm, what time is it in Chabarovsk? _____

42. In Russia, how many hours' difference is there between the time zone farthest east and the time zone farthest west? _____

ANSWER KEY

1. d	2. i	3. b	4. a	5. g
6. c	7. d	8. f	9. g	10. a
11. a	12. c	13. c	14. d	15. c
16. c	17. c	18. b	19. c	20. b
21. c	22. c	23. b	24. c	25. d
26. b	27. d	28. b		

29. Answers may vary. A possible answer: The continent of Europe juts out into the Atlantic Ocean. In addition, many smaller peninsulas provide bays and good harbors. The climate is milder in Europe than it is in Russia, because Europe receives the benefit of the North Atlantic Current. Mild weather and good harbors have enabled Western European countries to become world leaders in the shipping industry. Russia lies on the Arctic Ocean. Because of the cold climate there, the water is frozen for most of the year and cannot be used for shipping.

30. Answers may vary. A possible answer: Although Siberia makes up 75 percent of Russian territory, only 20 percent of the people live there. This is because of the area's harsh climate. More people live in the western part of Russia because the climate is milder. There is also more industry in the western part, even though Siberia has many natural resources. The country's harsh climate has made it difficult to develop the natural resources to the east of the Ural Mountains.

31. Answers may vary. A possible answer: Europe has a milder climate than Russia and its soil is fertile. Also, its location on a peninsula with many bays and harbors has provided easy access to other parts of the world, and its rivers can transport goods to and from many regions, allowing settlement there. As a result, Europe has a higher population density than most of the world. However, a region known as Siberia in eastern Russia makes up about 75 percent of Russian territory. Because of Siberia's poor soil and cold climate, only 20 percent of Russia's people are able to live there. As a result, Russia has a lower population density than Europe.

32. Answers may vary. A possible answer: Europe is a peninsula with many smaller peninsulas and bays that jut into the Atlantic Ocean. Because of the mild climate and good harbors, it was probably easy for Europeans to trade with other areas of the world by developing shipping routes. However, Russia lies on the Arctic Ocean which is frozen for most of the year and can't be used for shipping. As a result, trade between Russia and the countries of Europe and Asia occurred via overland routes.

33. five

34. west

35. 5 p.m.

36. It is also 6 p.m.

37. 4 hours' difference

38. 10

39. earlier

40. 4 p.m.

41. It is 11 p.m.

42. 9 hours' difference

A. KEY TERMS

Match the definitions with the terms. Write the correct letter in each blank. You will not use all the terms.

      a. alliance
      b. colony
      c. communism
      d. democracy
      e. empire
      f. feudalism
      g. humanism
      h. Renaissance
      i. westernization

1. _____ a kind of government that citizens run themselves

2. _____ a period of history in which there was a rebirth of interest in learning and art

3. _____ an agreement between countries to protect one another

4. _____ the process of becoming more like Western Europe

5. _____ a political theory that says all the people should own the farms and factories

Complete each sentence by writing the letter of the correct term in the blank. You will not use all the terms.

      a. alliance
      b. communism
      c. czar
      d. democracy
      e. empire
      f. humanism
      g. imperialism
      h. manor
      i. monarch

6. _____ In the Middle Ages, medieval lords owned a piece of land called a(n) _____ .

7. _____ During the Renaissance, people developed a new approach to knowledge called _____ , which focused on improving the world.

8. _____ During the age of _____ , many European countries took over other nations and turned them into colonies.

9. _____ The first Russian emperor, or _____ , Ivan IV, was crowned in 1547.

10. _____ Under _____ , everyone is supposed to share the work equally and receive an equal share of the rewards.

B. KEY CONCEPTS

Write the letter of the correct answer in each blank.

11. _____ One of ancient Rome's greatest contributions to the world was
   a. the concept of democracy.
   b. the idea of separate city-states.
   c. an organized system of written laws.
   d. a scientific way of gathering knowledge.

12. _____ During the Middle Ages, society was organized according to a system called
   a. democracy.
   b. dictatorship.
   c. feudalism.
   d. anarchy.

13. _____ Why did the Europeans begin to explore other lands during the Renaissance?
   a. They wanted to tax other countries.
   b. They wanted to conquer other countries.
   c. They were searching for trading wealth.
   d. They wanted to spread their religion.

14. _____ During the Scientific Revolution, scientists based their theories on information they had
   a. learned in church.
   b. learned from the Romans.
   c. tested.
   d. read about.

15. _____ One important result of the Industrial Revolution was the growth of
   a. small farms.
   b. wages paid to all factory workers.
   c. cities.
   d. family values.

16. _____ What was an effect of nationalism in Europe during the early 1900s?
   a. Countries learned to work together for the good of all Europe.
   b. Alliances between groups of nations resulted in World War I.
   c. Countries decided to adopt a common language.
   d. Countries formed a union to protect European political interests.

17. _____ What three themes often appear in Russia's history?
   a. scientific discovery, industrial invention, economic growth
   b. slow westernization, global colonization, democratic growth
   c. growing equality, enlightened rulers, influence in the West
   d. expansion, harsh treatment of common people, slow westernization

18. _____ What was one important factor that led to the overthrow of Nicholas II?
   a. war with the United States
   b. the spread of dictatorship
   c. a growing national debt
   d. mistreatment of the serfs

19. _____ What happened as a result of the Russian civil war?
    a. Stalin called for a general election.
    b. Lenin created a democratic state.
    c. Lenin created the Union of Soviet Socialist Republics.
    d. The Soviet empire collapsed.

20. _____ Alexander the Great spread Greek culture throughout the world by
    a. building universities.   c. establishing trade routes.
    b. conquering other lands.   d. making himself a Greek god.

21. _____ The idea of democracy came from
    a. Alexander the Great.   c. the ancient Greeks.
    b. feudal lords.   d. Marco Polo.

22. _____ How were people governed during the Middle Ages?
    a. by feudal lords   c. by the clergy
    b. by democratically elected leaders   d. by the local serfs

23. _____ What statement best describes the political situation during the Renaissance?
    a. Feudalism declined as kings became richer and more powerful.
    b. Feudalism grew as kings became weaker.
    c. The middle class took control of the governments.
    d. The lower classes revolted and overthrew the monarchs.

24. _____ Which war between the United States and Russia lasted from 1945 until 1991?
    a. World War I   c. World War II
    b. the Cold War   d. the Russian Revolution

25. _____ During the 1800s, a change in the way goods were produced resulted in the
    a. Pax Romana.   c. Industrial Revolution.
    b. Age of Revolution.   d. Age of Reason.

26. _____ Peter the Great changed Russia by
    a. refusing to pay taxes to the Mongols.
    b. bringing in Western European ideas and culture.
    c. freeing the serfs.
    d. conquering western Siberia.

27. _____ As a result of the mass killing known as Bloody Sunday, Czar Nicholas agreed to establish
    a. a kind of Russian congress.   c. a free educational system.
    b. an absolute monarchy.   d. an improved judicial system.

28. _____ What form of government did Lenin bring to Russia?
    a. absolute monarchy   c. democracy
    b. dictatorship   d. communism

C. CRITICAL THINKING

Answer the following questions in the space provided, on the back of this paper or on a separate sheet of paper.

29. **Making Comparisons:** How were people governed during the Roman Empire and during the Middle Ages?

30. **Identifying Central Issues:** Why were the 1600s and 1700s called the Age of Revolution? In your answer, name two revolutions that occurred during this time.

31. **Drawing Conclusions:** Why do you think that feudalism was an important part of people's lives during the Middle Ages? In your answer, briefly explain what feudalism was.

32. **Recognizing Cause and Effect:** How did the Russian serfs' living conditions lead to opposition to the czars? In your answer, describe the serfs' living conditions under the czars.

D. SKILL: INTERPRETING DIAGRAMS AND ILLUSTRATIONS

Use the illustration below of a medieval manor to answer the following questions. Write your answers on the lines provided.

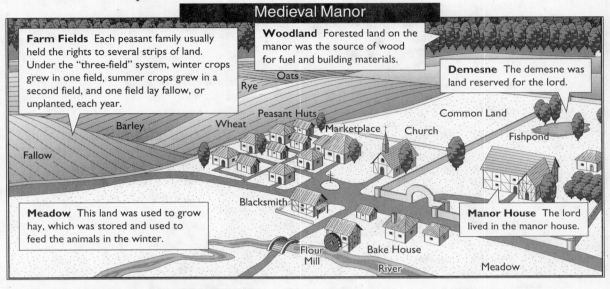

Medieval Manor

Farm Fields Each peasant family usually held the rights to several strips of land. Under the "three-field" system, winter crops grew in one field, summer crops grew in a second field, and one field lay fallow, or unplanted, each year.

Woodland Forested land on the manor was the source of wood for fuel and building materials.

Demesne The demesne was land reserved for the lord.

Meadow This land was used to grow hay, which was stored and used to feed the animals in the winter.

Manor House The lord lived in the manor house.

Oats
Rye
Barley
Wheat
Fallow
Peasant Huts
Marketplace
Church
Common Land
Fishpond
Blacksmith
Flour Mill
Bake House
River
Meadow

33. What does this diagram show? _____

_____

34. What is the difference between the demesne and the farm fields? _____

_____

35. Based on the labels on the diagram, what are three daily activities that took place on the manor? _____

_____

36. What was the meadow used for? _____

_____

37. How does this diagram help you understand what life on a medieval manor was like? _____

_____

_____

Use the illustration of the feudal social order to answer the following questions. Write your answer on the lines provided.

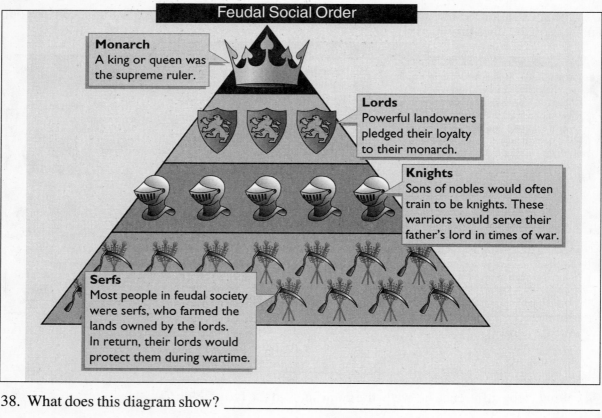

38. What does this diagram show? _____

_____

39. Who was at the top of feudal society? _____

_____

40. How were knights related to lords? _____

_____

41. Which group did most members of the population belong to? _____

_____

42. How does this diagram help you understand society under feudalism? _____

_____

ANSWER KEY

1. d	2. h	3. a	4. i	5. c
6. h	7. f	8. g	9. c	10. b
11. c	12. c	13. c	14. c	15. c
16. b	17. d	18. d	19. c	20. b
21. c	22. a	23. a	24. b	25. c
26. b	27. a	28. d		

29. Answers may vary. A possible answer: During the Roman Empire, an emperor ruled the people according to a system of well-organized written laws. After the fall of the Roman Empire, however, there was no central government. This period was called the Middle Ages. During the Middle Ages, people were ruled by feudal lords who controlled local areas. These lords, who were loyal to a more powerful leader, collected taxes, maintained order, and enforced the laws. The serfs who worked on the lords' manors could not leave without permission.

30. Answers may vary. A possible answer: During the 1600s and 1700s, far-reaching changes occurred in both government and science. Politically, it was the beginning of modern democracy as people began to question the absolute power traditionally held by monarchs. In the 18th century, there were revolutions in both America and France. There was also a Scientific Revolution, during which scientists learned to base their theories on facts that were tested via the scientific method.

31. Answers may vary. A possible answer: Feudalism was a method of organizing society when there was no central government. Under feudalism, leaders called lords ruled the local areas and owned land called a manor. The people who worked on the land were called serfs, and they depended on the lord for protection. Feudalism was important during this period because following the collapse of the Roman Empire, the powerful laws of the Roman government no longer protected people.

32. Answers may vary. A possible answer: Under the czars, there were two groups of people: the very rich and the very poor. The serfs were very poor. They could not own land and they were under the control of the person whose land they worked. When the serfs complained about their living conditions, the czars clamped down on them. Because they were unfairly treated, the serfs opposed the czars.

33. the buildings of a typical medieval manor

34. The demesne was land reserved for the lord of the manor. The farm fields were used by the peasant families to grow crops.

35. Answers may vary. A possible answer: People baked in the bake house, sold goods in the marketplace, and ground flour in the flour mill.

36. It was used to grow hay which fed the animals in the winter.

37. Answers may vary. A possible answer: The diagram helps me understand the different occupations of the people who lived on manors.

38. the feudal social order

39. the king or queen

40. Knights served their fathers' lords.

41. serfs

42. Answers may vary. A possible answer: This diagram helps me understand how a few people had power over many people during feudalism.

A. KEY TERMS

Match the definitions with the terms. Write the correct letter in each blank. You will not use all the terms.

        a. dialect
        b. ethnic group
        c. heritage
        d. immigrant
        e. migration
        f. multicultural
        g. propaganda
        h. repress
        i. urbanization

1. _____ the growth of cities

2. _____ a person who moves to one country from another

3. _____ a different version of a language that can be found only in a certain region

4. _____ movement from place to place by a group

5. _____ customs and practices that are passed from one generation to the next

Complete each sentence by writing the letter of the correct term in the blank. You will not use all the terms.

        a. dialect
        b. ethnic group
        c. heritage
        d. immigrant
        e. migration
        f. multicultural
        g. propaganda
        h. tariff
        i. urbanization

6. _____ Many different cultures influence the way of life in a(n) _____ country.

7. _____ Governments sometimes charge a fee, or a(n) _____ , on goods entering the country.

8. _____ People who share things such as a culture, a language, and a religion are called a(n) _____ .

9. _____ People who speak the same language may be unable to understand each other if they each speak a different _____ , or version of the language.

10. _____ Customs and practices that are passed from one generation to the next form a culture's _____ .

B. KEY CONCEPTS

Write the letter of the correct answer in each blank.

11. _____ In Western Europe 200 years ago, most people worked as
    a. merchants.   c. farmers.
    b. sailors.   d. manufacturers.

12. _____ Since World War II, what has happened to the movement of the population in Europe?
    a. Large numbers of people have left Western Europe.
    b. People have begun moving to Western Europe.
    c. People have left the large cities and moved to farms.
    d. People have moved to Eastern Europe and South Asia.

13. _____ What was one result of the Industrial Revolution?
    a. the development of small towns   c. the growth of large cities
    b. the growth of large farms   d. the increased need for farmworkers

14. _____ Although Slavs share the same customs, they have different
    a. languages and religions.   c. cultures and languages.
    b. cultures and economies.   d. religions and economies.

15. _____ The customs of Slavs have changed slowly because most Slavs live
    a. in urban areas.   c. close together.
    b. in one nation.   d. in rural areas.

16. _____ What happened when Czechoslovakia divided in 1993?
    a. Many ethnic communities fought each other.
    b. Two new countries were peacefully formed.
    c. The Magyars gained most of the land.
    d. One part of the country joined Russia.

17. _____ The largest ethnic group in Russia is the
    a. Mongolians.   c. Turks.
    b. Armenians.   d. Slavs.

18. _____ What is one important way in which Russians are reconnecting with their past?
    a. by forming separate countries   c. by practicing their religion
    b. by learning to read and write   d. by learning about Western culture

19. _____ To keep the country unified, the new Russian government has allowed ethnic groups to
    a. rule themselves.
    b. form new countries.
    c. join forces with other Eastern European countries.
    d. join forces with European countries.

20. _____ As a result of the Industrial Revolution, many people in Western Europe moved to
- a. large farms.
- c. cities.
- b. America.
- d. suburbs.

21. _____ Since World War II, many people have moved
- a. from Europe to North Africa and Asia.
- b. to Western Europe from Eastern Europe and South Asia.
- c. from Western Europe to the United States.
- d. to Eastern Europe from Western Europe.

22. _____ How is the European Union working to expand trade in Europe?
- a. by increasing taxes on imported goods
- b. by increasing the amount of imports
- c. by ending fees on goods entering the countries
- d. by ending taxes in different European countries

23. _____ Many Western European countries can be described as
- a. rural.
- c. poor.
- b. multicultural.
- d. isolated.

24. _____ Why do Slavs share many of the same customs?
- a. They live in urban areas where customs change slowly.
- b. They live mainly in one nation.
- c. They live in rural areas where customs change slowly.
- d. They live near large factories where they work.

25. _____ The Russian Orthodox religion and the Slavic ethnic group are two important influences on
- a. the old Soviet Union.
- c. Western tradition.
- b. communism.
- d. Russia's heritage.

26. _____ After the breakup of the Soviet Union, some non-Russian ethnic groups wanted to form
- a. their own religion.
- c. a permanent union with Russia.
- b. their own separate countries.
- d. an alliance with Eastern Europe.

27. _____ Under communism, the government only liked art that
- a. had been done during the Renaissance.
- c. supported communism.
- b. reflected Western traditions.
- d. supported the czar.

28. _____ Under the education system of the old Soviet Union, the nation increased
- a. the number of people who could read and write.
- b. the high school dropout rate.
- c. the number of religious schools.
- d. the number of private schools.

C. CRITICAL THINKING

Answer the following questions in the space provided, on the back of this paper or on a separate sheet of paper.

29. Recognizing Cause and Effect: What are two ways that the Industrial Revolution affected the culture of Western Europe?

30. Drawing Conclusions: This chapter explains that some non-Russian ethnic groups broke away from Russia and formed their own countries when the Soviet Union came apart. Why do you think this happened?

31. Recognizing Cause and Effect: How do you think the location of Western European countries and the ease of movement between them has affected the cultures of the region?

32. Identifying Central Issues: "Customs change more slowly in rural areas than in cities." What is the relationship between this idea and cultural change in Eastern and Western Europe?

D. SKILL: SUMMARIZING INFORMATION

Read the following paragraphs below from Chapter 3. Then answer the questions. Write your answers on the lines provided.

Immigrants do not simply leave their cultures when they leave their homelands. They bring along their languages, religious beliefs, values, and customs. But most immigrants make changes in their ways of life. They may change the way they dress. They may try new foods and discover new ways of cooking. Most of them learn the language of their new country.

In many ways, immigration has changed the cultures of Western Europe. In countries like Britain and France, people from many different backgrounds live and work together. They learn about one another's way of life. In the process, the cultures blend and change. In this way, many Western European countries have become multicultural. A multicultural country's way of life is influenced by many different cultures.

33. What is a main idea that you would include in a one-paragraph summary of the material you have just read? _____

_____

34. What is a detail you would include in your summary? _____

_____

35. What is a second detail you would include? _____

_____

36. What would be the first sentence of your summary? _____

_____

37. How does summarizing important information in a textbook help you prepare for a test? __

_____

_____

Read the following paragraphs below from Chapter 3. Then answer the following questions. Write your answers on the lines provided.

Let's focus on life in Germany for a moment. Most visitors to Germany think that the Germans are efficient. In other words, Germans do their work without waste or extra effort. Visitors get this idea from what they see. In Germany, cities, streets, and buses are clean. Hotels are well run. German cars are well designed and long lasting. Travel is swift on an excellent system of four-lane highways. Travel is equally fast on high-speed trains.

But life in Germany is not all hard work and fast-paced activity. Many workers enjoy up to six weeks of vacation each year. Outdoor recreation is popular. Mountains and highlands allow skiing, hiking, and camping. The country's many rivers, as well as the North and Baltic seas, are good for swimming and boating. Those who prefer city life enjoy the museums, concerts, and plays.

38. What is a main idea that you would include in a one-paragraph summary of the material you have just read? _____

_____

39. What is a detail you would include in your summary? _____

_____

40. What is a second detail you would include? _____

_____

41. What would be the first sentence of your summary? _____

_____

42. How might summarizing this information help you in your schoolwork? _____

_____

ANSWER KEY

1. i	2. d	3. a	4. e	5. c
6. f	7. h	8. b	9. a	10. c
11. c	12. b	13. c	14. a	15. d
16. b	17. d	18. c	19. a	20. c
21. b	22. c	23. b	24. c	25. d
26. b	27. c	28. a		

29. Answers may vary. A possible answer: As the factories' need for workers grew, more and more people moved to cities from rural areas. This resulted in the growth of cities, which increased after World War II. Also, as industry developed after World War II, immigrants moved to Western Europe from other countries, bringing their cultures with them.

30. Answers may vary. A possible answer: The non-Russian ethnic groups speak languages other than Russian and follow different religions. Also, they live far from the heavily populated western areas. As a result, they probably aren't closely tied to the culture and customs of Russian ethnic groups. This cultural diversity probably led to their decision to have their own homelands.

31. Answers may vary. A possible answer: Because European countries are small and close together, it's easy for travelers to get from one country to another quickly. Also, many people are moving to Western European countries from countries in Eastern Europe, North Africa, South Asia, and the Middle East. This ease of movement has enabled new ideas and cultures to be introduced into countries throughout the continent. As a result, cultures blend and change.

32. Answers may vary. A possible answer: In Eastern Europe, which has fewer factories than Western Europe, large numbers of people still live in rural areas and work as farmers. As a result, the people's culture and way of life has not changed very much. However, in Western Europe, which is more industrialized, more people live and work in the cities. As a result, the culture here has changed more quickly.

33. Answers may vary. A possible answer: "Immigration has changed the cultures of Western Europe."

34. Answers may vary. A possible answer: British and French people learn about each other's way of life.

35. Answers may vary. A possible answer: Immigrants bring their own languages and values when they leave their homelands.

36. Answers may vary. Possible answer: "When immigrants move to other countries, the old and new cultures blend and change."

37. Answers may vary; however, students may note that they can organize important information.

38. Answers may vary. A possible answer: "Life in Germany is a mixture of hard work and more leisurely activity."

39. Answers may vary. A possible answer: Many aspects of German life are efficiently run.

40. Answers may vary. A possible answer: People have time for leisurely activities, such as skiing, hiking, and camping.

41. Answers may vary. A possible answer: "Although life in Germany today is fast paced, many people also enjoy up to six weeks of vacation every year."

42. Answers may vary. A possible answer: Summarizing information about Germany could help me remember what I learned about it.

A. KEY TERMS

Match the definitions with the terms. Write the correct letter in each blank. You will not use all the terms.

a. benefit
b. constitutional monarchy
c. Holocaust
d. manufacturing
e. national debt
f. parliament
g. representative
h. reunification
i. welfare state

1. _____ a form of government in which the power of kings and queens is limited by a set of national laws

2. _____ a free service or payment

3. _____ a system in which many services are paid for by the government

4. _____ the process of turning raw materials into finished products

5. _____ the process of becoming unified again

Complete each sentence by writing the letter of the correct term in the blank. You will not use all the terms.

a. constitutional monarchy
b. emigrate
c. Holocaust
d. national debt
e. manufacturing
f. Parliament
g. representative
h. reunification
i. welfare state

6. _____ An elected official who stands for a group of people in a particular area of the country is called a(n) _____ .

7. _____ Since World War II, many people living in French colonies decided to move away, or _____ , from their homelands to France.

8. _____ Many services are paid for by the government in a(n) _____ .

9. _____ During the Industrial Revolution, _____ , which turned raw materials into finished products, became an important part of the economy of many European countries.

10. _____ The mass murder of six million Jews and other people during World War II is called the _____ .

B. KEY CONCEPTS

Write the letter of the correct answer in each blank.

11. _____ Which of the following statements about British democracy is true?
    a. It grants the king great power.
    b. Its roots go back hundreds of years.
    c. It began after World War II.
    d. It has caused a national debt.

12. _____ Great Britain's colonies provided the country with
    a. a new constitution and parliament.
    b. foreign debts to be paid.
    c. raw materials for its factories.
    d. manufactured goods to sell to the citizens.

13. _____ Great Britain became a member of the European Union in order to improve its
    a. educational system.
    b. economy.
    c. relationship with its colonies.
    d. welfare system.

14. _____ How has the French government reacted to foreign influences?
    a. It has made laws to encourage them.
    b. It has passed laws to discourage them.
    c. It has changed from a welfare state to a democracy.
    d. It is now similar to Sweden.

15. _____ In order to fulfill its promise of a better life for all Swedes, the Social Democratic party changed the country into
    a. a welfare state.
    b. a multicultural country.
    c. an absolute monarchy.
    d. an agricultural nation.

16. _____ One drawback to Sweden's current benefit system is that people spend
    a. too many hours working.
    b. too much time waiting for benefits.
    c. more money on goods than on education.
    d. less money on clothing and other goods.

17. _____ Compared to northern Italy, southern Italy is very
    a. nationalist and democratic.
    b. poor and traditional.
    c. agricultural and religious.
    d. wealthy and modern.

18. _____ The Italian government has helped the development of the southern region by
    a. decreasing taxes throughout the nation.
    b. refusing to join the European Union.
    c. building new schools and hospitals.
    d. decreasing the nation's foreign debt.

19. _____ What happened to Germany at the end of World War II?
    a. It was reunified.
    b. It joined the European Union.
    c. It was divided into two countries.
    d. It was governed by the United Nations.

20. _____ What are two things that helped make Britain a true democracy?
    a. raising taxes and providing benefits
    b. unifying with Scotland and Wales
    c. Parliament and representatives
    d. the changing of the guard and the crown jewels

21. _____ In Great Britain, the constitution limits the power of the
    a. monarchy.   c. absolute monarchy.
    b. Magna Carta.   d. welfare state.

22. _____ Because Great Britain is an island, it has limited
    a. educational facilities.   c. harbors.
    b. trade routes.   d. natural resources.

23. _____ Why has French culture changed since World War II?
    a. Children of immigrants are considered French citizens.
    b. People do not use foreign words in business.
    c. Immigrants have arrived from former French colonies.
    d. The government has refused to join the European Union.

24. _____ In order to pay for the benefits for Swedish citizens, the people must pay
    a. high taxes.   c. all educational expenses.
    b. all medical costs.   d. retirement benefits.

25. _____ What is one solution to Sweden's economic problems?
    a. spend more money on education
    b. increase the national debt
    c. increase taxes for all citizens and businesses
    d. make better use of the country's natural resources

26. _____ Italy's history is closely linked with the history of the
    a. Catholic Church.   c. fashion industry.
    b. Slavic people.   d. monarchy.

27. _____ What statement best describes the economy of northern Italy?
    a. The region is the center of the lumber industry.
    b. The region is a manufacturing center.
    c. The region is an agricultural center.
    d. The region is the center of the fishing industry.

28. ____ The United Kingdom is made up of
    a. England and Ireland.
    b. England, Scotland, Wales, and Northern Ireland.
    c. Great Britain and Scotland.
    d. England, Scotland, and Ireland.

C. CRITICAL THINKING

Answer the following questions in the space provided, on the back of this paper or on a separate sheet of paper.

29. Identifying Central Issues: What are two foreign influences on modern French culture?

30. Recognizing Cause and Effect: What effect did World War II have on Germany? In your answer, address Germany's past and present situations.

31. Expressing Problems Clearly: What are some of the problems faced by Sweden because of the country's government benefits program?

32. Making Comparisons: How are the problems faced by northern and southern Italy similar to those faced by a reunited Germany? How are they different?

D. SKILL: USING THE WRITING PROCESS

Use your knowledge about the writing process and the following diagram to answer the questions below. Write your answers on the lines provided.

The Writing Process

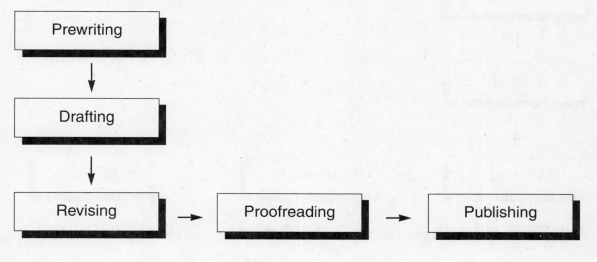

33. What two steps are involved in prewriting? _____

_____

34. What two steps are involved in drafting? _____

_____

35. Why do you make changes in your writing when you revise it? _____

_____

36. What do you correct in the proofreading step? _____

_____

37. What are two ways you can share your writing with an audience? _____

_____

The following diagram can be used to show the steps in the writing process. Fill in the boxes on the diagram as you write your answers to the following questions on the lines provided.

The Writing Process

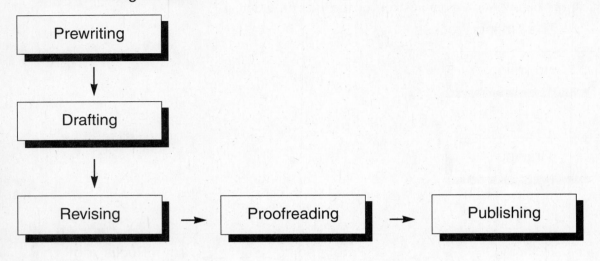

38. What is the first step in the writing process and what does it involve? _____

_____

39. What is the next step in the writing process? What does this step involve? _____

_____

40. What is the third step in the writing process? What does it involve? _____

_____

41. In what stage of the writing process do you check for small errors? _____

_____

42. What is the last step in the writing process? What does this step involve?_____

_____

ANSWER KEY

1. b	2. a	3. i	4. d	5. h
6. g	7. b	8. i	9. e	10. c
11. b	12. c	13. b	14. b	15. a
16. d	17. b	18. c	19. c	20. c
21. a	22. d	23. c	24. a	25. d
26. a	27. b	28. b		

29. Answers may vary. A possible answer: One foreign influence on French culture is the many people that have moved to France from the French colonies since World War II. In addition, when France joined the European Union, immigrants from other European countries moved there looking for work. A second foreign influence is represented by the EuroDisney theme park, which opened just outside of Paris in 1992.

30. Answers may vary. A possible answer: World War II divided Germany. When the Soviet Union, Britain, France, and the United States defeated Germany in the war, they divided the country. The American, British, and French sections were joined into a democratic country called West Germany. The Soviet Union installed a communist system in East Germany. Eventually, the two Germanys were reunited, but since each country had gotten used to a different style of government, differences between the two sides still exist today. Westerners are used to more freedom and economic opportunities. Easterners are used to things like free child care and guaranteed jobs.

31. Answers may vary. A possible answer: The country's economy has stalled. Since people pay such high taxes, they spend less money on clothing, food, and other goods. Also, medical care is not always available when it is needed. The government faces budgetary problems because to pay for the welfare benefits, it has borrowed heavily. As a result, the national debt has gotten out of control.

32. Answers may vary. A possible answer: Northern Italy and southern Italy have been united throughout Italy's history. The ways of life in northern and southern Italy set these two areas apart. Northern Italy is a manufacturing center; southern Italy is mostly agricultural. Also, northern Italy has more money than southern Italy. Northern Italy is paying for some of southern Italy's modernization. East and West Germany, however, were two separate countries until recently. East Germany was a communist nation; West Germany was a democracy. Their political differences set them apart. Since reunification, Germany has spent millions of dollars rebuilding the economy of what was East Germany. However, former East Germans have lost some of the economic benefits they enjoyed under communism, such as free child care and cheap housing.

33. deciding what you will write about; finding the information

34. making and revising an outline; writing a rough draft of your work

35. to make it clearer and more enjoyable to read

36. any errors in grammar, usage, spelling, and punctuation

37. turning it in to your teacher; posting it on the bulletin board

38. Prewriting is the first step. It involves deciding what you will write about and finding the information.

39. The second step is drafting. Drafting involves making and revising an outline as well as writing a rough draft of your work.

40. The third step is revising. That means you change your work so it's clearer and more enjoyable to read.

41. in the proofreading stage

42. The last step is publishing or sharing your work with an audience.

A. KEY TERMS

Complete each sentence by writing the letter of the correct term in the blank. You will not use all the terms.

- a. chernozem
- b. collective
- c. free enterprise
- d. icon
- e. investor
- f. shrine
- g. United Nations

1. _____ People open and run their own businesses under the system of _____ .

2. _____ A painting of a saint or a holy person is called a(n) _____ .

3. _____ The organization through which countries work to bring about peace and cooperation in the world is called the _____ .

4. _____ A rich, black soil called _____ covers half of Ukraine.

5. _____ Russia is now a country where an American _____ might spend money improving a business in the hopes of getting a profit.

Match the definitions with the terms. Write the correct letter in each blank. You will not use all the terms.

- a. chernozem
- b. collective
- c. communist
- d. free enterprise
- e. investor
- f. shrine
- g. United Nations

6. _____ an economic system in which people can open and run their own businesses

7. _____ a holy place

8. _____ rich, black soil

9. _____ a large, government-owned farm

10. _____ someone who spends money on improving a business in the hope of getting more money when it succeeds

B. KEY CONCEPTS

Write the letter of the correct answer in each blank.

11. _____ Since the fall of communism, Poland has adopted an economic system in which
   a. the government owns and runs most of the businesses.
   b. foreign countries own and run all the businesses.
   c. people own and run most of the businesses.
   d. Eastern European countries own and run all the businesses.

12. _____ For centuries, the center of Polish tradition has been the
   a. government.
   b. Catholic Church.
   c. Greek Orthodox Church.
   d. university system.

13. _____ Today, the standard of living in Poland is improving
   a. less rapidly than the educational system.
   b. less rapidly than in other Eastern European countries.
   c. more rapidly than in other Eastern European countries.
   d. more rapidly than the social security system.

14. _____ While most Serbians belong to the Christian Orthodox Church, most Bosnians practice
   a. Judaism.
   b. Roman Catholicism.
   c. the Muslim religion.
   d. Buddhism.

15. _____ What was a chief cause of the war in Bosnia-Herzegovina?
   a. No one political party wanted to form a government in Yugoslavia.
   b. No one ethnic group wanted to live in a country ruled by people from another group
   c. No one country wanted to take control of the region.
   d. No one ethnic group wanted to speak a different language.

16. _____ Other countries have invaded Ukraine because of
   a. the country's natural resources.
   b. the country's excellent universities.
   c. the country's foreign trade routes.
   d. the country's location in Europe.

17. _____ When the Soviet Union ruled Ukraine, individual farms were replaced with
   a. schools.
   b. large markets.
   c. collectives.
   d. factories.

18. _____ Many people in Ukraine suffered serious health problems because of
   a. the lack of meat and milk in their diet.
   b. the breakdown of the national health system.
   c. the nuclear accident at Chernobyl.
   d. the invasion by Soviet forces.

19. _____ What statement best describes life in Moscow?
   a. No one maintains any traditional ways.
   b. All the people live as their ancestors did.
   c. The free enterprise system has brought changes to the city, but Russian traditions still remain.
   d. Communism is helping people adapt to new ways.

20. _____ How has the Polish economy changed since the fall of the communist government?
   a. Collective farms were built.
   b. People own and run their own businesses.
   c. A socialist system was adopted.
   d. A foreign debt was paid.

21. _____ Two important Polish traditions are
   a. Greek Orthodoxy and Polish collective farms.
   b. Greek Orthodoxy and the Polish language.
   c. Polish Catholicism and the Polish language.
   d. Polish Catholicism and the Russian language.

22. _____ Serbians, Croatians, and Bosnians have different
   a. languages.   c. economies.
   b. religions.   d. educational systems.

23. _____ Croatia and Bosnia-Herzegovina used to be part of
   a. Russia.   c. Yugoslavia.
   b. Czechoslovakia.   d. Europe.

24. _____ Throughout its history, Ukraine's location and natural resources have attracted
   a. investors.   c. merchants.
   b. invaders.   d. scholars.

25. _____ One important economic change made by the Soviets in Ukraine was the creation of
   a. small family farms.   c. trade routes with the West.
   b. a free enterprise system.   d. large collectives.

26. _____ The accident at Chernobyl affected the environment by
   a. filling the air with poisonous gases.
   b. causing serious floods.
   c. causing serious droughts.
   d. lowering the temperature of the atmosphere.

27. _____ Which statement best describes life in Siberia today?
   a. Life in many Siberian villages is similar to life in American suburbs.
   b. Life in many Siberian villages is still very traditional.
   c. Life in Siberian villages has been changed by the free enterprise system.
   d. Life in Siberian villages is similar to life in Moscow.

28. _____ Although Moscow has been changed by the free market system, many people there are still influenced by
   a. Russian traditions.   c. the Siberian language.
   b. the Slavic educational system.   d. Ukrainian agricultural methods.

C. CRITICAL THINKING

Answer the following questions in the space provided, on the back of this paper or on a separate sheet of paper.

29. Draw Conclusions: Why do you think Ukraine wanted its independence from the Soviet Union?

30. Making Comparisons: How is life in the Polish countryside different from life in the cities? In your answer, explain what probably accounts for this difference.

31. Expressing Problems Clearly: What are three differences among Bosnians, Croatians, and Serbians that contributed to the conflict in Bosnia-Herzegovina?

32. Distinguishing Fact From Opinion: Give two facts and two opinions about life in Siberia.

D. SKILL: RECOGNIZING CAUSE AND EFFECT

Read the paragraph below. Then answer the questions. Write your answers on the lines provided.

Traditional ways still continue in Siberia. But the fall of communism and the arrival of free enterprise are starting to affect life in the region. Under the communist system, everyone was guaranteed a job. Now Siberians who work in factories and coal mines must worry about losing their jobs. On the other hand, for the first time in more than 70 years, Siberians are able to buy their own homes. Before, they had to live in houses that belonged to the state. People can also buy stock in the companies for which they work.

33. What was one effect of living under the communist system of government in Siberia? _____

_____

_____

34. What is one negative effect of the fall of communism in Siberia? _____

_____

_____

35. What is one positive effect of the fall of communism in Siberia? _____

_____

_____

36. Which of the above effects is the cause of something else? _____

_____

_____

37. What does that effect cause? _____

_____

_____

CHAPTER 5

Read the paragraphs below. Then answer the questions. Write your answers on the lines provided.

People like store owner Janusz Rajtar are doing well in the new Poland. To find the best products for his store, Rajtar rises at 4:00 a.m. to buy fruits and vegetables at the local farmers' market. By 7:00 a.m., he is behind his desk at a second job, working in an office. Then, at 3:00 p.m., he is back at the grocery store.

Janusz Rajtar is benefiting from his hard work. But people like Janusz's brother-in-law are working harder and are not benefiting. Farmers, with no government support, find it hard to compete in the European market. Many young people in rural areas feel that they have little chance to make a decent living. Some have moved to the city in the hope of finding jobs.

Migration to the cities, however, can cause overcrowding. Today, 60 percent of all Poles live in towns or cities, a huge increase from just 50 years ago. In response, the government is building apartment buildings and expanding suburban areas.

38. What is one effect of Janusz Rajtar's hard work? _____

_____

_____

39. What is one effect of the loss of government support for farms? _____

_____

_____

40. What is one effect of young people's loss of hope of making a living in the country? _____

_____

_____

41. Which of the above effects has been the cause of something else? _____

_____

_____

42. What has that effect caused? _____

_____

_____

ANSWER KEY

1. c	2. d	3. g	4. a	5. e
6. d	7. f	8. a	9. b	10. e
11. c	12. b	13. c	14. c	15. b
16. a	17. c	18. c	19. c	20. b
21. c	22. b	23. c	24. b	25. d
26. a	27. b	28. a		

29. Answers may vary. A possible answer: The Soviet Union dominated life in Ukraine for almost 70 years because of the area's vast natural resources. Under the Soviets, the official language was Russian. During this period Ukrainian industries grew, and the region eventually produced 25 percent of the country's goods as well as weapons and ships for the armed forces. However, the Soviets forced Ukrainian farmers to work on government-owned farms called collectives, which sent all the produce to the government. As a result, in the 1930s millions of Ukrainians died of hunger. The Ukrainians wanted to be independent of the Soviet Union and to go back to their own way of life, including reestablishing their ethnic identity by making Ukrainian the official language.

30. Answers may vary. A possible answer: In the countryside, traditions remain strong, but the economy is not good. Polish Catholicism has been at the center of Polish tradition, and the Polish language has also stood the test of time, but without government assistance, many farmers are struggling. Young people are moving out of the countryside to search for jobs. The cities show the strongest evidence of the new Poland. Small businesses have been started all over Warsaw and their owners are beginning to make good money. People are moving into the cities looking for opportunity. Because the cities are more likely to be influenced by foreign economies and cultural influences, the lifestyle there is probably less traditional. Also, change generally happens more slowly in rural areas, where modern communication and transportation are limited.

31. Answers may vary. A possible answer: Although the groups speak Serbo-Croatian, the Serbians and Croatians use different alphabets for this language. Also, while most Serbians belong to the Christian Orthodox Church, most Croatians are Roman Catholics, and most Bosnians are Muslims. Another difference is that the Serbians were in control of the government of Yugoslavia and the Croatians and Bosnians were not in control.

32. Answers may vary. A possible answer: Facts: Many of the factories in Siberia are outdated. Many Siberian homes have no running water. Opinions: People are foolish to live in Siberia. Life in Siberia is not as satisfying as life in Moscow.

33. Everyone here was guaranteed a job.

34. People are no longer guaranteed a job.

35. Siberians are able to buy their own homes.

36. People are no longer guaranteed a job.

37. It causes people to worry about losing their jobs.

38. He is benefiting economically.

39. Farmers find it hard to compete in the European market.

40. They move to cities.

41. Young people move to cities.

42. The cities are becoming overcrowded.

Chapter 6 ■ *Final Exam*

A. KEY TERMS

Complete each sentence by writing the letter of the correct term in the blank. You will not use all the terms.

- a. chernozem
- b. free enterprise
- c. icon
- d. immigrant
- e. imperialism
- f. manufacturing
- g. national debt
- h. tundra
- i. United Nations

1. _____ A treeless plain where grasses and mosses grow is a(n) _____ .

2. _____ The practice of one country turning another into a colony is called _____ .

3. _____ A person who moves from one country to another is a(n) _____ .

4. _____ Governments have to limit their _____ , or the money that is owed to another government.

5. _____ A thick, black soil called _____ is found in Ukraine.

Match the definitions in with the terms. Write the correct letter in each blank. You will not use all the terms.

- a. absolute monarch
- b. chernozem
- c. collective
- d. emigrate
- e. investor
- f. peninsula
- g. tariff
- h. tundra
- i. urbanization

6. _____ a body of land nearly surrounded by water

7. _____ a treeless plain where grasses and mosses grow

8. _____ a ruler who exercises complete power over his subjects

9. _____ the growth of cities

10. _____ to move from your homeland to another country

B. KEY CONCEPTS

Write the letter of the correct answer in each blank.

11. _____ More than half of Europe is covered by the
    a. Central Uplands.
    c. Northwestern Highlands.
    b. Alpine Mountain System.
    d. North European Plain.

12. _____ Two of Russia's most important resources are
    a. fossil fuels and iron ore.
    c. hydroelectric power and loess.
    b. loess and water.
    d. fossil fuels and water.

13. _____ Early European explorers searched for new routes to
    a. Russia and Ukraine.
    c. the Arctic Sea.
    b. rich lands in other parts of the world.
    d. the Central Uplands.

14. _____ How did the Industrial Revolution change the way of life in Europe in the 1800s?
    a. Large farms developed.
    c. People returned to their farms.
    b. Cities grew quickly.
    d. Wages quickly rose.

15. _____ What statement best describes the direction of human movement since World War II?
    a. Many people left Western Europe.
    b. Many people moved to Western Europe.
    c. Many people moved to Eastern Europe.
    d. Many people moved to South Asia.

16. _____ Today the Slavs of Eastern Europe have different
    a. languages and customs.
    c. religions and customs.
    b. religions and languages.
    d. customs and ethnic backgrounds.

17. _____ Which of the following countries served as one of the first models for modern democracy?
    a. Italy
    c. Yugoslavia
    b. Russia
    d. Great Britain

18. _____ In order to give Swedish citizens a better life, the government changed the country into a
    a. constitutional monarchy.
    c. communist state.
    b. welfare state.
    d. absolute monarchy.

19. _____ Many countries have invaded Ukraine because of the area's
    a. location on the Atlantic Ocean.
    c. natural resources.
    b. climate.
    d. manufacturing centers.

20. _____ Two major physical features of Russia are the
    a. North European Plain and the West Siberian Plain.
    b. North European Plain and the Alpine Mountain System.
    c. Northwestern Highlands and the Alpine Mountain System.
    d. West Siberian Plain and the Central Uplands.

21. _____ The warm waters and winds of the Atlantic Ocean bring
   a. harsh weather to southern Europe.   c. mild weather to eastern Russia.
   b. mild weather to northwestern Europe. d. harsh weather to northern Russia.

22. _____ Why did feudalism play an important role in the Middle Ages?
   a. It increased the power of the serfs and the farmers.
   b. It limited the power of the lords in the local areas.
   c. It organized society when there was no central government.
   d. It enabled people to have a written code of laws.

23. _____ The Industrial Revolution changed life across Europe by encouraging people to
   a. return to their villages.
   b. work in factories in the cities.
   c. work on large, government-owned farms.
   d. move to farms in other countries.

24. _____ European ideas and laws were influenced by
   a. climate and vegetation.
   b. Christopher Columbus.
   c. the ancient Greeks and Romans.
   d. Grigory Rasputin.

25. _____ How has Great Britain's status as an island nation influenced its political development?
   a. It is now a constitutional monarchy.
   b. It has a Parliament whose members can make laws.
   c. It built a large empire to provide its factories with raw materials.
   d. It became a welfare state.

26. _____ Compared to southern Italy, northern Italy is very
   a. poor.   c. traditional.
   b. modern.   d. religious.

27. _____ Two important traditions in Poland are
   a. Catholicism and the welfare state.
   b. Islam and the Polish language.
   c. Greek Orthodoxy and the Russian language.
   d. Catholicism and the Polish language.

28. _____ Why was Ukraine forced to become part of the Soviet Union?
   a. The Soviet Union agreed to provide the region with food.
   b. Ukraine needed the Soviet Union's natural resources.
   c. The Soviets wanted to control the area's natural resources.
   d. The Soviets had been invaded by the Ukrainians in the past.

CHAPTER 6

C. CRITICAL THINKING

Answer the following questions in the space provided, on the back of this paper or on a separate sheet of paper.

29. Identifying Central Issues: How did the existence of different ethnic groups contribute to the war in Bosnia-Herzegovina?

30. Making Comparisons: Compare the economic changes made by the Soviets in Ukraine with the economic changes made by the government of Sweden.

31. Drawing Conclusions: How do you think the location and physical features of Europe and Russia have affected the population densities of these two areas? In your answer explain what population density is.

32. Identifying Central Issues: Why were the 1600s and 1700s called the Age of Revolution? In your answer, describe two revolutions that happened during this time.

D. SKILL: SUMMARIZING INFORMATION

Use the paragraph below to answer the following questions. Write your answers on the lines provided.

As an island nation, Great Britain is more difficult to invade than other European countries. During World War II, it was one of the few European countries that was not captured by the Germans. But as an island, Britain has limited natural resources. It must trade with other nations for resources. For this reason, trade has always been important to Britain.

In the 1500s, Britain began building a large empire. Its empire grew to include colonies on six continents. The colonies provided Britain's factories with raw materials. They also provided places to sell the goods made in Britain's factories. The colonies, then, helped Britain become a world economic power.

33. What is one important main idea you would include in a summary of these paragraphs? ____

_____

_____

34. What is another important main idea you would include in a summary? _____

_____

_____

35. What is one important detail you would include in your summary? _____

_____

_____

36. What is another important detail you would include in your summary? _____

_____

_____

37. What would be the first sentence of your summary? _____

_____

_____

CHAPTER 6

Read the paragraphs below. Look for cause-and-effect relationships between events. Then answer the following questions. Write your answers on the lines provided.

Governments had to respond to workers' complaints. Making and selling goods was a big part of a country's economy. This meant that workers had become very important. As a result, the Industrial Revolution helped give working people a bigger voice in government. Many European nations became more democratic.

At the same time, though, European governments were becoming more aggressive abroad. During the 1800s, many European nations took over other countries and turned them into colonies. This is called imperialism. European nations were making more goods than their people could buy. They needed more customers. Colonies could supply those buyers. Colonies also provided raw materials that industry needed. These raw materials included such things as cotton, wood, and metals.

38. What was one effect of the important role that making and selling goods played in the economy? _____

_____

_____

39. What is one effect of European nations making more goods than their customers could buy?

_____

_____

40. What is one effect of European nations wanting more raw materials for their countries? ___

_____

_____

41. Which of the above effects had more than one cause, according to the passage above? ____

_____

_____

42. Which of the above effects became the cause for a second effect? What was the second effect? _____

_____

_____

ANSWER KEY

1. h	2. e	3. d	4. g	5. a
6. f	7. h	8. a	9. i	10. d
11. d	12. a	13. b	14. b	15. b
16. b	17. d	18. b	19. c	20. a
21. b	22. c	23. b	24. c	25. c
26. b	27. d	28. c		

29. Answers may vary. A possible answer: The tensions among different ethnic groups, the Serbs, Croatians, and Bosnians, led to a long and bitter war. When the Serbs controlled the government of Yugoslavia, the other ethnic groups wanted to form their own countries to rule themselves. But the groups distrusted each other and no group wanted to live in a country ruled by people of another ethnic group. This situation probably developed because the political leaders didn't reduce tensions and emphasized the religious and ethnic differences between the people who lived in the region.

30. Answers may vary. A possible answer: The economic changes made under the Soviet rule of Ukraine were very harsh. Ukrainian industries grew, but farmers were forced to work on large government-owned collectives instead of on individually owned farms. All the crops went to the government, and millions of Ukrainians died of hunger as a result. In Sweden, however, the government worked to provide benefits to the people by creating a welfare state. To pay for these services, the government collected high taxes.

31. Answers may vary. A possible answer: Population density is the average number of people living in an area. Europe has a much higher population density than most of the world due to its mild climate, rich farmland, and water access. Because the continent of Europe forms a peninsula, its harbors and bays have enabled countries to trade with other lands throughout history. A major landform in Europe, the North European Plain, has productive farmland. Because of Europe's location, warm water and winds bring mild weather to much of northwestern Europe. Russia, however, has a much lower population density. Russia lies on the Arctic Ocean, which is frozen for most of the year and cannot be used for shipping. Also, few people can live in the vast plains and mountains of eastern Russia, where the soil is poor and the climate is very harsh.

32. Answers may vary. A possible answer: During this period, there were revolutions in government and science. People began questioning the power of their governments and the English king was overthrown when he refused to share power with Parliament. The idea that the people, not their king or queen, should decide which type of government was best for them also spread to the American colonies and to France. In the French Revolution, the people overthrew the monarchs. In the Scientific Revolution, scientists began to base their theories on careful observation of the natural world. One result of this new approach was the development of the scientific method, in which ideas are tested with experiments and observations.

33. Answers may vary. A possible answer: Since it's an island, Great Britain is more difficult to invade than other European countries.

34. Answers may vary. A possible answer: Britain built a large empire because it needed raw materials and customers for its goods.

35. Answers may vary. A possible answer: During World War II, Great Britain was one of the few European countries that wasn't captured by the Germans.

36. Answers may vary. A possible answer: Britain's empire grew to include colonies on six continents.

37. Answers may vary. A possible answer: Great Britain became a world economic power even though its own natural resources were limited.

38. Workers were very important.

39. Europeans took over other countries and made them into colonies.

40. Europeans took over other countries and made them into colonies.

41. Europeans made other countries into colonies because they wanted more customers as well as more raw materials.

42. When workers became more important they were given a greater voice in government.

World Explorer

ASIA AND THE PACIFIC

BOOK 6

A. KEY TERMS

Complete each sentence by writing the letter of the correct term in the blank. You will not use all the terms.

   a. developing country
   b. peninsula
   c. loess
   d. developed country
   e. population density
   f. hydroelectricity
   g. deciduous
   h. archipelago
   i. monsoon

1. _____ A group of islands is called a(n) _____ .

2. _____ In East Asia, a(n) _____ blows across the region at certain times of the year.

3. _____ A nation that has low industrial production and little modern technology is a(n) _____ .

4. _____ The power of running water is used to generate electricity called _____ .

5. _____ A piece of land that is nearly surrounded by water is a(n) _____ .

Match the definitions with the terms. Write the correct letter in each blank. You will not use all the terms.

   a. developed country
   b. peninsula
   c. population density
   d. deciduous
   e. developing country
   f. plateau
   g. hydroelectricity
   h. aquaculture
   i. typhoon

6. _____ a raised area of mostly level land

7. _____ the average number of people living in a square mile

8. _____ a violent storm that develops over the Pacific Ocean

9. _____ a country with many industries and a well-developed economy

10. _____ sea farming

B. KEY CONCEPTS

Write the letter of the correct answer or ending in each blank.

11. _____ Unlike the other countries of East Asia, China's most important landforms include wide plains and
    a. plateaus.   c. mountains.
    b. rivers.   d. coasts.

12. _____ Which country takes up most of the territory of East Asia?
    a. Korea   c. China
    b. Japan   d. Nepal

13. _____ The North China Plain, one of the most fertile regions of China, is covered with deposits of
    a. gold.   c. ore.
    b. loess.   d. lava.

14. _____ The world's fourth-longest river, the Huang He, runs through a fertile region of East Asia called
    a. Tibet.   c. the North China Plain.
    b. Mongolia.   d. Shanghai.

15. _____ Much of the climate of East Asia is best described as
    a. cold.   c. varied.
    b. tropical.   d. mild.

16. _____ Which of the following is a strong influence on the climates of East Asia?
    a. snowstorms   c. rivers
    b. monsoons   d. vegetation

17. _____ Why is bamboo grown so widely in East Asia?
    a. It requires constant care.
    b. It is a strong plant that can survive dry spells.
    c. It is inexpensive to grow.
    d. It cannot withstand seasonal changes in rainfall.

18. _____ Although both Japan and South Korea are developed countries, both nations have few
    a. rivers.   c. manufacturing centers.
    b. large cities.   d. mineral resources.

19. _____ Why must the countries of East Asia farm all the available land?
    a. to export food products to other countries
    b. to feed the area's large population
    c. to encourage people to leave the manufacturing centers
    d. to make up for the small fishing industry

20. _____ All of the countries of East Asia include which landform?
   a. plains
   b. mountains
   c. plateaus
   d. steppes

21. _____ Two thirds of China's land is made up of high mountains and
   a. plateaus.
   b. coastal regions.
   c. deserts.
   d. highlands.

22. _____ Which country has the most extremes in vegetation?
   a. China
   b. Japan
   c. North Korea
   d. South Korea

23. _____ The Korean peninsula is surrounded by the Yellow Sea and the
   a. Pacific Ocean.
   b. Atlantic Ocean.
   c. Sea of Japan.
   d. Chang Jiang River.

24. _____ Because of East Asia's location near the Pacific Ocean,
   a. aquaculture has become an important industry.
   b. boating is a popular form of recreation.
   c. farming is not common in the region.
   d. all East Asians fish.

25. _____ Which statement describes how climate is related to vegetation throughout East Asia?
   a. Because the climate is very dry, little vegetation grows.
   b. Because the climate is very wet, no vegetation grows.
   c. Because the climate varies, the vegetation must be strong enough to survive.
   d. Because the climate is very hot, only desert shrubs grow.

26. _____ How have South Korea's limited mineral resources influenced its economy?
   a. It is a developing nation.
   b. It is one of East Asia's poorest countries.
   c. It must import coal, iron, and crude oil.
   d. It must import many food products.

27. _____ Which statement best compares the natural resources of China and its East Asian neighbors?
   a. China has fewer natural resources than other East Asian countries.
   b. China has many more natural resources than other East Asian countries.
   c. Unlike other East Asian countries, China has a small supply of coal.
   d. Unlike other East Asian countries, China has no copper, tin, or iron.

28. _____ Because mountains and plateaus cover so much of East Asia, people must farm
   a. only the most fertile land.
   b. only the land that is near the rivers.
   c. every bit of available land.
   d. only the land in the small villages.

C. CRITICAL THINKING

Answer the following questions in the space provided, on the back of this paper or on a separate sheet of paper.

29. **Making Comparisons:** Explain the difference in the population densities of the lowland and coastal areas and the deserts, highlands, and mountains of East Asia.

30. **Drawing Conclusions:** How do South Korea's limited resources affect its economy?

31. **Drawing Conclusions:** What do you think life is like for people who live along the banks of the Huang He in China?

32. **Drawing Conclusions:** If North and South Korea could get along and were willing to share, how do you think both countries would benefit?

D. SKILLS

Use the following four reading strategies as you read the paragraph below. Then answer the questions. Write your answers on the lines provided.

- Ask Questions
- Predict
- Connect
- Visualize

It was 6:00 p.m. on September 24, 1975, when British climbers Doug Scott and Dougal Haston reached the summit of Mount Everest, on the border of China and Nepal. Their feelings of triumph and joy were mixed with concern. It would soon be night, and they would have to spend the night in a quickly built snow cave near the summit. But what they saw made them forget their concerns. Looking toward the Plateau of Tibet, a huge highland region in southern China, they saw a vast range of small hills. Actually, these hills were mountains—some of which rose to 24,000 feet (7,315 m). They seemed so small next to Everest! Beyond those "hills," Everest cast a huge purple shadow some 200 miles (322 km) across Tibet. "The view was so staggering," Scott said, that it held them "in awe."

33. What does this selection describe? _____

_____

_____

34. Why were the mountain climbers feeling a little concerned? _____

_____

_____

35. If the passage continued, what do you think you would read about next? _____

_____

_____

36. What else do you know about Mount Everest? _____

_____

_____

37. What do you think it would be like to reach the summit of Mount Everest and look toward the Plateau of Tibet? _____

_____

_____

Use the following four reading strategies as you read the paragraph below. Then answer the questions. Write your answers on the lines provided.

- Ask Questions
- Predict
- Connect
- Visualize

On some days, oil workers in China's desert regions battle stinging sand and blowing pebbles. On other days, extreme temperatures may freeze or burn their skin. Trucks sink in the sand as they collect the oil. But no matter how terrible the conditions are, the oil drilling never stops. Scientists estimate that 74 billion barrels of oil may lie beneath the desert. This amount is three times the oil reserves of the United States. If this estimate is correct, China will have enough oil to fuel its economy. If not, China will have to keep importing the oil it needs. This will reduce its industrial development.

38. What does this selection discuss? _____

_____

_____

39. What conditions do oil workers face in China? _____

_____

_____

40. If the passage continued, what do you think you might read about next? _____

_____

_____

41. What else do you know about oil production? _____

_____

_____

32. What do you think it would be like to work in a Chinese oil field? _____

_____

_____

ANSWER KEY

1. h	2. i	3. a	4. f	5. b
6. f	7. c	8. i	9. a	10. h
11. a	12. c	13. b	14. c	15. c
16. b	17. b	18. d	19. b	20. b
21. c	22. a	23. c	24. a	25. c
26. c	27. b	28. c		

29. Answers may vary, but should include reference to the following: Few people can live in the deserts, highlands, and mountains of East Asia. As a result, most of the 1.5 billion people of the region crowd into the lowland and coastal areas, where it is easier to live and grow food. The population densities of these parts of East Asia are higher than those of the rest of the area.

30. Answers may vary, but should include reference to the need for South Korea to import coal, iron, crude oil, and the chemicals it needs for its industries from other countries. Despite its lack of mineral resources, however, South Korea has become one of East Asia's richest countries.

31. Answers may vary, but should include the following: Because the river runs through one of the most fertile regions of China, the wide North China Plain, the people who live here are able to farm the land. In addition to growing food for their own families, farmers here are probably able to sell farm produce to other areas in China. However, it is also a dangerous place to live because of the severe floods.

32. Answers may vary, but should include the following: South Korea would not have to import the resources, such as coal and iron, it needs for its industries from other countries. North Korea would benefit from South Korea's industrial production and modern technology and become a developed country.

33. It describes what Scott and Dougal Haston saw and felt when they climbed to the summit of Mount Everest.

34. They knew they would have to spend the night in a quickly built snow cave near the summit.

35. Answers may vary, however, students might say that they would read more about the mountain climbers' adventures.

36. Answers may vary, but students might note that Mount Everest is part of the Himalaya Mountains. It is the tallest mountain in the world.

37. Answers may vary; however, students might comment on the amazing view.

38. It discusses oil production in China.

39. The conditions are terrible. They include blowing sand and pebbles and extreme temperatures; however, the oil-drilling never stops.

40. Answers may vary; however, students might say that they would read more about the importance of oil to China's industrial development.

41. Answers may vary, but students might note that oil is an important natural resource.

42. Answers may vary; however, students might comment on the difficult working conditions and the harsh climate.

A. KEY TERMS

Complete each sentence by writing the letter of the correct term in the blank. You will not use all the terms.

    a. nomad
    b. cultural diffusion
    c. dynasty
    d. emperor
    e. famine
    f. dialect
    g. discrimination
    h. subsidize
    i. free enterprise

1. _____ Starting in ancient times, China was governed by a(n) _____ , or ruler.

2. _____ A person who moves from place to place in search of water and grazing for animals is a(n) _____ .

3. _____ Under the _____ economic system, people can start private businesses and make a profit.

4. _____ Workers sometimes face unfair treatment, or _____ , in their jobs.

5. _____ North Korea faced a huge food shortage, or _____ , in 1996.

Match the definitions with the terms. Write the correct letter in each blank. You will not use all the terms.

    a. subsidize
    b. ethnic
    c. civilization
    d. emperor
    e. dynasty
    f. incentive
    g. free enterprise
    h. famine
    i. commune
    j. migration

6. _____ a society that includes cities, a central government, workers who do specialized jobs, and social classes

7. _____ a community in which land is held in common and where members live and work together

8. _____ an economic system in which people can choose their own jobs, start private businesses, and make a profit

9. _____ to support economically

10. _____ a huge food shortage

B. KEY CONCEPTS

Write the letter of the correct answer or ending in each blank.

11. _____ Some of ancient China's most important inventions were paper, gunpowder, and
   a. the printing press.   c. pottery.
   b. armored warships.   d. hot-air heating of homes.

12. _____ Why did Japanese leaders keep their country isolated from the outside world for
   many hundreds of years?
   a. to protect citizens from disease   c. to keep the country united
   b. to protect their farmland   d. to strengthen the army

13. _____ Why did Commodore Matthew Perry come to Japan in 1853?
   a. to conquer the country
   b. to overthrow the emperor
   c. to establish American settlements
   d. to force the country to grant trading rights to the U.S.

14. _____ When the communist government came to power in China in 1949, one major
   change it made in the Chinese way of life was
   a. encouraging the idea of large families.
   b. encouraging women to stop working.
   c. creating farm communes.
   d. establishing private ownership of land.

15. _____ Which statement best describes the populations of Korea and Japan?
   a. There are many minority groups in both countries.
   b. The populations of both countries are homogeneous.
   c. The largest ethnic group in both countries is the Ainu.
   d. The smallest ethnic group in both countries is the Han.

16. _____ In the 1950s, the communist government in China began a policy called The "Great
   Leap Forward" in order to increase
   a. taxes.   c. cultural change.
   b. production in farms and factories.   d. the power of the people.

17. _____ Where did the Chinese Nationalists establish the Republic of China?
   a. Tibet   c. Mongolia
   b. Taiwan   d. South Korea

18. _____ What is one key factor that is responsible for Japan's great economic success?
   a. Japanese workers work shorter hours than Western workers.
   b. Japanese workers have longer vacations than Western workers.
   c. Japanese companies offer few benefits to their workers.
   d. Japanese workers are loyal and hard working.

19. _____ What is the main reason that North and South Korea remain divided?
   a. They have different cultural heritages. c. They have political differences.
   b. They do not speak the same language. d. They have economic differences.

20. _____ Three important contributions made by ancient Chinese engineers were digging canals, building dams, and
   a. printing with movable type.   c. hot-air heating of homes.
   b. setting up irrigation systems.   d. building armored warships.

21. _____ Why do Korea and China have close historical ties?
   a. In ancient times, Chinese settled in the Korean peninsula.
   b. Korea invaded and conquered China.
   c. China invaded Korea.
   d. Migrations led to a transfer of Korean customs to China.

22. _____ Why did Japanese leaders isolate their country for many hundreds of years?
   a. They wanted to protect their farmland.
   b. They wanted to keep the country united.
   c. They wanted to build the Great Wall.
   d. They wanted to protect the emperor.

23. _____ Dynasties are used to describe the history of which country?
   a. Mongolia   c. China
   b. North Korea   d. Japan

24. _____ One reason North Korea's economy is slow is that
   a. the country lacks mineral resources.
   b. it depends too much on aid from South Korea.
   c. it is not diversified.
   d. communist countries cannot succeed economically.

25. _____ Why did Mao begin a government policy called "The Great Leap Forward" in China?
   a. to create a completely new society
   b. to conquer Korea
   c. to seize land from large landowners
   d. to increase production on farms and in factories

26. _____ How do Japan's workers contribute to the nation's economic success?
   a. by working shorter hours than Western workers
   b. by taking more vacations than Western workers
   c. by being loyal and committed to their companies
   d. by working toward individual rather than group goals

CHAPTER 2

27. _____ How has South Korea's economy changed since the end of World War II?
   a. It has changed from a farming to an industrial economy.
   b. It has focused on the development of its many natural resources.
   c. It has changed from an industrial to an agricultural economy.
   d. It has stopped importing raw materials for its industries.

28. _____ What important historical event affected life in the two Koreas in 1950?
   a. The two countries were united.
   b. South Korea invaded North Korea.
   c. The Communists took over North Korea.
   d. North Korea invaded South Korea.

C. CRITICAL THINKING

Answer the following questions in the space provided, on the back of this paper or on a separate sheet of paper.

29. Making Comparisons: Explain the similarities and differences in the opening up of Japan and China to Western countries.

30. Drawing Conclusions: Why do you think the old traditions survive more strongly in the rural areas of China and Korea?

31. Identifying Central Issues: Explain the political changes that took place in both China and Korea after World War II.

32. Drawing Conclusions: How does the loyalty of Japanese companies to their workers influence the Japanese economy?

D. SKILLS

Study the route map below. Then answer the following questions. Write your answers on the lines provided.

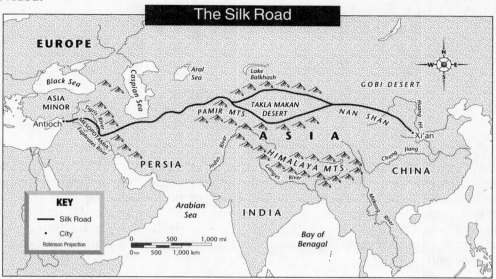

The Silk Road

33. What is the title of the map? _____

    _____

34. How does the map key help you read the map? _____

    _____

35. How is the Silk Road indicated on the map? _____

    _____

36. What are two major landforms that the Silk Road passes? _____

    _____

37. Why do you think the Silk Road divides and then meets again? _____

    _____

38. What title would you give the map? _____

    _____

39. What does the map key indicate? _____

    _____

40. To get to the Tigris River from the Pamir Mountains, what direction would you travel? ____

    _____

41. What two cities does the Silk Road connect? _____

    _____

42. Why do you think the Silk Road divides and then meets again? _____

    _____

CHAPTER 2

ANSWER KEY

1. d	2. a	3. i	4. g	5. e
6. c	7. i	8. g	9. a	10. h
11. a	12. c	13. d	14. c	15. b
16. b	17. b	18. d	19. c	20. b
21. a	22. b	23. c	24. c	25. d
26. c	27. a	28. d		

29. Answers may vary, but should include reference to the following: Western countries could not be kept away from China and Japan because they needed outlets for their manufactured goods. When U.S. Commodore Matthew Perry came to Japan in 1853, he forced the country to grant trading rights to the United States. Many foreign countries wanted to control parts of China and its wealth. Since China wasn't strong enough to protect itself, these countries gained control of parts of the country until the United States declared an open trade policy.

30. Answers may vary, but should include reference to the importance of industry and business in the cities of both countries, which would also increase contact with the cultures of Western countries. In the rural areas, the people are more likely to be farmers who have more limited economic and educational opportunities than city dwellers.

31. Answers may vary, but should include reference to the following: In China, civil war broke out after World War II between the Nationalists and the Communists. The Communists won the civil war in 1949 and made China a communist nation; the Nationalists set up a government on the island of Taiwan. After World War II, Korea was divided into two parts. The Communists ruled North Korea, and South Korea turned to Western nations for support. In 1950, the Koreas fought a bloody civil war, and neither side won.

32. Answers may vary, but should include reference to the following: By offering incentives such as free housing, education, and medical care, Japanese companies can attract workers and keep them happy and productive. The workers are loyal to their companies and work hard. Their productivity has a positive effect on the country's economy.

33. the Silk Road

34. It explains the symbols used for cities and the Silk Road.

35. with a black line

36. Answers will vary. Possible answers include the Black Sea, the Tigris River, the Caspian Sea, the Pamir Mountains, the Takla Makan Desert, and the Huang He River.

37. It divides to go around the Takla Makan Desert.

38. the Silk Road

39. the symbols used for cities and the Silk Road

40. east

41. Antioch and Xi´an

42. It divides to go around the Takla Makan Desert.

A. KEY TERMS

Complete each sentence by writing the letter of the correct term in the blank. You will not use all the terms.

    a. surplus
    b. Ring of Fire
    c. subcontinent
    d. Himalaya Mountains
    e. cash crop
    f. Ghat Mountains
    g. Bangladesh
    h. reserve
    i. rain forest
    j. monsoon

1. _____ At one time, the landmass that is now called the Indian _____ was attached to the east coast of Africa.

2. _____ A tropical _____ receives at least 60 inches of rain a year.

3. _____ Some countries on mainland Southeast Asia have produced a rice _____ , or more than the people need.

4. _____ In South and Southeast Asia, tea, cotton, or rubber may be raised as a _____ to be sold for money on the world market.

5. _____ The _____ is a region of volcanoes surrounding the Pacific Ocean.

Match the definitions with the terms. Write the correct letter in each blank. You will not use all the terms.

    a. cash crop
    b. Himalaya Mountains
    c. Southeast Asia
    d. rain forest
    e. monsoon
    f. Ring of Fire
    g. subcontinent
    h. landform
    i. surplus

6. _____ a large landmass that is a major part of a continent

7. _____ a thick forest that receives at least 60 inches of rain a year

8. _____ more than is needed

9. _____ a plant, such as tea or cotton, that is raised to be sold for money on the world market

10. _____ a region of volcanoes surrounding the Pacific Ocean

B. KEY CONCEPTS

Write the letter of the correct answer or ending in each blank.

11. _____ About 40 million years ago, the Indian subcontinent collided with Asia and formed the
a. Bay of Bengal.
b. Indus River.
c. Himalaya Mountains.
d. Indian Ocean.

12. _____ Which important South Asian rivers begin high in the Himalaya Mountains?
a. the Ganges and the Brahmaputra
b. the Indus and the Brahmaputra
c. the Indus and the Ganges
d. the Nile and the Ganges

13. _____ The nations of Vietnam, Cambodia, Laos, Myanmar, and Thailand form
a. island Southeast Asia.
b. South Asia.
c. the Indian subcontinent.
d. mainland Southeast Asia.

14. _____ The river valleys of South and Southeast Asia are more heavily populated than the mountain regions because of
a. the fertile farmland.
b. the industrial centers.
c. the many rain forests.
d. the cold weather.

15. _____ The single most important factor that affects the climate of South Asia is
a. the Himalaya Mountains.
b. the monsoons.
c. the Ghat Mountains.
d. the Bay of Bengal.

16. _____ Much of Southeast Asia has a climate that is described as
a. mild.
b. warm.
c. arid.
d. tropical wet.

17. _____ How do the Himalaya Mountains affect the weather during the winter months in South Asia?
a. They block the bitter cold air from reaching the region.
b. They cause heavy rains throughout the region.
c. They create extremely hot weather throughout the region.
d. They allow the dry, cold air to reach the region.

18. _____ One danger facing the rain forests of South and Southeast Asia is
a. lack of water.
b. logging.
c. extreme cold.
d. monsoon rains.

19. _____ The natural resources of South and Southeast Asia include land, minerals, and
a. industries.
b. water.
c. medicines.
d. chemicals.

20. _____ Malaysia, Brunei, Singapore, Indonesia, and the Philippines form
   a. South Asia.
   b. island Southeast Asia.
   c. the Indian subcontinent.
   d. mainland Southeast Asia.

21. _____ Winter in much of Southeast Asia can be described as
   a. snowy.
   b. rainy.
   c. cold.
   d. dry.

22. _____ The economy of people living in the Himalayas depends on
   a. cash crops.
   b. aquaculture.
   c. yak herds.
   d. trade.

23. _____ Why are mountains the most important landform in South Asia?
   a. They affect where rain falls in the region.
   b. They form a barrier between India and Sri Lanka.
   c. They prevent rivers from flooding.
   d. They contain the most fertile farmland in the region.

24. _____ The single most important factor in determining the climate of South Asia is
   a. the rivers of the region.
   b. the monsoons.
   c. the vegetation.
   d. the typhoons.

25. _____ Because of Southeast Asia's tropical wet climate the region is covered with
   a. plateaus.
   b. highlands.
   c. mountains.
   d. rain forests.

26. _____ During the winter months in Asia, what keeps the dry, cold air from reaching South Asia?
   a. the Himalaya Mountains
   b. the monsoons
   c. the rivers
   d. the plateaus

27. _____ Why do the majority of South Asians live in the river valleys of the region?
   a. because the land is cheap
   b. because the land is fertile
   c. because the land is dry
   d. because the land is flat

28. _____ Logging in South and Southeast Asia is threatening
   a. mineral resources.
   b. farming.
   c. the rain forests.
   d. the Himalayas.

CHAPTER 3

C. CRITICAL THINKING

Answer the following questions in the space provided, on the back of this paper or on a separate sheet of paper.

29. Identifying Central Issues: Explain the difference in population distribution between the river valleys and the mountainous regions of South and Southeast Asia.

30. Expressing Problems Clearly: What is one problem that is caused by using the mineral resources of South and Southeast Asia? What is one problem caused by using the rain forest resources of South and Southeast Asia?

31. Drawing Conclusions: Why are the rivers of South and Southeast Asia so important to the people who live in these regions?

32. Identifying Central Issues: Why are the rain forests of South and Southeast Asia considered a "fragile resource"?

D. SKILLS

Use the precipitation map to answer the following questions. Write your answers on the lines provided.

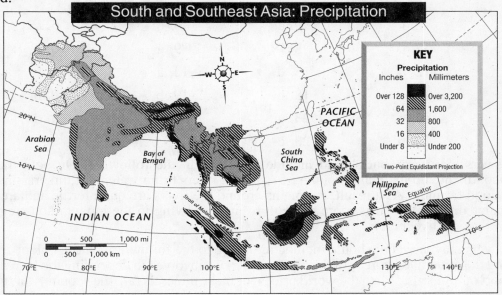

33. What is the amount of precipitation between 120°E and 130°E on the map? _____

_____

34. How much rain falls in the region between 10°N and 0°? _____

_____

35. How much rain falls just north of the Arabian Sea?_____

_____

36. As you move southeast of the Bay of Bengal, what happens to precipitation? _____

_____

37. How can you tell where little rain falls? _____

_____

38. What is the amount of precipitation between 70°E and 80°E on the map? _____

_____

39. How much rain do the rainiest parts of Southeast Asia receive each year? _____

_____

40. How much rain do the driest parts of Southeast Asia receive? _____

_____

41. Between what longitude lines are the driest parts of Southeast Asia? _____

_____

42. How does the key help you read the map? _____

_____

ANSWER KEY

1. c	2. i	3. a	4. e	5. b
6. g	7. d	8. i	9. a	10. f
11. c	12. c	13. d	14. a	15. b
16. d	17. a	18. b	19. b	20. b
21. b	22. c	23. a	24. b	25. d
26. a	27. b	28. c		

29. Answers may vary, but should include reference to the following: On both the Indian subcontinent and mainland Southeast Asia, the rivers bring water and minerals necessary for good farming. As a result, the plains around the rivers are quite fertile and are heavily populated. However, it is more difficult to make a living in the mountainous regions, so fewer people live there.

30. Answers may vary, but should include reference to the following: One problem caused by using the mineral resources of the region is the risk involved in depending too heavily on the export of minerals. When the world prices for these minerals fall, the economy of the area is adversely affected. Another serious problem is destroying too many trees in the Asian rain forests through logging, without giving the forests a chance to grow back.

31. Answers may vary, but should include the following: The river valleys are extremely fertile because rivers carry the water and minerals from the mountains that are necessary for good farming. As a result, the plains around the rivers are heavily populated in South Asia. Similarly, the fertile river valleys between the mountain ranges of mainland Southeast Asia are home to millions of people who live in small villages and grow their own food.

32. Answers may vary, but should include the following. The rain forests are an important resource because they contain a variety of plant and animal life and are valuable sources of raw materials, such as bamboo and timber. However, the rain forests are fragile because they are being destroyed by logging carried out with modern equipment. Because so many trees are being destroyed so quickly, the forests do not have a chance to grow back.

33. over 32 inches (800 mm)

34. over 64 inches (1,600 mm)

35. under 32 inches (800 mm)

36. It gets heavier.

37. You can look for the areas shaded with the pattern that indicates less than 8 inches (200 mm) of rainfall.

38. under 128 inches (3,200 mm)

39. over 128 inches (3,200 mm)

40. over 32 inches (800 mm)

41. 60°E and 80°E

42. It identifies each pattern and the amount of precipitation each indicates.

Chapter 4 ■ South and Southeast Asia: Physical Geography

A. KEY TERMS

Complete each sentence by writing the letter of the correct term in the blank. You will not use all the terms.

a. nationalist
b. caste
c. parliament
d. colony
e. textile
f. quota
g. boycott
h. drought
i. refugee

1. _____ A territory ruled by another nation, usually one far away, is a _____ .

2. _____ A _____ is someone who is devoted to the interests of his or her country.

3. _____ A _____ is a certain portion of something, such as jobs, that is set aside for a group.

4. _____ A long period without rain is a _____ .

5. _____ A _____ is someone who flees his or her country because of war.

Match the definitions with the terms. Write the correct letter in each blank. You will not use all the terms.

a. dictator
b. textile
c. colony
d. boycott
e. drought
f. refugee
g. purdah
h. partition
i. parliament

6. _____ a refusal to buy or use goods and services

7. _____ a leader who has absolute power

8. _____ a lawmaking body

9. _____ the Indian custom of covering women's heads and faces with veils

10. _____ cloth

B. KEY CONCEPTS

Write the letter of the correct answer or ending in each blank.

11. _____ The Aryan invaders influenced the culture of northern India by introducing
    a. Christianity.
    b. the caste system.
    c. a monarchy.
    d. democratic government.

12. _____ Which European nation took over most of South Asia, including India?
    a. Spain
    b. Germany
    c. Great Britain
    d. Italy

13. _____ Why did a variety of cultures develop in Southeast Asia?
    a. The mountains in the region prevented contact among the different peoples here.
    b. Many countries invaded the area.
    c. People easily communicated with those who lived outside their own valley.
    d. Many people from the region traveled throughout Europe.

14. _____ Traders from India influenced Southeast Asia by introducing
    a. Christianity to the region.
    b. farming to the area.
    c. Confucian teachings to the region.
    d. Hinduism to the region.

15. _____ How did colonial rule affect the economy of Southeast Asia?
    a. The ruling powers encouraged farmers to grow their own food.
    b. The ruling powers encouraged private ownership of land.
    c. The ruling powers forced farmers to grow cash crops.
    d. The ruling powers forced farmers to sell their land.

16. _____ After India became independent, how did the caste system change?
    a. The new government strengthened the caste system.
    b. The new government added new subcastes to the system.
    c. The new government added the lowest caste to the system.
    d. The new government passed laws protecting the rights of Untouchables.

17. _____ What is one way in which the lives of Indian women have changed since the country became independent?
    a. They are not allowed to vote.
    b. They cannot inherit property.
    c. They cannot take part in business.
    d. They can participate in public life.

18. _____ Both Pakistan and India claim Kashmir in order to control
    a. trade routes.
    b. the rich farmland.
    c. the waters of the Indus River.
    d. the mountain regions.

19. _____ What European colonial power did the Vietnamese Communists, led by Ho Chi Minh, defeat?
    a. Great Britain
    b. Italy
    c. Spain
    d. France

20. _____ The Mauryan emperor Chandragupta changed India politically by
   a. dividing the country into many small kingdoms.
   b. uniting many of the small kingdoms to create a great empire.
   c. establishing a monarchy.
   d. destroying the Indian empire.

21. _____ Which religions began in India?
   a. Hinduism and Christianity   c. Buddhism and Hinduism
   b. Christianity and Judaism   d. Buddhism and Shintoism

22. _____ Which European country ruled India until its independence?
   a. Great Britain   c. Germany
   b. France   d. Italy

23. _____ The kingdoms of Southeast Asia were invaded from time to time by their strong northern neighbor,
   a. Pakistan.   c. Tibet.
   b. China.   d. Thailand.

24. _____ After independence, how did the new government of India begin to change the social system?
   a. by passing laws that strengthened the caste system
   b. by adding new subcastes to the caste system
   c. by passing laws that protected the rights of Untouchables
   d. by passing laws forbidding women to vote

25. _____ In the past and today, Pakistan's most important industry has been
   a. aquaculture.
   b. herding.
   c. agriculture.
   d. computer technology.

26. _____ More than half of Pakistan's industrial output is based on
   a. producing electronic equipment.
   b. turning crops into manufactured goods.
   c. producing cars.
   d. manufacturing chemicals.

27. _____ Under leader Ho Chi Minh, the Vietnamese Communists defeated their colonial ruler,
   a. Germany.   c. China.
   b. Great Britain.   d. France.

28. _____ After the United States pulled out of Vietnam, what happened to the country?
   a. It was reunited under a communist government.
   b. It was divided into two countries.
   c. It was reunited under a democratic government.
   d. It established colonies in other Southeast Asian countries.

C. CRITICAL THINKING

Answer the following questions in the space provided, on the back of this paper or on a separate sheet of paper.

29. Drawing Conclusions: Why do you think nationalists were organizing independence movements throughout Southeast Asia by the early 1900s?

30. Identifying Central Issues: What are three ways in which early invaders influenced the cultures of South Asia?

31. Identifying Central Issues: What were two important influences on the early cultures of Southeast Asia?

32. Drawing Conclusions: Why do you think the Indian caste system has been slower to change in the rural areas of the country?

D. SKILLS

Read the selection below. Then answer the following questions. Write your answers on the lines provided.

Hinduism is unlike other major world religions. It has no one single founder. However, it has many great religious thinkers. Also, Hindus worship many gods and goddesses, but they believe in a single spirit. To Hindus, the various gods and goddesses represent different parts of this spirit. As an old Hindu saying states: "God is one, but wise people know it by many names."

33. What is the central issue or most important idea of this selection? _____

_____

34. What is one detail that supports the central issue? _____

_____

35. What is another detail from the paragraph that supports the central issue? _____

_____

36. What is a third detail from the paragraph that supports the central issue? _____

_____

37. How would you title this selection? _____

_____

Read the selection below. Then answer the following questions. Write your answers on the lines provided.

Problems and Solutions
Irrigation solves many farming problems. But it creates others. For example, river water contains small amounts of salts. When water evaporates, the salts are left behind. Over time, salts build up in the soil. Plant growth slows. Pakistani scientists are trying to find a way to treat the salt-damaged soil. They are also working to develop a type of wheat that can grow in salty soil.

38. What is the central issue or most important idea in the paragraph? _____

_____

39. What is one detail that supports this central issue? _____

_____

40. What is another detail that supports this central issue? _____

_____

41. What is a third detail that supports this central issue? _____

_____

42. What relationship do you see between the title of the selection and the central issue? _____

_____

ANSWER KEY

1. d	2. a	3. f	4. h	5. i
6. d	7. a	8. i	9. g	10. b
11. b	12. c	13. a	14. d	15. c
16. d	17. d	18. c	19. d	20. b
21. c	22. a	23. b	24. c	25. c
26. b	27. d	28. a		

29. Answers may vary, but should include reference to the following: Although colonial nations did improve transportation in the region and built schools and universities, they built economic and political systems that did not benefit the local people. By the early 1900s, educated Southeast Asians, who wanted their countries to be independent of colonial rule, were ready to lead the struggle for independence.

30. Answers may vary, but should include reference to the following: The Aryan conquerors, who ruled northern India for more than 1,000 years, introduced the caste system to Indian society. A new system of belief, Hinduism, also emerged from Aryan religious ideas. During the rule of the Mauryan emperor Asoka, Buddhism spread throughout his empire and beyond its borders.

31. Answers may vary, but should include the following: Periodically Chinese armies from the north invaded Southeast Asia. In 111 B.C. the Chinese conquered Vietnam, and the Vietnamese adopted Chinese ways of farming. The Indians were another influence on the region. Nearly 2,000 years ago, Indian traders sailed across the Indian Ocean to Southeast Asia, and introduced Hinduism to the region. Later, Indians brought Buddhism to the region.

32. Answers may vary, but should include reference to the fact that it's harder to enforce laws protecting Untouchables in the villages of India. Also, the people in the rural areas are more likely to follow Indian traditions than city dwellers who have been exposed to more modern social views and who are better educated.

33. Hinduism is different from other major world religions.

34. Hinduism has no one single founder.

35. Hindus worship many gods and goddesses, but they believe in a single spirit.

36. To Hindus, the different gods and goddesses represent different parts of this spirit.

37. Answers may vary. Possible title: Differences Between Hinduism and Other World Religions

38. Irrigation solves many farming problems but creates others.

39. River water contains small amounts of salts.

40. When water evaporates, the salts are left behind.

41. Over time, salts build up in the soil.

42. The selection focuses on one of the problems caused by irrigation and how Pakistani scientists are trying to solve it.

A. KEY TERMS

Complete each sentence by writing the letter of the correct term in the blank. You will not use all the terms.

   a. petroleum
   b. reserves
   c. peninsula
   d. nonrenewable resource
   e. crossroads
   f. oasis
   g. standard of living
   h. irrigation
   i. wadi

1. _____ At a(n) _____ , fresh water is available from an underground spring or well.

2. _____ A waterway that fills up in the rainy season but is dry the rest of the year is called a(n) _____ .

3. _____ The source of gasoline and other fuels is _____ .

4. _____ Once it is used, a(n) _____ cannot be replaced.

5. _____ Many countries work hard to improve the quality of life, or _____ , of their people.

Match the definitions in with the terms. Write the correct letter in each blank. You will not use all the terms.

   a. petroleum
   b. renewable resource
   c. reserves
   d. oasis
   e. natural resource
   f. nonrenewable resource
   g. hydroelectricity
   h. wadi
   i. arable land

6. _____ a place where fresh water is available from an underground spring or well

7. _____ a waterway that fills up in the rainy season

8. _____ land that can produce crops

9. _____ a resource that cannot be replaced once it is used

10. _____ the source of gasoline and other fuels

B. KEY CONCEPTS

Write the letter of the best answer or ending in each blank.

11. _____ Why are Southwest and Central Asia called "the Dry World"?
   a. The region contains many dry riverbeds.
   b. The region contains some of the world's largest deserts.
   c. The region contains land that is arid for part of the year.
   d. The region contains many mountains.

12. _____ The land along the Tigris, Euphrates, and Ural rivers is very
   a. dry.   c. sparsely populated.
   b. fertile.   d. difficult to farm.

13. _____ How are the mountains of Central Asia and the seas of Southwest Asia alike?
   a. They both provide trade routes between regions and countries.
   b. They both provide communication routes between regions and countries.
   c. They both separate regions and countries.
   d. They both contribute to the economies of the countries in the regions.

14. _____ What is the best description of the climates in Southwest and Central Asia?
   a. very dry   c. given to climate extremes
   b. mild all year   d. very rainy

15. _____ What must farmers do in order to grow crops in Southwest and Central Asia?
   a. import seeds from other countries   c. move to the mountainous areas
   b. irrigate their land   d. rotate their crops

16. _____ Most people in Southwest and Central Asia earn their living by
   a. working in factories.   c. cutting down the forests.
   b. working in the mines.   d. working on farms.

17. _____ What is the relationship between petroleum production in Southwest Asia and the people's standard of living there?
   a. All the countries have the same high standard of living.
   b. Countries with oil have higher standards of living than those countries without oil reserves.
   c. Countries that import oil have a higher standard of living than other countries.
   d. Countries that export oil have a lower standard of living than other countries.

18. _____ Why are many countries helping Central Asia develop a larger oil industry by providing equipment and loans?
   a. to share the wealth in return
   b. to improve the standard of living of the people
   c. to get higher interest on the loans
   d. to establish settlements in Central Asia

CHAPTER 5

19. _____ The resource that people in Southwest and Central Asia need the most is
   a. coal.
   c. farmland.
   b. gas.
   d. water.

20. _____ Why is the Rub al-Khali an important landform of the Arabian peninsula?
   a. It is the largest highland area in the region.
   b. It is the largest all-sand desert in the world.
   c. It is the highest mountain range in the region.
   d. It is the narrowest coastal plain in the world.

21. _____ Why is Southwest Asia often called the Middle East?
   a. because it is in the middle of a continent
   b. because it is in the eastern part of a continent
   c. because it is at the crossroads of Africa, Asia, and Europe
   d. because it is an island

22. _____ Which body of water forms Southwest Asia's western border?
   a. the Black Sea
   c. the Red Sea
   b. the Caspian Sea
   d. the Mediterranean Sea

23. _____ Which statement best describes the climates of Southwest and Central Asia?
   a. Both regions have a mild climate, with warm summers and cool winters.
   b. Both regions have huge climate extremes with frequent droughts.
   c. Both regions have mild winters and hot summers.
   d. Both regions have moderate temperatures year-round and a lot of rain.

24. _____ Which plants grow well in Southwest and Central Asia?
   a. Plants that require constant watering.
   b. Plants that require moderate temperatures.
   c. Plants that require warm climates.
   d. Plants that adapt to the harsh climate.

25. _____ People in Southwest and Central Asia tend to settle near
   a. mountain valleys.
   c. river valleys and oases.
   b. hilly regions.
   d. sandy deserts.

26. _____ Most of the borders of regions and countries in Southwest Asia are formed by
   a. rivers.
   c. roads.
   b. mountains.
   d. sand dunes.

27. _____ The largest oil-producing region in the world is
   a. Central Asia.
   c. Southwest Asia.
   b. Africa.
   d. East Asia.

28. _____ To increase the amount of arable land, Turkey
   a. built wadis.
   c. uses heavy fertilizers.
   b. built large dams.
   d. imports water.

C. CRITICAL THINKING

Answer the following questions in the space provided, on the back of this paper or on a separate sheet of paper.

29. **Identifying Central Issues:** What are the reasons for the population distribution of Southwest and Central Asia?

30. **Draw Conclusions:** Why is the petroleum mined in Southwest Asia described as "black gold"?

31. **Recognizing Cause and Effect:** What are two ways in which the vast desert regions of Southwest and Central Asia affect the lives of the people who live here?

32. **Draw Conclusions:** As the countries of Central Asia develop more of their oil reserves, how might the lives of the people change?

D. SKILLS

Use the bar graph below to answer the following questions. Write your answers on the lines provided.

33. What is the subject matter of the graph?

_____

_____

34. What information does the horizontal axis show? _____

_____

35. What information does the vertical axis show? _____

_____

36. Which country produces the most oil?

_____

37. Which country produces the least oil?

_____

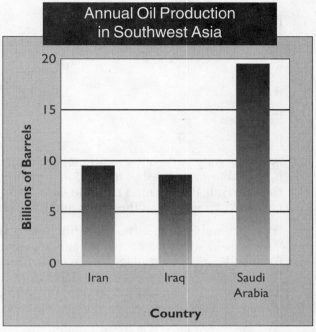

Annual Oil Production in Southwest Asia

Use the bar graph below to answer the following questions. Write your answers on the lines provided.

38. What area of the world does this graph cover?_____

_____

39. What information does the vertical axis show? _____

_____

40. What information does the horizontal axis show? _____

_____

41. About how much oil does Iraq produce per year?_____

_____

42. About how much more oil does Saudi Arabia produce than Kuwait per year?

_____

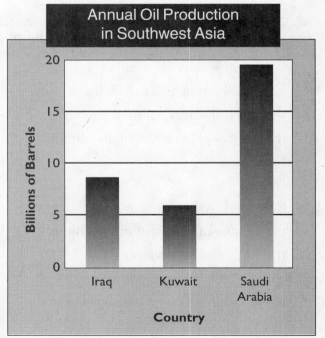

Annual Oil Production in Southwest Asia

ANSWER KEY

1. f	2. i	3. a	4. d	5. g
6. d	7. h	8. i	9. f	10. a
11. b	12. b	13. c	14. c	15. b
16. d	17. b	18. a	19. d	20. b
21. c	22. d	23. b	24. d	25. c
26. b	27. c	28. b		

29. Answers may vary, but should include reference to the following: People live where water is available since most of the region is extremely dry and water is necessary for farming and for survival. People tend to settle near coasts, oases, and rivers. The Mediterranean Coast and the river valleys of the Tigris and Euphrates are heavily populated.

30. Answers may vary, but should include reference to the following: Petroleum is called "black gold" because of its tremendous value. Petroleum deposits take millions of years to form and cannot be replaced once used. Since petroleum is the source of gasoline and other fuels, people all over the world depend on it to fuel cars, provide energy for industry, and heat homes. Petroleum is found in only a few places around the globe, and Southwest Asia is the largest oil-producing region in the world.

31. Answers may vary but should include reference to the following: 1. Because most of this region gets so little rain, water is extremely valuable. To grow crops in many areas, people must irrigate their land. 2. Few plants grow in the desert so people must farm the fertile land along the river banks of the major rivers. More people in these regions live in the river valleys than anywhere else in the region because of the fertile land and the proximity to water.

32. Answers may vary, but should include reference to the relationship between the oil wealth of a country and the standard of living of the citizens. Since oil rich Southwest Asian countries have increased the standard of living of their citizens, the quality of life of Central Asian citizens will probably rise.

33. annual oil production in Southwest Asia

34. the oil-producing countries

35. the number of barrels of oil in billions

36. Saudi Arabia

37. Iraq

38. Southwest Asia

39. the number of barrels of oil in billions

40. the oil-producing countries

41. about 8 billion barrels per year

42. about 13 billion barrels more per year

A. KEY TERMS

Complete each sentence by writing the letter of the correct term in the blank. You will not use all the terms.

    a. collective
    b. hajj
    c. desalination
    d. diversify
    e. muezzin
    f. radiation poisoning
    g. steppe
    h. deity
    i. moshavim

1. _____   Christians, Jews, and Muslims all worship the same _____ , or god.

2. _____   The person who summons Muslims to pray is the _____ .

3. _____   A treeless plain is called a _____ .

4. _____   The process of removing salt from water is called _____ .

5. _____   The pilgrimage to Mecca is called the _____ .

Match the definitions with the terms. Write the correct letter in each blank. You will not use all the terms.

    a. steppe
    b. radiation poisoning
    c. deity
    d. muezzin
    e. desalination
    f. hajj
    g. collective
    h. diversify
    i. kibbutz

6. _____   a person whose job is to summon Muslims to pray

7. _____   a treeless plain

8. _____   a kind of cooperative settlement found in Israel

9. _____   the pilgrimage to Mecca

10. _____   a sickness caused by exposure to radiation produced by nuclear explosions

B. KEY CONCEPTS

Write the letter of the best answer in each blank.

11. _____ Which ancient people invented the sailboat, produced a system of written laws, and irrigated their fields?
    a. Egyptians   c. Syrians
    b. Mesopotamians   d. Chinese

12. _____ Judaism, Christianity, and Islam all have their beginnings in
    a. Central Asia.   c. China.
    b. Egypt.   d. Southwest Asia.

13. _____ The Silk Road influenced the culture of the people of Central Asia by bringing them into contact with
    a. people of East and Southwest Asia and Europe.
    b. people from Africa.
    c. people of North America
    d. people of South America.

14. _____ In the 1800s, which foreign power gained control of Central Asia?
    a. England   c. Russia
    b. France   d. the United States

15. _____ Which landform makes up the southern two thirds of Israel?
    a. the Negev Desert   c. Galilee
    b. the Jordan River   d. the Dead Sea

16. _____ Why is the Jordan River important to both Israel and its Arab neighbors?
    a. They use the river for trade.
    b. They have built many factories along the riverbanks.
    c. They use the water from the river for irrigation.
    d. They want to build large cities along the river.

17. _____ The country that exports more petroleum than any other country on the Earth is
    a. Israel.   c. Kazakstan.
    b. Saudi Arabia.   d. Syria.

18. _____ Despite changes in Saudi Arabia, men and women are usually
    a. separate.   c. in competition for jobs.
    b. in the same schools.   d. together.

19. _____ One serious problem facing Kazakstan today that can be traced to Soviet rule is
    a. radiation sickness caused by nuclear fallout.
    b. the overproduction of cotton plants.
    c. the flooding of the Aral Sea.
    d. the lack of factories and skilled workers.

20. _____ What is one important achievement of the ancient Mesopotamian civilization?
    a. settlements in the New World
    b. a written code of law
    c. trade with China
    d. the discovery of gold

21. _____ A million Central Asians starved to death during the 1930s because
    a. there was a famine.
    b. their crops failed.
    c. Soviet collectives did not produce enough food.
    d. they couldn't afford to import food.

22. _____ Tensions between Arabs and Jews started because of
    a. Jewish settlement in Palestine after World War I.
    b. the unification of Palestine.
    c. Arab settlement in Palestine after World War I.
    d. the migration of Jews from Palestine to Europe.

23. _____ Which statement best describes the ethnic groups living in Central Asia?
    a. The Kazaks are the only ethnic group.
    b. There are many ethnic groups.
    c. There are no Russians living there.
    d. Only Uzbeks and Cossacks live there.

24. _____ The Silk Road was an ancient trade route linking
    a. South Asia to Africa.
    b. China to Europe.
    c. Europe to North America.
    d. Africa to Europe.

25. _____ Why have Israel and its Arab neighbors fought over Galilee?
    a. Each country wants to control the trade routes there.
    b. Each country wants to establish settlements there.
    c. Each country depends on the water from the Jordan River.
    d. Each country depends on the industry in the region.

26. _____ The country that exports more petroleum than any other nation on the Earth is
    a. China.
    b. Russia.
    c. Saudi Arabia.
    d. Israel.

27. _____ The traditional values of the Sunni branch of Islam forbid
    a. department stores.
    b. cellular phones.
    c. hotels.
    d. movie theaters.

28. _____ Until recently, which country controlled Kazakstan?
    a. China
    b. the Soviet Union
    c. Saudi Arabia
    d. Afghanistan

CHAPTER 6

C. CRITICAL THINKING

Answer the following questions in the space provided, on the back of this paper or on a separate sheet of paper.

29. Identifying Central Issues: What is one important influence on the early cultures of Southwest and Central Asia?

30. Drawing Conclusions: How do you think the discovery of oil has influenced life in Saudi Arabia?

31. Drawing Conclusions: How do you think Southwest Asia's location at a crossroads of Asia, Africa, and Europe has affected its development?

32. Making Comparisons: How does the presence of oil in Saudi Arabia and Kazakstan affect life in those countries?

D. SKILLS

Use the topics listed below to answer the following questions. Write your answers on the lines provided.

- Life in Ancient Mesopotamia
- The History of Kazakstan
- The Economy of Israel

33. What are two key words that you would use to search the Internet and the World Wide Web for information about "Life in Ancient Mesopotamia"? _____

_____

34. How will the search engine respond to your key words? _____

_____

35. What are two key words that you would use to search for information about "The History of Kazakstan"? _____

36. Why is it important to use key words in your search? _____

_____

37. What are two key words that you would use to search for information about "The Economy of Israel"? _____

Use the topics listed below to answer the following questions. Write your answers on the lines provided.

- Hammurabi's Code
- The Silk Road
- The Negev Desert

38. What are two key words that you would use to search the Internet and the World Wide Web for information about "Hammurabi's Code"? _____

_____

39 How will the search engine respond to your key words? _____

_____

40. What are two key words that you would use to search for information about "The Silk Road"? _____

41. Why is it important to use key words in your search? _____

_____

42. What are two key words that you would use to search for information about "The Negev Desert"? _____

_____

ANSWER KEY

1. h	2. e	3. g	4. c	5. b
6. d	7. a	8. i	9. f	10. b
11. b	12. d	13. a	14. c	15. a
16. c	17. b	18. a	19. a	20. b
21. c	22. a	23. b	24. b	25. c
26. c	27. d	28. b		

29. Answers may vary, but should make reference to the fact that Judaism, Christianity, and Islam all had their roots in Southwest Asia. The followers of these major religions all worship the same god and include the Bible as part of their heritage. Of the three, Islam has the most followers in this region, and as the religion spread, so did the Arabic language. Another important influence on the early cultures of Central Asia is the trade route called the Silk Road, which linked China to Europe. The traders exchanged ideas and inventions. Cities that became wealthy centers of trade and learning developed along this route.

30. Answers may vary, but should include reference to the following: Saudi Arabia became a wealthy nation. As a result, its standard of living is high. It has the most important oil economy in the world and exports more petroleum than any other nation on the Earth. Because its economy is linked so directly to oil, any change in the price of oil will affect Saudi Arabia. Also, since petroleum is such an important nonrenewable resource to every nation on the Earth, Saudi Arabia's oil reserves makes it important politically, both in the region and in the world.

31. Answers may vary, but should include reference to the following: Since Southwest Asia is at a crossroads the country has a diverse ethnic background. Many groups have settled here and continue to live here today. This area was the site of the beginnings of Judaism, Christianity, and Islam. The ethnic diversity has led to an exchange of ideas; however, this same ethnic diversity has also resulted in religious and ethnic conflicts.

32. Answers may vary, but should include reference to the tremendous impact that the discovery of oil in Saudi Arabia in the 1930s had on the country. The nation that was one of the poorest nations in the world became extremely rich. Kazakstan, however, is an example of a country with tremendous oil reserves that have yet to be developed. Kazakstan has signed an agreement with an American company to begin developing the Tengiz oil field. Like Saudi Arabia did, it will use its future oil wealth to improve the country. For example, it may begin cleaning its environment.

33. Mesopotamia; Hammurabi's Code

34. With the names of articles or Web pages

35. Kazakstan; the Silk Road

36. Specific key words will narrow the topic and give better research results.

37. Negev Desert; Galilee

38. Mesopotamia; Hammurabi

39. With the names of articles or Web pages

40. caravans; Samarkand

41. Specific key words will narrow the topic and give better research results.

42. Israel; moshavim

A. KEY TERMS

Complete each sentence by writing the letter of the correct term in the blank. You will not use all the terms.

    a. artesian well
    b. coral
    c. tectonic plate
    d. marsupial
    e. fiord
    f. station
    g. penal colony
    h. geyser
    i. atoll

1. _____ An animal that carries its young in a body pouch is called a(n) _____ .

2. _____ A small coral island in the shape of a ring is a(n) _____ .

3. _____ A place settled by convicts or prisoners is a(n) _____ .

4. _____ A farmer will dig a(n) _____ deep into the Earth to tap porous rock filled with ground water.

5. _____ A huge piece of the outer "skin" of the Earth, or the crust, is called a(n) _____ .

Match the definitions with the terms. Write the correct letter in each blank. You will not use all the terms.

    a. penal colony
    b. high island
    c. artesian well
    d. fiord
    e. tectonic plate
    f. coral
    g. station
    h. low island
    i. atoll

6. _____ a narrow inlet

7. _____ a small coral island in the shape of a ring

8. _____ a place settled by convicts or prisoners

9. _____ an island that usually has mountains

10. _____ a rocklike material made up of the skeletons of tiny sea creatures

CHAPTER 7

B. KEY CONCEPTS

Write the letter of the correct answer or ending in each blank.

11. _____ What is one effect of Australia and New Zealand's isolated location on the development of plant and animal life?
   a. Most of their plants and animals are found all over the world.
   b. Many of their plants and animals are found nowhere else on the Earth.
   c. Many of their plants and animals require little water to survive.
   d. Many of their plants and animals are found on islands in the Pacific and Atlantic oceans.

12. _____ While Australia's east coast has fertile farmland, the rest of the country is made up of
   a. semiarid plateaus, desert, and dry grasslands.
   b. mountains and river valleys.
   c. fertile plateaus.
   d. hills and wet grasslands.

13. _____ Why is the Canterbury Plain important to the people who live on South Island, New Zealand?
   a. Most of the country's factories are located there.
   b. Farmers produce most of New Zealand's crops there.
   c. Most minerals are mined there.
   d. All the major cities are located there.

14. _____ The three major areas of the Pacific island region are Melanesia, Micronesia, and
   a. New Zealand.   c. Tasmania.
   b. Australia.   d. Polynesia.

15. _____ Why do more people live on high islands than on low islands?
   a. because of the mountains   c. because of their fertile soil
   b. because of their small size d. because of their sandy soil

16. _____ The most important resource in the Pacific island region is
   a. palm grasses.   c. small shrubs.
   b. coconut palms.   d. phosphate deposits.

17. _____ Which European country took control of both Australia and New Zealand?
   a. France   c. Germany
   b. Italy   d. Great Britain

18. _____ Scientists think that the Aborigines of Australia and the Maori of New Zealand originally came from
   a. Africa.   c. South America.
   b. Asia.   d. Europe.

19. _____ Australia has close ties with Pacific Rim nations, including Japan, South Korea, China, and
   a. the United States.   c. Great Britain.
   b. Brazil.   d. Italy.

20. ____ Why are so many of New Zealand's and Australia's animals and plants found nowhere else on the Earth?
   a. because of the countries' closeness to other islands
   b. because of the countries' great distance from other large land masses
   c. because of the climate
   d. because of the landforms

21. ____ The land along the east coast of Australia is
   a. fertile farmland.   c. high plateau.
   b. dry desert.   d. mountainous.

22. ____ The Pacific island region is made up of Melanesia, Polynesia, and
   a. New Zealand.   c. Tasmania.
   b. Australia.   d. Micronesia.

23. ____ The landforms of New Zealand were shaped by
   a. typhoons.   c. fiords.
   b. volcanoes.   d. glaciers.

24. ____ Most Pacific islands
   a. are dry.   c. have many natural resources.
   b. are heavily populated.   d. receive year-round rainfall.

25. ____ The main goal of Aborigines is to
   a. fit into Australian society.
   b. create rock paintings.
   c. gain political office.
   d. gain rights and re-gain their ancestral lands.

26. ____ How were the people of the Pacific region affected by the distances between the islands?
   a. They communicated with one another frequently.
   b. They developed the same language and customs.
   c. They developed distinct languages and customs.
   d. They visited different islands regularly.

27. ____ Some of Australia's trading partners in the Pacific Rim include the United States, China, Taiwan, and
   a. Egypt.   c. India.
   b. Japan   d. Italy.

28. ____ Australia is one of the world's leading growers and exporters of
   a. sugar cane.   c. wheat.
   b. oats.   d. coconuts.

CHAPTER 7

C. CRITICAL THINKING

Answer the following questions in the space provided, on the back of this paper or on a separate sheet of paper.

29. Recognizing Cause and Effect: How has the fact that most of Melanesia's large islands are high islands affected the size of its population?

30. Making Comparisons: Compare the ways in which the European settlers impacted on the lives of the Aborigines and the Maori.

31. Identifying Central Issues: Why do you think Australia's economy depends more and more on trade with Pacific Rim countries?

32. Expressing Problems Clearly: What problems of the native peoples were caused by the European settlement of Australia and New Zealand?

D. SKILLS

Use the selection below to answer the following questions. Write your answers on the lines provided.

This plain has Australia's most fertile farmland and receives ample rain. Winds flowing westward across the Pacific Ocean pick up moisture. As the winds rise to cross the Great Dividing Range—mountains just to the west of the coastal plain—the moisture falls as rain. These winds not only bring rain, they also help make the climate mild and pleasant. Also, Australia's most important rivers, the Murray and Darling, flow through the region.

33. What is one fact about the east coast of Australia included in this selection? _____

_____

34. What is another fact about the east coast of Australia included in this selection? _____

_____

35. What fact about the climate of the east coast of Australia is included in this selection? _____

_____

36. What do you already know about the population distribution of regions with plenty of water and fertile farmland? _____

_____

37. What conclusions can you draw about the population distribution of Australia's east coast?

_____

Use the selection below to answer the following questions. Write your answers on the lines provided.

The rest of Australia is very different. Just west of the Great Dividing Range is a rain shadow. This is a region that gets little precipitation because of a mountain range. This area is made up of semiarid plateaus and desert lands. As rain seldom falls here and there are few rivers, people depend on wells for fresh water. Farther west, the huge central plain called the Outback is desert and dry grassland.

38. What is one fact about the land west of the Great Dividing Range of Australia that is given in this selection? _____

39. What is another fact about the type of land that is found in this area? _____

_____

40. What is one fact about the bodies of water found in this region? _____

_____

41. What do you already know about the population of land that is very dry and has few rivers?

_____

42. What conclusion can you draw about the size of the population in this part of Australia? __

_____

CHAPTER 7

ANSWER KEY

1. d	2. i	3. g	4. a	5. c
6. d	7. i	8. a	9. b	10. f
11. b	12. a	13. b	14. d	15. c
16. b	17. d	18. b	19. a	20. b
21. a	22. d	23. b	24. d	25. d
26. c	27. b	28. c		

29. Answers will vary, but should include reference to the fact that high islands support larger populations than low islands. This is because high islands are larger and have fertile soil that consists of volcanic ash and that is useful for growing crops.

30. Answers may vary but should include reference to the following: After the arrival of the Europeans in Australia, the Aborigines were forced from their land and made to adopt European ways. Many died from disease. Recently, however, life for the Aborigines has begun to improve. They have started to play an important role in the economic life of the country and to regain their ancestral land. Similarly, after the British defeated the Maoris in New Zealand, they forced them to adopt English ways, and Maori culture seemed in danger of being destroyed. However, the Maoris of New Zealand, like the Aborigines of Australia, have recovered their traditional land and are gaining more political power in the country.

31. Answers may vary, but should include reference to the following: These countries are located in the same region as Australia and reflect the country's own cultural diversity. Several of them have invested large amounts of money in Australia's economy and have set up banks, insurance companies, and other businesses there. Australia's farm products, minerals, and livestock are important exports that could be traded with other Pacific Rim countries.

32. Answers will vary, but should include reference to the following: The European settlers of New Zealand and Australia inflicted great hardships on the native peoples there. In Australia, settlers forced Aborigines off their lands; thousands of Aborigines died of European diseases. They also began to lose their own customs and traditions. Similarly, in New Zealand, Great Britain promised to protect Maori land when the island became a British colony. However, settlers broke that promise and finally defeated the Maori in 1872. The Maori were forced to adopt English ways, and their native culture was in danger of being destroyed.

33. It has Australia's most fertile farmland and has ample rain.

34. Australia's most important rivers flow through the region.

35. The climate is mild and pleasant.

36. It tends to be high.

37. Most of Australia's people probably live here.

38. This region gets little rain.

39. The area is made up of semiarid plateaus and desert lands.

40. There are few rivers.

41. Generally, few people live in this kind of environment.

42. Probably few Australians live here because it is so dry and would be difficult to farm.

Chapter 8 ▪ Final Exam

A. KEY TERMS

Complete each sentence by writing the letter of the correct term in the blank. You will not use all the terms.

a. partition
b. collective
c. tectonic plate
d. peninsula
e. atoll
f. steppe
g. cash crop
h. oasis
i. ethnic group

1. _____ The Korean _____ , which is a piece of land nearly surrounded by water, juts into the Yellow Sea and the Sea of Japan.

2. _____ People who share the same languages, religions, and cultural traditions belong to the same _____ .

3. _____ Tea is an example of a(n) _____ , which can be raised to be sold on the world market.

4. _____ In 1947, a division, or _____ , established the countries of India and Pakistan.

5. _____ At a(n) _____ , fresh water is available from an underground spring or well.

Match the definitions with the terms. Write the correct letter in each blank. You will not use all the terms.

a. communism
b. tectonic plate
c. aquaculture
d. petroleum
e. subcontinent
f. boycott
g. desert
h. atoll
i. collective

6. _____ a dry region of extreme temperatures and little vegetation

7. _____ a form of government in which the government owns large industries, businesses, and most of the country's land

8. _____ a large landmass that is a major part of a continent

9. _____ a refusal to buy or use goods and services

10. _____ a nonrenewable resource formed from the remains of ancient plants and animals

© Prentice-Hall, Inc.

Chapter 8 ▪ **311**

CHAPTER 8

B. KEY CONCEPTS

Write the letter of the correct answer or ending in each blank.

11. _____ What is the largest nation in East Asia?
    a. Japan   c. China
    b. North Korea   d. Mongolia

12. _____ What is a very strong influence on the climates of East Asia?
    a. monsoons   c. forests
    b. plains   d. volcanoes

13. _____ Which ancient East Asian culture invented the magnetic compass, the printing press, and the water wheel?
    a. Mongolian   c. North Korean
    b. Chinese   d. South Korean

14. _____ The rain forests of South and Southeast Asia are being destroyed by
    a. too little rain.   c. rapid logging.
    b. extremely cold temperatures.   d. severe storms.

15. _____ What is one way in which Indian society has changed since the country became independent?
    a. Women no longer have the right to business.
    b. Women cannot vote.
    c. The government passed laws to protect the rights of Untouchables.
    d. The government eliminated the caste system.

16. _____ What happened to Vietnam after the Vietnamese Communists defeated the French?
    a. The country was united.
    b. The communist government was overthrown.
    c. A democratic government ruled the country.
    d. The country was divided into northern and southern parts.

17. _____ More people live in the river valleys of Southwest and Central Asia than elsewhere in the region because of
    a. the inexpensive land.   c. the fertile farmland.
    b. the manufacturing centers.   d. the many oases.

18. _____ In the 1930s, the lives of Saudi Arabian citizens changed permanently because of
    a. war with Israel.   c. invasion by the Chinese.
    b. the collapse of the government.   d. the discovery of oil.

19. _____ What continent did the Aborigines of Australia and the Maori of New Zealand originally come from?
    a. South America   c. Africa
    b. Europe   d. Asia

20. _____ The Himalaya Mountains, the plateau of Tibet, and the North China Plain are three major landforms in
   a. South Asia.
   b. Central Asia.
   c. East Asia.
   d. Southeast Asia.

21. _____ Because large areas of South and Southeast Asia have a tropical climate, what resource is found here?
   a. copper
   b. wheat
   c. rain forests
   d. oil

22. _____ What is a strong influence on the climates of East Asia?
   a. lakes
   b. longitude
   c. monsoons
   d. rivers

23. _____ Which statement best describes the populations of East Asian countries?
   a. The populations of Korea and Japan are homogeneous, while China has many minority groups.
   b. Korea and China have many minority groups; Japan is homogeneous.
   c. Korea, China, and Japan are made up of many different ethnic groups.
   d. Korea, China, and Japan have no minority groups.

24. _____ One effect that the Aryan invasion had on the culture of northern India was introducing
   a. a democratic form of government.
   b. Islam to the area.
   c. the caste system.
   d. laws requiring people to treat each other with humanity.

25. _____ Where in Asia are the Rub al-Khali desert, the Euphrates River, and the Hindu Kush mountains?
   a. South and Southeast Asia
   b. East Asia
   c. Southwest and Central Asia
   d. Australia and New Zealand

26. _____ What is one important benefit resulting from the oil reserves of Southwest Asia?
   a. Few people from other countries work there.
   b. Governments have increased the standard of living of citizens.
   c. Governments have built fewer schools.
   d. The countries use the oil for their own needs.

27. _____ One of the most important accomplishments of the early Mesopotamians was
   a. the invention of paper.
   b. the invention of the spinning wheel.
   c. the use of silk weaving.
   d. the development of Hammurabi's code of law.

28. _____ Scientists believe that the unique plant and animal life of Australia and New Zealand resulted from
   a. the countries' rivers and mountains.
   b. the countries' great distance from other large land masses.
   c. the countries' climate.
   d. the countries' soil.

C. CRITICAL THINKING

Answer the following questions in the space provided, on the back of this paper or on a separate sheet of paper.

29. Making Comparisons: Describe the major landforms in China and in India.

30. Identifying Central Issues: Why did European nations colonize Asia during the 1700s, 1800s, and 1900s? In your answer, briefly discuss the European colonization of two Asian countries.

31. Making Comparisons: Compare the population distribution of South and Southeast Asia with that of Australia. Where do most of the people live and why?

32. Cause and Effect: How did efforts by foreign countries to control China and India bring about political change in both Asian countries?

D. SKILLS

Use the selection below to answer the following questions. Write your answers on the lines provided.

The Effect of Location

New Zealand and Australia are so far from other large land masses that many of their animals and plants are found nowhere else on the Earth. Only in New Zealand can you find kiwis and yellow-eyed penguins. Eighty-four percent of the vegetation in New Zealand's forests grows nowhere else. Australia has many unique creatures, such as the kangaroo and the koala. These animals are biologically distinctive, too. They are marsupials, or animals that carry their young in a body pouch. Marsupials are found elsewhere in the world. The opossum of North America, for instance, is a marsupial. But in Australia, almost all mammals are marsupials. This is not true anywhere else on the Earth.

33. What is the central issue of this selection? _____

_____

34. What is one detail that supports this central issue? _____

_____

35. What is another detail that supports this central issue? _____

_____

36. Name a third detail that supports this central issue? _____

_____

37. What is the relationship between the title of the selection and the central issue? _____

_____

Use the selection below to answer the following questions. Write your answer on the lines provided.

Towering mountains and deserts take up over two thirds of China. Western and southwestern China are home to some of the highest mountains anywhere. Only the Nile and the Amazon are longer than the Chang Jiang and the Huang He. More than four million people live along the banks of the Huang He, the world's fourth-longest river. It runs through one of the most fertile regions of China, the wide North China plain. This plain is covered with deposits of a brownish yellow fertile soil.

38. What is one detail in this selection about the geography of China? _____

_____

39. What is another detail in this selection about the geography of China? _____

_____

40. What detail is given in this selection about the North China Plain? _____

_____

41. What do you already know about the relationship between geography and human settlement? _____

42. What conclusions can you draw about where Chinese might farm and choose to live? _____

_____

CHAPTER 8

ANSWER KEY

1. d	2. i	3. g	4. a	5. h
6. g	7. a	8. e	9. f	10. d
11. c	12. a	13. b	14. c	15. c
16. d	17. c	18. d	19. d	20. c
21. c	22. c	23. a	24. c	25. c
26. b	27. d	28. b		

29. Answers may vary but should include reference to the following: China's landscape is dominated by mountains, highlands, and plateaus. Mountains and deserts take up over two thirds of China. Part of the Himalaya Mountain range is located in an area of China called Tibet. Only the Nile and the Amazon are longer than China's Chang Jiang and Huang He rivers. The Indian subcontinent is dominated by the Himalaya Mountains, which extend about 1,500 miles from east to west. The Ganges and the Indus rivers, the two most important rivers in India, begin in the Himalaya Mountains.

30. Answers may vary but should include reference to the following: In general, European countries wanted to establish colonies in Asia in order to control the wealth produced by these countries, including valuable raw materials and fertile land. For example, Great Britain took over most of South Asia, including India, because of the riches it produced. Similarly, Great Britain controlled both Australia and New Zealand. Although Australia was originally used as a penal colony, after the discovery of gold in the mid-1800s, the population soared. A third example is the European control of most of Southeast Asia in the 1700s and 1800s in order to control the economy of the region.

31. Answers may vary but should include reference to the following: Most of the people of South and Southeast Asia make their living from the land. Three out of four South Asians live in the countryside, and most are crowded into fertile river valleys. Similarly, millions of people live in the river valleys between the mountain ranges of mainland Southeast Asia, which are also very fertile. In Australia, most Australians live on the east coast, a plain that has the country's most fertile farmland and important rivers, and receives ample rain.

32. Answers may vary, but should include reference to the following: Foreign countries entered China to control parts of the country and its wealth. Many Chinese blamed the emperor for the growing foreign influence and, in 1911, a revolution broke out in China. The rule of emperors ended, and a republic was set up. Britain, which had the largest colonial empire in the world, took over most of South Asia, including India. A strong independence movement grew up, and in 1947 Great Britain was forced to grant India its freedom.

33. Because New Zealand and Australia are so far from other large land masses, many of their animals and plants are found nowhere else on the Earth.

34. Only in New Zealand can you find kiwis and yellow-eyed penguins.

35. Australia has many unique creatures, such as the kangaroo and the koala.

36. These animals are biologically distinctive, too.

37. The title, "Effect of Location," sums up the central issue, which is how location affects the development of animals and plants in New Zealand and Australia.

38. Mountains and deserts take up over two thirds of China.

39. The Chang Jiang and Huang He are some of the longest rivers in the world.

40. It is a very fertile region of China and is covered with a brownish yellow fertile soil.

41. People generally settle in areas that are fertile, where they can farm to support themselves.

42. The Chinese would probably live and farm in the North China Plain, where the land is extremely fertile. They would be unable to farm in the area of China covered by mountains and deserts.

World Explorer

THE UNITED STATES AND CANADA

BOOK 7

A. KEY TERMS

Complete each sentence by writing the letter of the correct term in the blank. You will not use all the terms.

        a. tundra
        b. rain shadow
        c. Continental Divide
        d. glacier
        e. alluvial
        f. tributary
        g. prairie
        h. agribusiness
        i. permafrost

1. _____ A huge, slow-moving sheet of ice is called a(n) _____ .

2. _____ In the Arctic, a cold, dry region called the _____ is covered with snow for more than half the year.

3. _____ The surface of _____ , which is permanently frozen subsoil, thaws only during the Arctic summer.

4. _____ A region of flat or rolling land covered with grasses is a(n) _____ .

5. _____ The silt that is left by rivers after a flood forms is _____ soil.

Match the definitions with the terms. Write the correct letter in each blank. You will not use all the terms.

        a. glacier
        b. alluvial
        c. Continental Divide
        d. agribusiness
        e. hydroelectricity
        f. irrigation
        g. tundra
        h. tributary
        i. prairie

6. _____ the boundary separating rivers flowing toward opposite sides of the continent

7. _____ a huge, slow-moving sheet of ice

8. _____ a region of flat or rolling land covered with tall grasses

9. _____ watering farmland by artificial methods

10. _____ composed of silt deposited by water

B. KEY CONCEPTS

Write the letter of the correct answer or ending in each blank.

11. _____ One major landform that is found in both the United States and Canada is
    a. the Kilauea Volcano.   c. the Great Basin.
    b. the Rocky Mountains.   d. Mount Logan.

12. _____ Why are the Great Lakes important to both the United States and Canada?
    a. They form the Continental Divide.
    b. They are an important link to the Pacific Ocean.
    c. They are major shipping routes.
    d. They form a boundary with Alaska.

13. _____ How do the huge plains areas in Canada and the United States affect the way people live here?
    a. The rich soil is good for farming.
    b. The tall mountains provide lumber.
    c. The volcanic soil hardens into new land.
    d. The very rugged land makes settlement difficult.

14. _____ Because Canada is a long way from the Equator, much of the country has a climate that is
    a. moderate.   c. cool.
    b. warm.   d. very cold.

15. _____ Factors that influence the climate in both the United States and Canada include oceans, mountains, and
    a. agriculture.   c. latitude.
    b. population.   d. volcanoes.

16. _____ Geographers identify four major kinds of plant life in the United States and Canada: tundra, grassland, desert scrub, and
    a. prairie.   c. savanna.
    b. desert.   d. forest.

17. _____ The major natural resources of the United States are soil, water, timber, farmland, and
    a. solar energy.   c. manufactured goods.
    b. minerals.   d. agribusinesses.

18. _____ Much of Canada's mineral wealth is found in the
    a. Prairie Provinces.   c. St. Lawrence Lowlands.
    b. Canadian Shield.   d. Great Lakes.

19. _____ The rivers of Quebec Province are used to make
    a. solar energy.   c. thermal energy.
    b. hydroelectric power.   d. petroleum.

20. ____ How do the United States and Canada appear from outer space?
   a. as two separate countries
   b. as different continents
   c. as one landmass
   d. as a landmass divided by the Atlantic Ocean

21. ____ The landform that lies between the Rockies and the Appalachians is
   a. a huge plains area.
   b. the St. Lawrence River.
   c. the Great Lakes.
   d. the Laurentian Highlands.

22. ____ Why do so few people live on the land covered by the Canadian Shield?
   a. The land is too warm.
   b. The land is too rugged.
   c. The land is too dry.
   d. The land is too wet.

23. ____ Because much of Canada is a long way from the Equator, the climate is
   a. tropical.
   b. moderate.
   c. cold.
   d. warm.

24. ____ Which statement best compares the climates in the United States and Canada?
   a. The climate in the United States is colder than the climate in Canada.
   b. The climate in Canada is milder than the climate in the United States.
   c. There is a greater variety of climates in the United States.
   d. The climates in both countries are the same.

25. ____ One of North America's greatest transportation routes is
   a. the Atlantic Ocean.
   b. the Continental Divide.
   c. the St. Lawrence Seaway.
   d. the Great Lakes.

26. ____ The area from Texas through Kansas is known for
   a. hurricanes.
   b. tornadoes.
   c. heavy snowfall.
   d. heavy rainfall.

27. ____ Where are the largest oil reserves in North America?
   a. along the eastern coast
   b. near the Great Lakes
   c. in the Canadian Shield
   d. along the northern coast of Alaska

28. ____ Why are the Prairie Provinces and the St. Lawrence Lowlands important to the economy of Canada?
   a. They are major agricultural regions.
   b. They are major mineral regions.
   c. They are major manufacturing regions.
   d. They are major forest regions.

C. CRITICAL THINKING

Answer the following questions in the space provided, on the back of this paper or on a separate sheet of paper.

29. Cause and Effect: Consider what you have learned about the geography and climate of Canada and the United States. Why do you think the United States has 10 times more people than Canada?

30. Identifying Central Issues: Imagine that you are a farmer from England who comes to Canada or the United States to live in the 1800s. In what area of Canada or the United States will you settle and start a farm? Explain your choice.

31. Drawing Conclusions: Think about the landforms that act as natural divisions between the United States and Canada. What conclusions can you draw about the effect of these natural divisions on the relationship between the two nations?

32. Identifying Central Issues: If you looked down at the United States and Canada from outer space, what major landforms common to both countries would you see?

D. SKILLS

Use the population map below to answer the following questions. Write your answers on the lines provided.

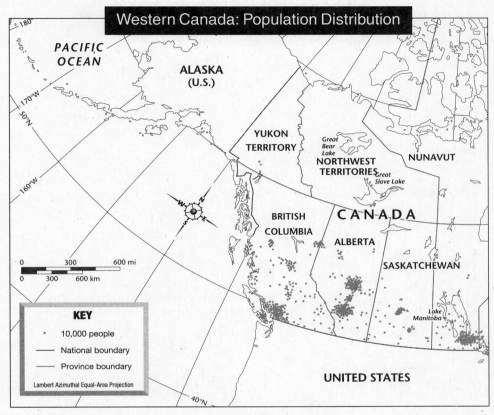

Western Canada: Population Distribution

33. What information does the title of this map provide? _____

_____

34. How is the population represented on the map? _____

_____

35. How many people does each symbol stand for? _____

_____

36. Which area of western Canada has the highest population density? _____

_____

37. Consider the climate and vegetation of western Canada. Why do you think so much of this region is sparsely populated? _____

_____

Use the population map below to answer the following questions. Write your answers on the lines provided.

Central and Eastern Canada: Population Distribution

KEY
· 10,000 people
— National boundary
---- Province boundary

Lambert Azimuthal Equal-Area Projection

38. What information does the title of this map provide? _____

_____

39. How is the population represented on the map? _____

_____

40. How many people does each symbol stand for? _____

_____

41. Which area of Central and Eastern Canada has the highest population density? _____

_____

42. Which area of Central and Eastern Canada has the lowest population density? _____

_____

ANSWER KEY

1. d	2. a	3. i	4. g	5. e
6. c	7. a	8. i	9. f	10. b
11. b	12. c	13. a	14. d	15. c
16. d	17. b	18. b	19. b	20. c
21. a	22. b	23. c	24. c	25. c
26. b	27. d	28. a		

29. Answers may vary, but should include reference to the following: Canada's geography and climate make vast areas of the country difficult for people to live in. The Canadian Shield, a huge region of ancient rock, is very rugged. As a result, more than half of the country's population lives in the smallest land region, the St. Lawrence Lowlands. Also, the very cold climate in much of the country limits population growth.

30 Answers may vary, but should include the following: A farmer in the United States would have settled in an area with rich soil, a mild climate, and access to rivers or other bodies of water. Possible areas include: the eastern and southern coastal plains or the Great Plains. In Canada, a farmer would probably have settled in the St. Lawrence Lowlands, where the soil is fertile and there is access to water routes for trade and shipping.

31. Answers may vary, but should include the following: The two landforms are the St. Lawrence River and the Great Lakes. Since these waterways are important transportation and manufacturing centers for both countries, the United States and Canada would be more likely to work together as trade partners.

32. Answers may vary, but should include the following: The Rocky Mountains extend north to south along the western section of the continent; in the East, the Appalachian Mountains stretch about 1,500 miles. The Appalachians become the Laurentian Highlands in Canada. Between these two mountain systems lies a huge plains area, called the Great Plains and the Central Plains in the United States and the Interior Plains in Canada. You would also see the Great Lakes.

33. The title identifies the map as a population distribution map of western Canada.

34. Population is represented by dots.

35. Each symbol stands for 10,000 people.

36. The southern half of this area has the highest population density.

37. The more northern part of the region is much colder and has less rainfall. Also, it is largely covered with forests or tundra.

38. The title identifies the map as a population distribution map of central and eastern Canada.

39. Population is represented by dots.

40. Each symbol stands for 10,000 people.

41. Most people live in the southeastern areas of the country, along the border with the United States.

42. The northern area has the lowest population density.

A. KEY TERMS

Complete each sentence by writing the letter of the correct term in the blank. You will not use all the terms.

a. dominion
b. clear-cutting
c. bilingual
d. boycott
e. fossil fuel
f. indigenous
g. interdependent
h. labor force
i. abolitionist

1. ____ Before the Revolutionary War, the American colonists decided to ____ , or refuse to buy, British goods.

2. ____ A person who wanted to end slavery in the United States was called a(n) ____ .

3. ____ After the Industrial Revolution, many poor immigrants joined the ____ , or supply of workers.

4. ____ In 1867, Canada became a(n) ____ , or self-governing area.

5. ____ When logging companies practice ____ , they cut down all the trees in an area.

Match the definitions with the terms. Write the correct letter in each blank. You will not use all the terms.

a. immigrant
b. bilingual
c. indentured servant
d. abolitionist
e. dominion
f. indigenous
g. communism
h. tariff

6. ____ a person who has to work for a period of years to gain his or her freedom

7. ____ a person who moves from one country to another

8. ____ a form of government in which the state owns all industries

9. ____ a self-governing area

10. ____ a fee charged on an import

B. KEY CONCEPTS

Write the letter of the correct answer or ending in each blank.

11. ____ Some scientists think that Native Americans migrated from
    a. Europe.   c. Spain.
    b. Asia.   d. England.

12. ____ What was the purpose of the United States Constitution that was approved in 1789?
    a. It set up the framework of the government.
    b. It officially ended the Revolutionary tariff system.
    c. It inspired many colonists to fight for their independence.
    d. It demanded an end to the British War.

13. ____ Which statement best explains why the Louisiana Purchase of 1803 was important to the development of the United States?
    a. It created new taxes on imported goods.
    b. It resulted in immigration from France to the United States.
    c. It doubled the size of the country.
    d. It encouraged Native Americans to settle more land in the West.

14. ____ Why did some Southern states withdraw from the United States in 1860?
    a. They wanted to avoid the Civil War.
    b. They didn't believe in Manifest Destiny.
    c. They wanted to trade freely with Great Britain.
    d. They feared they would have little say in the government.

15. ____ What was one event that helped make the United States a world power?
    a. The country experienced the Great Depression.
    b. The country fought in World War I.
    c. The country signed the Peace of Paris.
    d. The country fought in the French and Indian War.

16. ____ The United States feared that the Soviets were trying to expand their power throughout the world. This fear resulted in
    a. World War II.   c. World War I.
    b. the Cold War.   d. the NAFTA agreement.

17. ____ As a result of the Treaty of Paris, Great Britain gained complete control over
    a. Newfoundland.   c. Quebec.
    b. Canada.   d. the United States.

18. ____ What was one important political result of the Canadian constitution of 1982?
    a. Quebec became an independent nation.
    b. English became the official language of Canada.
    c. Canada became completely independent.
    d. A monarchy was established in Canada.

19. _____ The United States and Canada have worked to solve environmental problems such as water pollution, soil erosion, and
   a. acid rain.
   b. tariffs on imported goods.
   c. free trade.
   d. the North American Free Trade Agreement.

20. _____ Why did English settlers come to America?
   a. to find gold
   b. to become fur traders
   c. to start a new life
   d. to become missionaries

21. _____ Why did American colonists object to the taxes on British goods?
   a. Great Britain was boycotting American-made goods.
   b. They preferred to buy goods made in France.
   c. They were being taxed without having any representation in Parliament.
   d. They wanted to use goods made in America.

22. _____ How did the doctrine of Manifest Destiny in the United States affect the development of the country in the 1800s?
   a. Many Americans moved westward across the continent to settle new territories.
   b. Many Americans moved to European countries looking for work.
   c. Americans encouraged Native Americans to move eastward across the country.
   d. Americans wanted to develop the eastern coast of the United States.

23. _____ Why were the Southern states displeased when California was admitted to the Union as a free state?
   a. Slaves were escaping from California to Canada.
   b. More slaves were needed to work on the Southern plantations.
   c. The Fugitive Slave Act would not be passed.
   d. The Southern states wanted slavery to spread into the new territories.

24. _____ After Lincoln's election as President, why did some Southern states withdraw from the United States?
   a. to abolish slavery
   b. to found a new country
   c. to establish closer ties with Great Britain
   d. to become part of Mexico

25. _____ How did the Industrial Revolution affect the poor in the late 1800s?
   a. The city slums emptied.
   b. Poverty was eliminated.
   c. The life of the poor did not improve.
   d. The life of the poor improved greatly.

26. _____ The United States entered the Cold War because it was afraid of
    a. social problems in other countries.
    b. another world war with Germany and Japan.
    c. an economic decline after World War II.
    d. Soviet expansion throughout the world.

27. _____ The French and Indian War was fought between
    a. France and Native Americans.   c. the United States and France.
    b. Britain and the United States.   d. Britain and France.

28. _____ As a result of the British North American Act of 1867, Canada had its own
    a. monarch.   c. language.
    b. central government.   d. economy.

C. CRITICAL THINKING

Answer the following questions in the space provided, on the back of this paper or on a separate sheet of paper.

29. Making Comparisons: Explain the similarities and differences between the American Revolution and Canada's "peaceful revolution." What did each revolution accomplish?

30. Identifying Central Issues: Former President John F. Kennedy, in describing the relationship between Canada and the United States, said that "economics has made us partners." Explain how the development of the St. Lawrence Seaway illustrates this economic partnership.

31. Identifying Central Issues: Select one of the environmental issues facing both the United States and Canada. Explain how the countries have worked together to solve this problem.

32. Making Comparisons: Explain the similarities and differences between how the Spanish and French dealt with the indigenous peoples in North America.

D. SKILLS

Use the diagram below to answer the following questions. Write your answers on the lines provided.

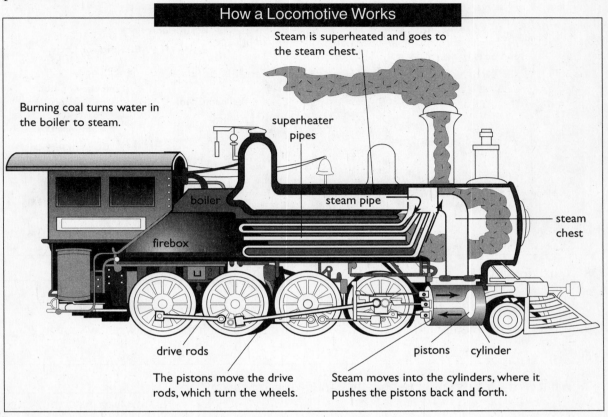

How a Locomotive Works

Steam is superheated and goes to the steam chest.

Burning coal turns water in the boiler to steam.

superheater pipes

boiler

steam pipe

firebox

steam chest

drive rods

pistons   cylinder

The pistons move the drive rods, which turn the wheels.

Steam moves into the cylinders, where it pushes the pistons back and forth.

33. What is the purpose of this diagram?_____

_____

34. What does the picture tell you about how a locomotive works? _____

_____

35. What do the labels in the diagram identify? How is movement shown? _____

_____

36. What are the names of three parts of a locomotive?_____

_____

37. How does the combination of words and pictures make this diagram a useful study tool? __

_____

Use the diagram below to answer the following questions. Write your answers on the lines provided.

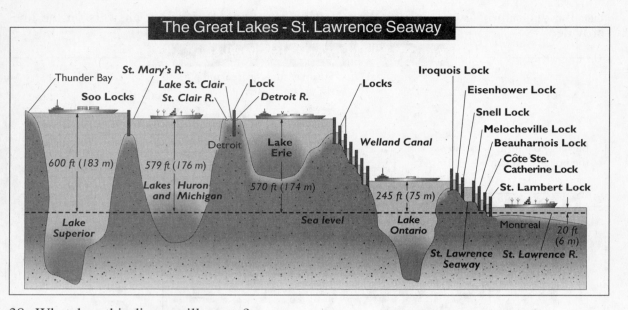

The Great Lakes - St. Lawrence Seaway

38. What does this diagram illustrate? _____

_____

39. What does the picture tell you about how ships pass through the St. Lawrence Seaway? ___

_____

40. What do the labels tell you about the St. Lawrence Seaway? _____

_____

41. Between which two lakes is there the greatest drop in elevation? _____

_____

42. How does this diagram help you understand the St. Lawrence Seaway?_____

_____

ANSWER KEY

1. d	2. i	3. h	4. a	5. b
6. c	7. a	8. g	9. e	10. h
11. b	12. a	13. c	14. d	15. b
16. b	17. b	18. c	19. a	20. c
21. c	22. a	23. d	24. b	25. c
26. d	27. d	28. b		

29. Answers may vary, but should include reference to the following: The American Revolution was an armed conflict between Great Britain and the American colonies. At the end of the war, the colonies won their independence from Great Britain, and the United States of America was established as a separate country. Canada's peaceful revolution did not involve violence. Instead, after the British Parliament accepted the British North American Act, Canada became a dominion. It was still subject to Great Britain, but a central government would run the country.

30. Answers may vary, but should include reference to the following: The United States and Canada worked together to solve the problem of moving ships from one water level to another by building the St. Lawrence Seaway. It is a system of locks, canals, and dams that allows water transportation from the Great Lakes all the way to the Atlantic Ocean. The St. Lawrence Seaway, completed in 1959, makes it easier for both countries to trade with each other and with Europe.

31. Answers may vary, but should include reference to one of the following issues: protecting the whales from extinction; water pollution of the Cuyahoga River; acid rain; or renewing forests.

32. Answers may vary, but should include reference to the following: The Spanish settlers spread out across the United States and often enslaved Native Americans. Spanish missionaries tried to make Native Americans more like Europeans. French explorers, however, claimed land along the St. Lawrence and Mississippi rivers. French traders and missionaries often lived among the Native Americans and learned their languages. Unlike the Spanish, they did not take over Native American land.

33. The diagram shows how a locomotive works.

34. The pictures illustrate how the steam travels through the engine and makes the wheels turn.

35. The labels identify the main parts of a locomotive and how they work. Movement is shown by arrows and labels.

36. any three: boiler, firebox, steam pipe, superheater pipes, steam chest, cylinder, pistons, drive rods

37. Answers may vary, but students should note that while the pictures illustrate the different parts of a locomotive, the labels explain what the parts are and how they work together.

38. the St. Lawrence Seaway

39. Ships move from higher water levels to lower ones through a series of steps over several bodies of water.

40. They tell you the names of the lakes, rivers, locks, and canals that make up the St. Lawrence Seaway. They also tell the water level of each lake.

41. Lake Erie and Lake Ontario

42. Answers may vary, but students may note that the labels and illustration help them understand how ships can move from one water level to another on the St. Lawrence Seaway, as well as the bodies of water that it covers.

A. KEY TERMS

Complete each sentence by writing the letter of the correct term in the blank. You will not use all the terms.

    a. immigrant
    b. reserve
    c. cultural diversity
    d. custom
    e. ethnic group
    f. cultural exchange
    g. mosaic
    h. Nunavut

1. _____ A group of people who share a language, a history, or a culture is a(n) _____ .

2. _____ A process in which different cultures share ideas and ways of doing things is a(n) _____ .

3. _____ A place with a wide variety of cultures has _____ .

4. _____ In Canada, native peoples were sent to a special area, called a(n) _____ , that the government had set aside for them.

5. _____ Canada's Inuits call their new homeland _____ .

Match the definitions with the terms. Write the correct letter in each blank. You will not use all the terms.

    a. cultural exchange
    b. Nunavut
    c. immigrant
    d. cultural diversity
    e. cultural identity
    f. ethnic group
    g. regional difference
    h. reserve
    i. Chippewa

6. _____ a process in which different cultures share ideas and ways of doing things

7. _____ a wide variety of cultures

8. _____ an area set aside by a government for native peoples

9. _____ a group of people who share a language, a history, and a culture

10. _____ the Inuits' new homeland

CHAPTER 3

B. KEY CONCEPTS

Write the letter of the correct answer or ending in each blank.

11. _____ What is one example of cultural exchange during the settlement of North America?
    a. The Spanish introduced horses to North America.
    b. Native Americans ate a great deal of fish.
    c. European settlers took Native American lands.
    d. Spanish and French explorers came to North America looking for wealth.

12. _____ How did the contributions of Russian settlers in the Midwest change American life here?
    a. They learned how to trap and hunt forest animals.
    b. They developed a new language.
    c. They invented a kind of work pants.
    d. They introduced a type of wheat that could grow well in the Midwestern climate.

13. _____ Before the Europeans arrived, the culture of Native Americans living in North America was influenced by
    a. where they lived.   c. the clothes they made.
    b. the crops they grew.   d. the types of houses they built.

14. _____ In the United States, foods, accents, pastimes, and music
    a. are the same everywhere.   c. vary from region to region.
    b. all originated in Russia.   d. are the same as in Canada.

15. _____ The two national languages of Canada are
    a. Spanish and English.   c. French and English.
    b. French and Spanish.   d. Dutch and English.

16. _____ Because many French Canadians of Quebec are worried about preserving their heritage, they want Quebec to become
    a. the capital of the country.   c. a separate country.
    b. a French colony.   d. part of the United States.

17. _____ How do Canada's native peoples intend to preserve their cultures?
    a. by becoming independent
    b. by moving to reserves
    c. by using their own languages in their schools
    d. by using English on the street signs in their communities

18. _____ In order to preserve their cultural identity, Canada's Inuits moved
    a. to Newfoundland.   c. to the United States.
    b. to their new homeland.   d. to Quebec.

19. _____ What country, according to most Canadians, has too much influence on their culture?
    a. Great Britain   c. the United States
    b. France   d. Spain

CHAPTER 3

20. _____ How did Native American groups influence each other's cultures?
   a. by trading with each other
   b. by living in different areas of the country
   c. by growing crops
   d. by hunting animals for food

21. _____ Native Americans teaching English settlers how to grow local foods is an example of
   a. regional differences.   c. ethnic groups.
   b. cultural exchange.   d. cultural similarities.

22. _____ One way in which immigrants change American life is by
   a. studying American laws.
   b. learning English.
   c. refusing to speak their native languages.
   d. bringing their ethnic customs with them.

23. _____ How did Russian settlers change the Midwest?
   a. by bringing iron cooking pots
   b. by bringing a kind of hardy wheat from their homeland
   c. by creating a popular kind of work pants
   d. by developing a new language

24. _____ Which region is known as "America's Breadbasket?"
   a. the Midwest   c. Saskatchewan
   b. the South   d. the West

25. _____ Many French Canadians want to preserve their heritage by
   a. adopting the French constitution.
   b. making French the official language of Canada.
   c. making Quebec a separate country.
   d. becoming part of France.

26. _____ How do Canada's new laws help native peoples to preserve their culture?
   a. by finding them new homes on reserves
   c. by allowing English in their schools
   b. by forcing schools to teach French Canadian history
   d. by allowing them to use their own languages in their schools

27. _____ Nunavut is
   a. a city in Yukon.   c. Canada's most populated area.
   b. Canada's newest province.   d. a French-speaking province.

28. _____ Groups who trade with each other also take part in
   a. migration.   c. music.
   b. preservation of their language.   d. cultural exchange.

C. CRITICAL THINKING

Answer the following questions in the space provided, on the back of this paper or on a separate sheet of paper.

29. Identifying Central Issues: Describe one example of cultural exchange in your community involving people from different ethnic groups.

30. Making Comparisons: Explain a similarity and a difference in the ways different ethnic groups live in the United States and Canada.

31. Identifying Central Issues: In what ways is your community like a cultural kaleidoscope? In your answer, identify and briefly discuss two different cultural influences in your community.

32. Expressing Problems Clearly: What are two ways in which Canada's indigenous peoples are preserving their cultures?

D. SKILLS

Complete the concept map below to show contributions of people from Spanish and Chinese ethnic groups to cultural diversity.

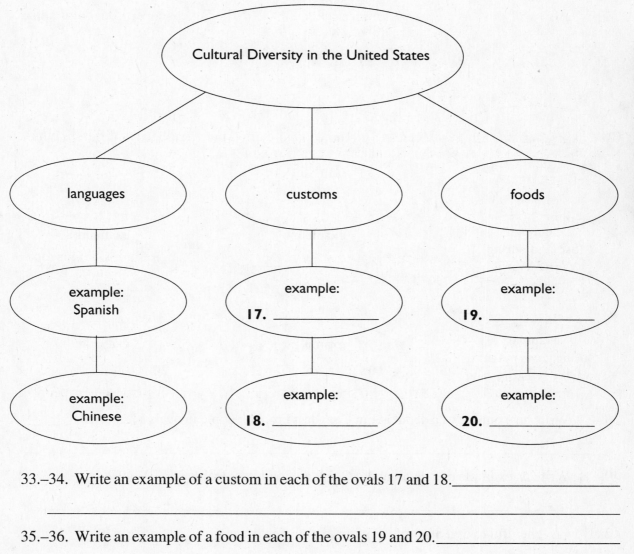

33.–34. Write an example of a custom in each of the ovals 17 and 18._____

_____

35.–36. Write an example of a food in each of the ovals 19 and 20._____

_____

37. How is it helpful to organize information in a concept map?_____

_____

CHAPTER 3

Complete the concept map below to show details about Canada's people.

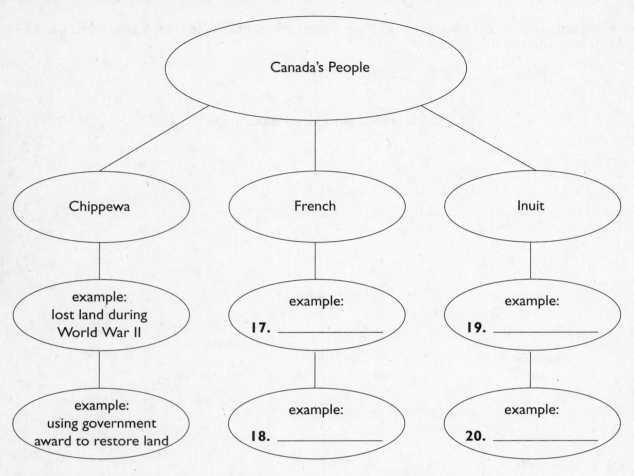

Canada's People

Chippewa

French

Inuit

example:
lost land during
World War II

example:
17. _____

example:
19. _____

example:
using government
award to restore land

example:
18. _____

example:
20. _____

38.–39. Write an example of a detail about Canada's French people in ovals 17 and 18. _____

_____

40.–41. Write an example of a detail about Canada's Inuit people in ovals 19 and 20. _____

_____

42. How is it helpful to organize information in a concept map? _____

_____

ANSWER KEY

1. e	2. f	3. c	4. b	5. h
6. a	7. d	8. h	9. f	10. b
11. a	12. d	13. a	14. c	15. c
16. c	17. c	18. b	19. c	20. a
21. b	22. d	23. b	24. a	25. c
26. d	27. b	28. d		

29. Answers may vary, but might include an ethnic restaurant that includes more traditional American food on its menu.

30. Answers may vary, but might include reference to the following: Similarity: Immigrants came to both countries in search of better lives. Difference: In the United States, members of different ethnic groups may disagree, but they do not talk about forming separate states. However, many French Canadians of Quebec want to form a separate country.

31. Answers may vary, but should include references to two cultural influences, such as ethnic music and ethnic restaurants.

32. Answers may vary, but could include reference to new laws that allow native peoples to use their own languages in their schools. Also, the Inuits, who were fearful of losing their cultural identity, are moving to a new homeland in the Northwest Territory.

33.–34. Answers may vary, but could include music, dancing, and dragon parades.

35.–36. Answers may vary, but could include paella, rice, and stir fry.

37. Answers may vary. Possible answer: It sometimes helps to see information mapped out rather than reading it in a paragraph. It works like an outline.

38.–39. Answers may vary, but could include the fact that Quebeckers speak French, many street signs are in French, and certain laws promote French culture and heritage.

40.–41. Answers may vary, but could include the fact that Inuits used to live in the Arctic and they will soon move into their new homeland, Nunavut.

42. It sometimes helps to see information mapped out rather than reading it in a paragraph. It works like an outline.

CHAPTER 3

Chapter 4 ■ *Exploring the United States*

A. KEY TERMS

Complete each sentence by writing the letter of the correct term in the blank. You will not use all the terms.

        a. corporate farm
        b. mass transit
        c. population density
        d. industrialization
        e. Sun Belt
        f. corporate farm
        g. megalopolis
        h. forty-niner
        i. mixed-crop farm

1. _____ In a(n) _____ , cities and suburbs are so close together that they form one big urban area.

2. _____ The South is part of the _____ .

3. _____ A farmer grows several different kinds of crops on a(n) _____ .

4. _____ To counter the problems caused by freeways and air pollution, San Jose built a(n) _____ system.

5. _____ A region's _____ is the average number of people per square mile.

Match the definitions with the terms. Write the correct letter in each blank. You will not use all the terms.

        a. petrochemicals
        b. urban sprawl
        c. industrialization
        d. mass transit
        e. recession
        f. commute
        g. forty-niners
        h. megalopolis
        i. mixed-crop farm

6. _____ to travel to work each day

7. _____ substances, like plastics, paint, and asphalt

8. _____ the process of changing to an industry-based economy from an agriculture-based economy

9. _____ a farm that grows several different kinds of crops

10. _____ the first miners of the Gold Rush

B. KEY CONCEPTS

Write the letter of the best answer in each blank.

11. _____ What is the most densely populated region of the United States?
    a. the South   c. the Northeast
    b. the Midwest   d. the West

12. _____ From the 1890s to the 1940s, most immigrants entering the United States arrived at
    a. cities in the Midwest.   c. cities in the West.
    b. port cities in the Northeast. d. port cities in the South.

13. _____ Features that make much of the South a great place for growing crops include
    a. ports and industry.   c. industry and climate.
    b. rich soil and climate.   d. trade routes.

14. _____ Over the past 50 years, the South has changed from an agriculture-based economy to
    a. a trade-based economy.   c. a forestry-based economy.
    b. a mining-based economy.   d. an industry-based economy.

15. _____ Many farmers have sold or left their lands since 1980 because of
    a. a population decline in the Midwest. c. an economic recession.
    b. an increase in mixed-crop farms.   d. environmental problems.

16. _____ What factor contributed to Chicago's rise as a steel-making and manufacturing center in the late 1800s?
    a. Railroads were built.   c. Corporate farms declined.
    b. The population increased.   d. Mixed-crop farms increased.

17. _____ The natural resources of the West include animals, plants, soil, and
    a. thermal energy.   c. communication systems.
    b. trade routes.   d. minerals.

18. _____ How did the California Gold Rush affect the region?
    a. Few towns developed.
    b. The population quickly increased.
    c. People quickly returned to the East.
    d. People did not develop the area's natural resources.

19. _____ Where is the District of Columbia located?
    a. in Georgia
    b. between the states of North Carolina and South Carolina
    c. between the states of Maryland and Virginia
    d. in the West

20. _____ Today, the economic centers of the Northeast are its
    a. timberlands.   c. farming communities.
    b. small fishing ports.   d. cities.

21. _____ Which word best describes the Northeast?
   a. rural   c. underpopulated
   b. urban   d. agricultural

22. _____ What is one factor that contributed to the tremendous growth of industry in Philadelphia?
   a. its location near land and water transportation routes
   b. its size
   c. its historical importance during the American Revolution
   d. its reputation as the nation's "money capital"

23. _____ As a result of the South's rich soil and climate, its early economy focused on
   a. industry.   c. farming.
   b. trade.   d. mining.

24. _____ Which city hosted the 1996 Summer Olympic Games?
   a. Boston   c. San Francisco
   b. Atlanta   d. Miami

25. _____ For the past few decades, the population of the Sun Belt has been
   a. decreasing.   c. staying the same.
   b. rising.   d. moving to the Northeast.

26. _____ Millions of immigrants entered the United States at
   a. Philadelphia.   c. Ellis Island.
   b. Boston.   d. Atlanta.

27. _____ The textile industry is an important industry in which region?
   a. the Northeast   c. the Midwest
   b. the South   d. the West

28. _____ Early settlers came to the West because of the region's
   a. location.   c. industry.
   b. natural resources.   d. trade routes.

CHAPTER 4

C. CRITICAL THINKING

Answer the following questions in the space provided, on the back of this paper or on a separate sheet of paper.

29. **Making Comparisons:** Explain the similarities and differences between corporate farms and mixed-crop farms.

30. **Drawing Conclusions:** Identify three problems resulting from urban sprawl in the western region of the United States. If these problems are not solved, what will the outcome likely be?

31. **Drawing Conclusions:** Why do you think colonists founded the cities of the Northeast along rivers or near the Atlantic Ocean?

32. **Identifying Central Issues:** How has industrialization affected the South over the past 50 years?

D. SKILLS

Use the circle graph below to answer the following questions. Write your answer on the lines provided.

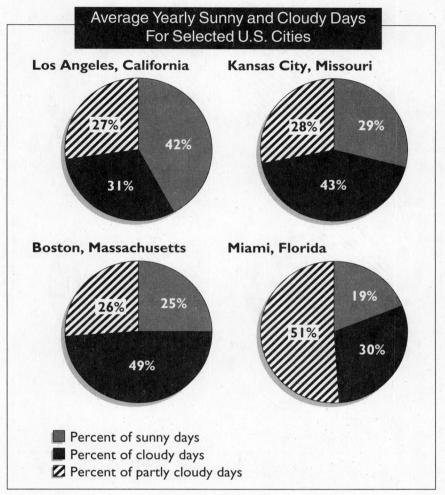

Average Yearly Sunny and Cloudy Days For Selected U.S. Cities

Los Angeles, California
27% 42% 31%

Kansas City, Missouri
28% 29% 43%

Boston, Massachusetts
26% 25% 49%

Miami, Florida
19% 51% 30%

- Percent of sunny days
- Percent of cloudy days
- Percent of partly cloudy days

33. What U.S. cities are shown on the circle graphs? _____

_____

34. What information do the circle graphs show? _____

_____

35. Which city has the most sunny days? Which city has the fewest? _____

_____

36. Which city has the most cloudy days? Which city has the fewest? _____

_____

37. Describe the weather in Los Angeles. _____

_____

Use the circle graph below to answer the following questions. Write your answer on the lines provided.

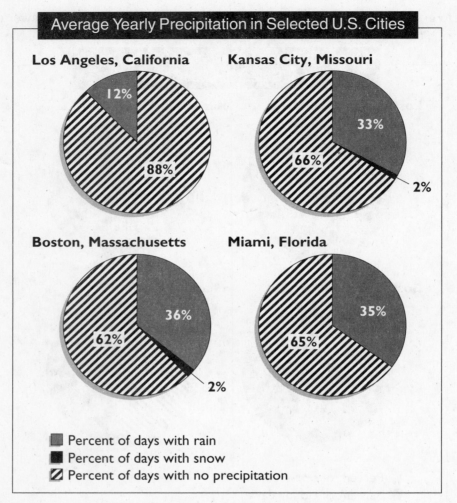

Average Yearly Precipitation in Selected U.S. Cities

Los Angeles, California
12%
88%

Kansas City, Missouri
33%
66%
2%

Boston, Massachusetts
36%
62%
2%

Miami, Florida
35%
65%

Percent of days with rain
Percent of days with snow
Percent of days with no precipitation

38. What U.S. cities are shown on the circle graphs? _____

_____

39. What information is shown on the circle graphs? _____

_____

40. Which city has the most rainy days? Which city has the fewest?_____

_____

41. Which cities have the most snowy days?_____

_____

42. Compare the amount of precipitation in Los Angeles to the amount in the other cities. ____

_____

ANSWER KEY

1. g	2. e	3. i	4. b	5. c
6. f	7. a	8. c	9. i	10. g
11. c	12. b	13. b	14. d	15. c
16. a	17. d	18. b	19. c	20. d
21. b	22. a	23. c	24. b	25. b
26. c	27. b	28. b		

29. Answers may vary, but should include reference to the following: Mixed-crop farms are operated by families. These farms grow several different kinds of crops. However, corporate farms are large farms that are operated by agricultural companies. Corporate farmers use machines and computers to do much of the farmwork and employ fewer workers than the mixed-crop farms.

30. Answers may vary, but should include reference to the following: Three problems include air pollution, traffic congestion, and water pollution from industrial waste. If these problems are not corrected through mass transit systems and anti-pollution legislation, the quality of life in these cities will deteriorate.

31. Answers may vary, but should include reference to the importance of water transportation for the early colonists. Water routes enabled them to travel and transport goods from one colony to another; being near the Atlantic Ocean gave the colonial cities access to boats from England and other European countries.

32. Answers may vary, but should include reference to the following: Most people in the South today live in cities; more people work in industry-related jobs than in agriculture-based jobs; textiles, technology, transportation, and tourism are all important to the South's economy today.

33. Los Angeles; Boston; Kansas City; and Miami

34. percentage of sunny, cloudy, and partly cloudy days each year for Los Angeles, Boston, Kansas City, and Miami

35. Los Angeles; Miami

36. Boston; Miami

37. Students may conclude that the weather in Los Angeles is sunnier than in most other areas of the country; Los Angeles has the greatest number of sunny days and the second lowest number of cloudy and partly cloudy days.

38. Los Angeles; Boston; Kansas City; and Miami

39. average number of days each year with and without precipitation for Los Angeles, Boston, Kansas City, and Miami

40. Boston; Los Angeles

41. Boston and Kansas City

42. Students may conclude that Los Angeles is drier, while Boston has the most precipitation of the cities shown.

CHAPTER 4

A. KEY TERMS

Complete each sentence by writing the letter of the correct term in the blank. You will not use all the terms.

   a. referendum
   b. boomtown
   c. Francophone
   d. separatist
   e. Quiet Revolution
   f. totem pole
   g. Montreal
   h. immunity
   i. Pacific Rim

1. _____ A person living in Quebec who wants the province to break away from Canada is a _____ .

2. _____ Voters cast ballots for or against an issue in a _____ .

3. _____ A natural resistance to a disease is a(n) _____ .

4. _____ A giant, carved _____ includes the symbols for a group, a clan, or a family.

5. _____ A person who speaks French as his or her first language is a(n) _____ .

Match the definitions with the terms. Write the correct letter in each blank. You will not use all the terms.

   a. referendum
   b. separatist
   c. Francophone
   d. totem pole
   e. Quiet Revolution
   f. boomtown
   g. Pacific Rim
   h. Victoria
   i. immunity

6. _____ a person who speaks French as a first language

7. _____ a vote by the people on an issue

8. _____ natural resistance to a disease

9. _____ a settlement whose only purpose was to meet the needs of miners

10. _____ a carved object with the symbols for a group, a clan, or a family

B. KEY CONCEPTS

Write the letter of the correct answer or ending in each blank.

11. _____ What happened to the region now known as Quebec as a result of the Seven Years' War?
    a. The territory went to France.
    b. The territory went to the United States.
    c. The territory went to Great Britain.
    d. The territory went to Spain.

12. _____ How did the new government in Quebec, elected in 1976, change life in that Canadian province?
    a. The government voted to separate from Canada.
    b. The government made Quebec a part of France.
    c. The government made French the official language.
    d. The government made English the official language.

13. _____ Today, the majority of Quebec's population is made up of descendants of
    a. English colonists.
    b. Spanish colonists.
    c. American colonists.
    d. French colonists.

14. _____ One way in which European settlers changed the lives of the native peoples in the Plains region was by
    a. exposing them to diseases such as measles.
    b. building schools for their children.
    c. giving them free land.
    d. teaching them how to farm their land.

15. _____ What happened after Canada advertised free land in European newspapers in the late 1800s and early 1900s?
    a. Immigration decreased.
    b. Immigration increased.
    c. People left Canada for Europe.
    d. Canadians moved from the farms to the cities.

16. _____ Why is Saskatchewan called "Canada's Breadbasket"?
    a. It's a major manufacturing center.
    b. It's a major wheat-growing center.
    c. It's a major mining center.
    d. It's a major shipping center.

17. _____ Early Spanish, British, and Russian explorers of what is now British Columbia came to the region in order to
    a. settle.
    b. farm.
    c. trade.
    d. mine.

18. _____ What was one effect of the gold rush of 1858 on Vancouver Island?
    a. Farming increased.
    b. Manufacturing decreased.
    c. The population increased.
    d. Immigration decreased.

19. _____ What was the purpose of the Canadian Pacific Railway?
   a. to unify the United States
   b. to increase settlement in Britain
   c. to unite Canada
   d. to help the native peoples of Canada

20. _____ The largest cultural group living in Quebec today are the descendants of
   a. British settlers.   c. Spanish explorers.
   b. French colonists.   d. American loyalists.

21. _____ What is one change brought about by the Quiet Revolution in Quebec's government?
   a. The government made English the official language.
   b. The government kept immigrants from living in Quebec.
   c. The government made French the official language.
   d. The government made Quebec a separate nation.

22. _____ Jacques Cartier claimed the region he discovered near the Gulf of St. Lawrence for his nation,
   a. Great Britain.   c. the United States.
   b. Spain.   d. France.

23. _____ Immigrants from Central and Eastern Europe came to Saskatchewan in the late 1800s and early 1900s in response to an offer of
   a. free transportation to Canada.   c. free land in the Prairie Provinces.
   b. an education for their children.   d. jobs in factories.

24. _____ Why did the ways of life of many indigenous peoples in the Plains region of North America end in the late 1870s?
   a. European descendants built factories on their land.
   b. European descendants built schools to educate them.
   c. European descendants began moving from Canada back to their homelands.
   d. European descendants began killing off the buffalo herds.

25. _____ Saskatchewan's main contribution to the Canadian economy is
   a. mining.   c. growing wheat.
   b. producing manufactured goods. d. trading with other countries.

26. _____ Why did Spanish, British, and Russian explorers first come to what is now British Columbia in the late 1500s?
   a. to settle   c. to farm
   b. to trade   d. to cut down forests

27. _____ In 1858, what event significantly changed life on Vancouver Island?
   a. the establishment of Victoria, a small trading village
   b. the discovery of a trade route to the Pacific Ocean
   c. the discovery of gold along Fraser River
   d. the arrival of Russian explorers

28. ____ British Columbia's geography and trade partners create a strong link with the area known as
    a. the Pacific Rim.
    b. Western Europe.
    c. Eastern Europe.
    d. South China.

C. CRITICAL THINKING

Answer the following questions in the space provided, on the back of this paper or on a separate sheet of paper.

29. Identify Central Issues:　Explain how the ways of life of many native peoples in the Plains region of North America ended in the late 1870s.

30. Recognizing Cause and Effect:　How did the completion of the Canadian Pacific Railway affect life in Canada?

31. Drawing Conclusions:　Why do you think the Canadian government is opposed to Quebec's becoming a separate nation? In your answer, briefly explain why Quebeckers want to break away from Canada.

32. Identifying Central Issues:　How did European settlers in Canada affect the indigenous peoples already living there?

D. SKILLS

Read the following topic ideas for a one-page paper. Then answer the questions below. Write your answers on the lines provided.

- Topic A: Jacques Cartier's discovery of what is now Quebec in 1535
- Topic B: The immigration of Central and Eastern European people to the Canadian prairies
- Topic C: A gold mine on Vancouver Island

33. Which topic would you choose to write about? Does the topic you chose describe a process, an event, or a thing? _____

_____

34. Who is your audience? _____

_____

35. What are two research sources you would use?_____

_____

36. How would you organize your paper?_____

_____

37. What would be your next step, before you begin writing your paper?_____

_____

Read the following topic ideas for a one-page paper. Then answer the questions below. Write your answers on the lines provided.

- Topic A: The arrival of James Cook, a British explorer, on Vancouver Island
- Topic B: The building of the Canadian Pacific Railway
- Topic C: The locomotive engine used on trains traveling on the Canadian Pacific Railway

38. Which topic would you choose to write about? Does the topic you chose describe a process, an event, or a thing? _____

_____

39. Who is your audience? _____

_____

40. What are two research sources you would use?_____

_____

41. How would you organize your paper?_____

_____

42. What would be your next step, before you begin writing your paper?_____

_____

ANSWER KEY

1. d	2. a	3. h	4. f	5. c
6. c	7. a	8. i	9. f	10. d
11. c	12. c	13. d	14. a	15. b
16. b	17. c	18. c	19. c	20. b
21. c	22. d	23. c	24. d	25. c
26. b	27. c	28. a		

29. Answers may vary, but should include reference to the following: Descendants of Europeans killed off the buffalo herds that were central to the lives of native peoples. At the same time, the governments of Canada and the United States took over the native peoples' land and sent them to live on reserves.

30. Answers will vary, but should include reference to the following: The railroad provided a way of uniting Canada from Montreal to Vancouver. Building the project attracted immigrants from all over the world. Towns grew up along the railroad, and more newcomers came to Canada.

31. Answers may vary, but should include reference to the following: Many people in Quebec who are of French descent are worried that their culture and language might die if Quebec remains part of Canada. Therefore, many Quebeckers demand independence for Quebec. Although the Canadian government did make some changes, such as making French the official language of Quebec, the separatists have warned that they will continue their struggle. If Quebec does separate, it would weaken Canada politically and economically. It might encourage other Canadian provinces to become separate nations as well.

32. Answers will vary, but should include reference to the following: The European settlers permanently changed the cultures of the native peoples by bringing European goods, such as pots and guns. Also, they introduced diseases to Canada that the native peoples had no immunity against. The Europeans destroyed the buffalo herds that were essential to the lives of the native peoples. Then the governments of Canada and the United States took the land that belonged to the native peoples and forced them to live on reserves.

33. Answers will vary. Topic A describes an event; Topic B describes a process; Topic C describes a thing.

34. teachers and classmates

35. Answers will vary, but students can refer to nonfiction books, encyclopedia articles, newspapers of the period, and magazine articles.

36. Topic A—chronological order; Topic B—the steps in the process; Topic C—its purpose and parts

37. writing an outline

38. Answers will vary. Topic A describes an event; Topic B describes a process; Topic C describes a thing.

39. teachers and classmates

40. Answers will vary, but students can refer to nonfiction books, encyclopedia articles, newspapers of the period, and magazine articles.

41. Topic A—chronological order; Topic B—the steps in the process; Topic C—its purpose and parts

42. writing an outline

A. KEY TERMS

Complete each sentence by writing the letter of the correct term in the blank. You will not use all the terms.

        a. glacier
        b. immunity
        c. separatist
        d. Industrial Revolution
        e. tributary
        f. commute
        g. industrialization
        h. reserve
        i. cultural diversity

1. _____ A huge, slow-moving sheet of ice is a(n) _____ .

2. _____ The change from making goods by hand to making them by machine is called the _____ .

3. _____ An area that the Canadian government set aside as a place for native peoples to live is called a(n) _____ .

4. _____ The process of changing from an agriculture-based economy to an industry-based economy is called _____ .

5. _____ A natural resistance to disease is a(n) _____ .

Match the definitions with the terms. Write the correct letter in each blank. You will not use all the terms.

        a. indentured servant
        b. glacier
        c. recession
        d. tributary
        e. megalopolis
        f. separatist
        g. ethnic group
        h. geographic diversity
        i. abolitionist

6. _____ a river that flows into a larger river

7. _____ a person who had to work for a number of years to gain freedom

8. _____ a person who wanted to end slavery

9. _____ a group of people who share a language, a history, and a culture

10. _____ a region in which cities and suburbs are so close that they form one big urban area

CHAPTER 6

B. KEY CONCEPTS

Write the letter of the best answer in each blank.

11. _____ The landform that lies between the Rocky and Appalachian mountains is a
   a. low mountain range.   c. coastal area.
   b. huge plains area.   d. swamp.

12. _____ Which statement best describes the climates of the United States and Canada?
   a. Most of the United States is very cold, while Canada has a mild climate.
   b. The United States and Canada have the same climate.
   c. Much of Canada is very cold, while the United States has a more varied climate.
   d. The United States has a warm climate, while the climate of Canada is mild.

13. _____ Why did English settlers come to America?
   a. to find wealth   c. to start a new life
   b. to enslave the Native Americans   d. to find new trade routes to Asia

14. _____ After Abraham Lincoln was elected President in 1860, some Southern states
   a. withdrew from the United States.
   b. wanted to abolish slavery.
   c. became colonies of Great Britain.
   d. issued the Emancipation Proclamation.

15. _____ One way in which the Spanish changed Native American life was by
   a. building schools in North America.
   b. bringing horses to North America.
   c. teaching Native Americans how to farm.
   d. teaching Native Americans about medicinal plants.

16. _____ After the recession of the 1980s, mixed-crop farms in the American Midwest were replaced by
   a. industries.   c. corporate farms.
   b. mines.   d. plantations.

17. _____ Explorers were first attracted to the American West because of the region's
   a. trade routes.   c. natural resources.
   b. different ethnic cultures. d. industries.

18. _____ In order to preserve their French culture, many people in Quebec want to
   a. become a colony of France.   c. require immigrants to learn English.
   b. get better-paying jobs.   d. separate from Canada.

19. ____ Why did the ways of life of many native peoples in the Plains region of North America end in the late 1870s?
    a. Many native peoples left the United States for Europe.
    b. The government encouraged native peoples to move to the cities.
    c. descendants of Europeans began killing off the buffalo herds.
    d. The population of the native peoples grew at a tremendous rate.

20. ____ What is the largest mountain system in North America?
    a. the Appalachian Mountains   c. the Sierra Nevada
    b. the Rocky Mountains   d. the Cascades

21. ____ Geographers have identified four major kinds of plant life in the United States and Canada: tundra, grassland, desert scrub, and
    a. desert.   c. forest.
    b. rain forest.   d. plains.

22. ____ Spanish and French explorers came to North America looking for
    a. wealth.   c. freedom of religion.
    b. settlements.   d. a new life.

23. ____ How did the idea of Manifest Destiny influence settlement in the United States?
    a. Americans began traveling to the eastern cities to live.
    b. Americans began traveling to Canada to settle.
    c. Americans began traveling to the West to settle.
    d. Americans began traveling to Mexico to live.

24. ____ The way of life of Native Americans changed after the Spanish introduced
    a. public schools.   c. ways of growing local foods.
    b. medicinal plants.   d. horses.

25. ____ In order to regain their cultural identify, Canada's Inuits are moving to
    a. Quebec.   c. the United States.
    b. reserves.   d. their new homeland.

26. ____ During the California Gold Rush of 1849, what happened to the population of the region?
    a. It increased.   c. People moved away from California.
    b. It decreased.   d. It stayed the same.

27. ____ British Columbia's geography, ethnic diversity, and trade link the province to
    a. Eastern Europe.   c. South America.
    b. the Pacific Rim.   d. Russia.

28. ____ The two official languages of Canada are
    a. English and Spanish.   c. English and French.
    b. French and Spanish.   d. French and German.

C. CRITICAL THINKING

Answer the following questions in the space provided, on the back of this paper or on a separate sheet of paper.

29. **Making Comparisons:** Explain the similarities and differences between the Civil War in the United States and the Quiet Revolution in Quebec.

30. **Identifying Central Issues:** How did the arrival of European settlers in North America affect the lives and the cultures of the indigenous peoples there? Use two facts from the book in your answer.

31. **Drawing Conclusions:** Canada has more land than the United States, but the United States has 10 times more people than Canada. Why do you think this is so?

32. **Making Comparisons:** Explain the similarities and differences in the ways the United States and Canada each achieved independence.

D. SKILLS

Use the population distribution map of Canada below to answer the questions. Write your answers on the lines provided.

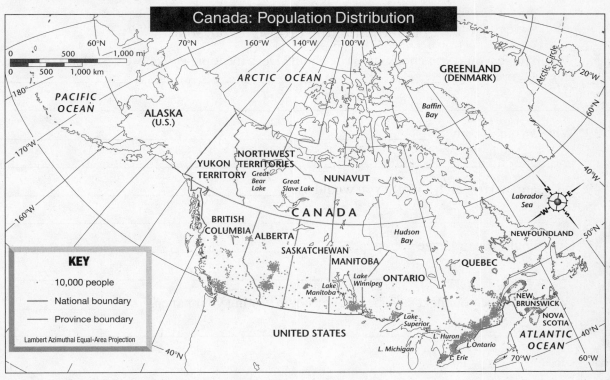

Canada: Population Distribution

KEY

· 10,000 people

— National boundary

— Province boundary

Lambert Azimuthal Equal-Area Projection

33. What country is shown on the map? _____

_____

34. How is the population represented on the map? How many people does each symbol stand for? _____

_____

35. Where do the people of Canada live? _____

_____

36. Where do most of the people of Canada live? _____

_____

37. Why do you think the population of Canada is distributed the way it is? _____

_____

Read the following topic ideas for a one-page paper. Then answer the questions below. Write your answers on the lines provided.

- Topic A: The arrival of European explorers and settlers in North America
- Topic B: The start of the Civil War
- Topic C: A plantation in the pre–Civil War South

38. Which topic would you choose to write about? Does the topic you chose describe a process, an event, or a thing? _____

_____

39. Who is your audience? _____

_____

40. What are two research sources you would use?_____

_____

41. How would you organize your paper?_____

_____

42. What would be your next step, before you begin writing your paper?_____

_____

ANSWER KEY

1. a	2. d	3. h	4. g	5. b
6. d	7. a	8. i	9. g	10. e
11. b	12. c	13. c	14. a	15. b
16. c	17. c	18. d	19. c	20. b
21. c	22. a	23. c	24. d	25. d
26. a	27. b	28. c		

29. Answers will vary, but should include reference to the following: The Civil War was an armed struggle between the Union and the Confederacy that started when the Southern states seceded from the United States. The states left the Union because they thought that President Lincoln would abolish slavery, a system that was central to the Southern economy. However, the Quiet Revolution was a peaceful change in government in which the political party that supported Quebec's separation from Canada won control of the provincial legislature. The new government made French the official language of Quebec. However, Quebec still remained a province of Canada.

30. Answers may vary, but should include reference to the following: Descendants of Europeans destroyed the culture of the native peoples by taking their land and forcing them to live on reserves, by destroying the buffalo herds that they depended upon, and by introducing diseases to which they had no immunity.

31. Answers may vary, but should include reference to Canada's cold climate, which makes it difficult for people to live in much of the country, and the more varied and generally milder climate of the United States. Also, the Canadian Shield covers about half of Canada. Because the land on the Canadian Shield is so rugged, few people live here.

32. Answers may vary, but should include reference to the following: The American colonies fought the Revolutionary War against Great Britain to gain their independence. Canada also wanted to be independent of British rule. However, it happened gradually, beginning with the British North American Act of 1867, which made Canada a dominion, or self-governing area. At that time, Canada was still subject to Great Britain. However, in 1982, the Canadians wrote a new constitution. It enabled Canadians to change their constitution without Great Britain's permission. At that point, Canada was completely independent.

33. Canada

34. by dots; 10,000

35. throughout the country, with the exception of the extreme north

36. along the southern border

37. The climate is milder in the south.

38. Answers will vary. Topic A describes an event; Topic B describes a process; Topic C describes a thing.

39. teachers and classmates

40. Answers will vary; however, students can refer to nonfiction books, encyclopedia articles, newspapers of the period, and magazine articles.

41. Topic A—chronological order or steps in the process; Topic B—the steps in the process or chronological order; Topic C—its purpose and parts

42. writing an outline

CHAPTER 6

World Explorer

MEDIEVAL TIMES to TODAY

BOOK 8

Chapter 1 ▪ *The Byzantine and Muslim Empires*

A. KEY TERMS

Complete each sentence by writing the letter of the correct term in the blank. You will not use all the terms.

   a. hajj
   b. nomad
   c. hijra
   d. tolerance
   e. Ramadan
   f. patriarch
   g. Quran
   h. strait
   i. icon

1. _____ The leader of the Christian Church in Constantinople was called the _____ .

2. _____ A person who constantly moves from place to place is called a(n) _____ .

3. _____ All Muslims who can afford to do so make the _____ , or sacred journey to Mecca, at least once.

4. _____ Many Muslims know their holy book, the _____ , by heart.

5. _____ During the golden age, Muslim rulers treated Jews and Christians with _____ , accepting their differences.

Match the definitions with the terms. Write the correct letter in each blank. You will not use all the terms.

   a. hajj
   b. caliph
   c. hijra
   d. tolerance
   e. Ramadan
   f. patriarch
   g. Quran
   h. icon
   i. strait

6. _____ the leader of the Church in Constantinople during the Byzantine empire

7. _____ the chief ruler of Islam

8. _____ the sacred journey each Muslim tries to make at least once in his or her life

9. _____ a special month in which Muslims fast

10. _____ the holy book of Islam

B. KEY CONCEPTS

Write the letter of the correct answer in each blank.

11. _____ Constantinople grew rich because it
    a. borrowed money from the Roman Empire.
    b. was located in a natural crossroads of trade.
    c. used "Greek fire" to defend its capital against attacks.
    d. had an unpredictable ruler.

12. _____ The Byzantines recorded and saved the knowledge of
    a. ancient China.   c. ancient Greece and Rome.
    b. only ancient Rome.   d. only ancient Greece.

13. _____ Mecca lay on a trade route on the edge of the desert that takes up most of
    a. the Red Sea.   c. the Kabah.
    b. Syria.   d. the Arabian Peninsula.

14. _____ Why was Islam so attractive to the peoples of the Arabian Peninsula?
    a. Islam offered people a way of life in contrast to the oppressive rules of the
       nearby Byzantine and Persian empires.
    b. Islam tried to enforce complicated law codes.
    c. Islamic beliefs spread out over North Africa, Spain, and southern France.
    d. Islam could not compete with Medina in trade.

15. _____ Islam quickly spread to Asia, North Africa, and the Mediterranean Coast because
    a. people in those areas had no religion.
    b. Muhammad migrated to those regions.
    c. Muslim traders took their religion there.
    d. Mecca was no longer an important religious center.

16. _____ Which of the following is one of the Five Pillars of Islam?
    a. prophecy   c. prayer
    b. caliphs   d. memorizing

17. _____ What do followers of Islam and the Jewish and Christian religions all believe in?
    a. one God alone   c. Ramadan
    b. Muhammad   d. journeying to Mecca

18. _____ Scholars see Islam's golden age as
    a. one of the worst periods in world history.
    b. a period when the arts suffered.
    c. a period when many gold objects were made.
    d. one of the most brilliant periods in world history.

19. _____ One great contribution of the Islamic golden age was
    a. algebra.   c. singing stars.
    b. taxes.   d. golden goblets.

20. _____ The Byzantine empire lasted a long time because it
    a. had no religious disputes.
    b. had rulers with limited power.
    c. grew rich from trade.
    d. had little contact with the rest of the world.

21. _____ The Code of Justinian clearly stated
    a. the history of Byzantium.   c. the laws and what they meant.
    b. future events.   d. how to make "Greek fire."

22. _____ Which statement best describes the Bedouins?
    a. They moved from one place to another.
    b. They lived in walled cities.
    c. They followed the Code of Justinian.
    d. They were farmers.

23. _____ Why did Islam spread so fast?
    a. The Byzantine and Persian empires had good roads.
    b. Muslims were expert traders and traveled widely.
    c. Islam divided Arabs into separate communities that moved away.
    d. People of all religions made pilgrimages to Mecca.

24. _____ Islam treated Jews and Christians with respect, but did make them
    a. pay higher taxes.   c. follow the nomadic way of life.
    b. worship Abraham and Moses.   d. work together.

25. _____ The saying, "There is no god but God," expresses the importance of the Muslim belief in
    a. prophets.   c. one God.
    b. muezzins.   d. tolerating others.

26. _____ Muslims must pray five times
    a. a day.   c. a week.
    b. an hour.   d. a year.

27. _____ In the A.D. 600s, the Islamic world split into two groups: the Shiites and the
    a. Meccans.   c. Muslims.
    b. Sunnis.   d. Greek Orthodox.

28. _____ Harun ar-Rashid was a great supporter of
    a. the arts.   c. the army at Mecca.
    b. the Code of Justinian.   d. the Sufis.

C. CRITICAL THINKING

Answer the following questions in the space provided, on the back of this paper or on a separate sheet of paper.

29. Making Comparisons: What did the Byzantine empire and the Islamic world have in common?

30. Recognizing Cause and Effect: How did the Islamic world benefit from tolerance?

31. Identifying Central Issues: Why can Islam be described as a way of life?

32. Making Comparisons: How can you compare the life of women in the Islamic world with the life of women in your community today?

D. SKILL: READING TABLES

Use the table below to answer the following questions. Write your answers on the lines provided.

Key Figures in Byzantine and Islamic History

	Justinian	Muhammad	Harun ar-Rashid
Years of Rule	A.D. 527–A.D. 565	A.D. 611–A.D. 632	A.D. 786–A.D. 809
Place of Rule	Constantinople	Arabian Peninsula	Baghdad
Major Accomplishment	ordered the writing of the Code of Justinian	brought Islam to the world	ruled during the golden age of Islam

33. Which leader ruled the longest? _____

_____

34. Which leader ruled from Baghdad? _____

_____

35. Which leader ruled during the golden age of Islam? _____

_____

36. If the table did not give the years each leader ruled, how could you tell that Harun ar-Rashid came after Muhammad? _____

_____

37. What was Muhammad's major accomplishment?_____

_____

Use the table below to answer the following questions. Write your answers on the lines provided.

Byzantine and Muslim Empires

	Byzantine Empire	Muslim Empire
Time Period	A.D. 527–A.D. 1453	A.D. 640–A.D. 1750
Location	surrounding the Mediterranean Sea in Southwest Asia, southeastern Europe, and North Africa	North Africa, Southwest Asia, and southern Europe
Major City	Byzantium/Constantinople	Mecca
Religion	Christianity	Islam
Source of Wealth	trade	trade
Scientific and Mathematical Contributions	records of Greek and Roman advances in science, mathematics, and health care	Avicenna's medical discoveries, algebra, an improved decimal system, and scientific classification

38. What was the source of wealth for both empires? _____

_____

39. Which empire lasted longer? _____

_____

40. Which empire extended into Europe? _____

_____

41. In which row of the table can you find information about mathematics?_____

_____

42. What does the table tell you about religion? _____

_____

ANSWER KEY

1. f	2. b	3. a	4. g	5. d
6. f	7. b	8. a	9. e	10. g
11. b	12. c	13. d	14. a	15. c
16. c	17. a	18. d	19. a	20. c
21. c	22. a	23. b	24. a	25. c
26. a	27. b	28. a		

29. Answers will vary, but should include discussion of the importance of trade in both the Byzantine empire and the Islamic world.

30. Answers will vary, but should mention that Islam's tolerance of other religions resulted in increased peace and an increase in intellectual work of scholars of other religions.

31. Answers will vary, but should mention the Five Pillars of Islam and explain how they affect the everyday life of Muslims.

32. Answers will vary, but should discuss the balance of work inside and outside the home.

33. Justinian

34. Harun ar-Rashid

35. Harun ar-Rashid

36. On the line of the table showing the major accomplishment of each leader, Muhammad is listed as the person who brought Islam to the world, and Harun ar-Rashid is listed as someone who ruled during the golden age of Islam. Therefore, Harun ar-Rashid must have ruled after Muhammad.

37. He brought Islam to the world.

38. trade

39. the Muslim empire

40. both empires

41. the last row: Scientific and Mathematical Contributions

42. The table tells that the religion in the Byzantine empire was Christianity; in the Muslim empire, the religion was Islam.

A. KEY TERMS

Complete each sentence by writing the letter of the correct term in the blank. You will not use all the terms.

    a. clan
    b. oasis
    c. migration
    d. savanna
    e. silent barter
    f. province
    g. city-state
    h. Swahili

1. _____ Much of the area north and south of Africa's rain forests is _____ , a rolling grassland.

2. _____ Desert travelers can rest at a(n) _____ , an area of vegetation fed by springs.

3. _____ Not even physical barriers can stop a great _____ , or movement of people.

4. _____ Merchants in Africa bought gold by means of _____ , or trading without speaking.

5. _____ Kilwa was a(n) _____ , having its own independent government and controlling the land around it.

Match the definitions with the terms. Write the correct letter in each blank. You will not use all the terms.

    a. city-state
    b. oasis
    c. migration
    d. savanna
    e. silent barter
    f. clan
    g. province
    h. Swahili

6. _____ a mass movement of people

7. _____ a process of trading goods without speaking

8. _____ a group of families who trace their roots to the same ancestor

9. _____ an area of gently rolling land covered by grasses

10. _____ an area of vegetation fed by springs and underground water

CHAPTER 2

B. KEY CONCEPTS

Write the letter of the correct answer in each blank.

11. _____ Africa's rain forests are located on either side of the
    a. Equator.   c. Sahara.
    b. coastal plains.   d. deserts.

12. _____ The Bantu migrations lasted for
    a. about 5,000 years.   c. about 2,000 years.
    b. about 1,000 years.   d. about 100 years.

13. _____ Historians study the Bantu migrations by examining
    a. records of metalworking.   c. cattle raising.
    b. old maps of migration routes.   d. where Bantu-speakers live today.

14. _____ The two most important products that were traded in West Africa were gold and
    a. wheat.   c. slaves.
    b. iron.   d. salt.

15. _____ Muslim scholars in the empire of Mali taught students to read
    a. the Christian Bible.   c. the Quran.
    b. Swahili writings.   d. Bantu poems.

16. _____ With the help of a Muslim architect, Mansa Musa built the city of
    a. Ghana.   c. Tombouctou.
    b. Mali.   d. Kumbi Saleh.

17. _____ The people who finally drove the rulers of Aksum from the coast of Africa were
    a. Muslim traders.   c. Christian kings.
    b. Jewish refugees.   d. Bantu farmers.

18. _____ Cut off from the rest of the world, the Ethiopians developed their own form of
    a. gold-salt trade.   c. metalworking.
    b. Christianity.   d. farming.

19. _____ The port cities of East Africa traded with
    a. China, India, and Southwest Asia.   c. Europe and the Americas.
    b. Songhai.   d. Portugal.

20. _____ What is the largest desert in Africa and in the world?
    a. the savanna   c. Swahili
    b. the Sahara   d. Songhai

21. _____ The Bantu-speaking people probably began to migrate because of
    a. rainy weather.   c. lack of gold.
    b. failing oases.   d. population growth.

22. _____ What did the Bantu-speaking people spread across Africa as they migrated?
   a. their language and culture
   b. bronze-making skills
   c. Christianity
   d. Islam

23. _____ What item did the people of West Africa usually trade to get salt?
   a. gold
   b. bronze
   c. silk
   d. water

24. _____ One sign of the Muslim influence in Mali was
   a. gold dust.
   b. mosques.
   c. camels.
   d. Sundiata.

25. _____ Mansa Musa wanted Tombouctou to be a leading center of
   a. Muslim learning.
   b. military power.
   c. Christian learning.
   d. agriculture.

26. _____ During the A.D. 300s, what became the official religion of Aksum?
   a. Islam
   b. Judaism
   c. Christianity
   d. Swahili

27. _____ Kilwa was a Muslim city that thrived because of
   a. offshore fishing.
   b. raising yams.
   c. trade with foreign lands.
   d. Swahili scholars.

28. _____ Most of the gold that was brought to the Swahili city-states came from around
   a. Ethiopia.
   b. Portugal.
   c. Kenya.
   d. Great Zimbabwe.

C. CRITICAL THINKING

Answer the following questions in the space provided, on the back of this paper or on a separate sheet of paper.

29. Recognizing Cause and Effect: What effect did Muslims have on the history of ancient Africa?

30. Drawing Conclusions: Why do you think the Portuguese captured and looted the Swahili cities?

31. Expressing Problems Clearly: If you were a historian, how would you go about studying a migration in Africa that took place more than 1,000 years ago?

32. Recognizing Cause and Effect: How did Ethiopia's location affect the development of religion in the kingdom?

D. SKILL: ORGANIZING YOUR TIME

Study the homework assignment plan below to answer the following questions. Write your answers on the lines provided.

Assignment: Study Chapter 2 for a chapter test.

Steps	Estimated Time
1. Take notes on Lesson 1	20 minutes
2. Take notes on Lesson 2	20 minutes
3. Take notes on Lesson 3	20 minutes
4. Review notes	15 minutes
5. Memorize information in notes	20 minutes
6. Self-check of information	15 minutes
TOTAL TIME:	**1 hour 50 minutes**

33. How much time is allowed for taking notes on each lesson? _____
_____

34. How much time is allowed for reviewing notes? _____
_____

35. How much time is allowed for memorizing information? _____
_____

36. If you already had taken notes on your reading, how long would it take to study for the test using this plan? _____
_____

37. Do you think the study plan is good? Explain your reasoning. _____
_____

Study the homework assignment plan below to answer the following questions. Write your answers on the lines provided.

Assignment: Write a report on the Swahili port cities.

Steps	Estimated Time
1. Go to the library and choose a topic	40 minutes
2. Read and take notes on topic	2 hours 50 minutes
3. Create outline from notes	40 minutes
4. Write first draft from notes	2 hours
5. Do final research if needed	20 minutes
6. Write final draft of report	1 hour 30 minutes
TOTAL TIME:	**8 hours**

38. How much time is allowed for choosing the topic? _____

_____

39. How much time is allowed for reading and taking notes? _____

_____

40. According to the homework plan, which would take longer, writing the first draft or the final draft? _____

_____

41. Considering the total number of hours in the plan, how long would it take you to write the report if you set aside two hours a week for it? _____

_____

42. Do you think the study plan is good? Explain your reasoning. _____

_____

ANSWER KEY

1. d	2. b	3. c	4. e	5. g
6. c	7. e	8. f	9. d	10. b
11. a	12. b	13. d	14. d	15. c
16. c	17. a	18. b	19. a	20. b
21. d	22. a	23. a	24. b	25. a
26. c	27. c	28. d		

29. Answers will vary, but should discuss one or more of the following topics: the positive contributions of Muslim scholars in Mali; Muslim traders in East Africa; the negative effect of trade competition that drove the people of Aksum inland.

30. Answers will vary, but should mention the desire to take over profitable trade routes.

31. Answers will vary, but should focus on the need to investigate where the language of the people you are studying is spoken today.

32. Answers will vary, but should include the fact that Ethiopia was surrounded by Muslim areas and cut off from most of the rest of the Christian world. This caused the Ethiopians to develop their own distinctive form of Christianity.

33. 20 minutes

34. 15 minutes

35. 20 minutes

36. 50 minutes

37. Answers will vary, but may express the thought that the period allowed is too lengthy or too short, or that a different study method might be more productive.

38. 40 minutes

39. 2 hours 50 minutes

40. writing the first draft

41. four weeks

42. Answers will vary, but may express the thought that the period allowed is too lengthy or too short, or that a different research and writing method might be more productive.

Chapter 3 ■ The Ancient Americas

A. KEY TERMS

Complete each sentence by writing the letter of the correct term in the blank. You will not use all the terms.

a. quipu
b. causeway
c. maize
d. pueblo
e. aqueducts
f. artisan
g. terrace
h. hieroglyphics

1. _____ The most important crop of the Mayas was _____ , a type of corn.

2. _____ Aztecs approached their capital by boat or by _____ , a raised roadway.

3. _____ Drinking water reached the Aztec capital by _____ .

4. _____ A steplike ledge for growing crops is called a(n) _____ .

5. _____ An Anasazi village, or _____ , might be built on a mesa.

Match the definitions with the terms Write the correct letter in each blank. You will not use all the terms.

a. quipu
b. hieroglyphics
c. maize
d. pueblo
e. causeway
f. artisan
g. terrace
h. aqueduct

6. _____ a system of writing using signs and symbols

7. _____ a type of corn

8. _____ a roadway raised above water

9. _____ a skilled worker

10. _____ the village of the Anasazi people

B. KEY CONCEPTS

Write the letter of the correct answer in each blank.

11. _____ To honor the gods, the Mayas held great
      a. mound-building contests.   c. festivals.
      b. quipus.   d. sacrifices.

12. _____ The Mayas developed a system of writing using
      a. 365 characters.   c. the same letters we use.
      b. hieroglyphs.   d. stone pens.

13. _____ Who was at the bottom of Aztec society?
      a. artisans   c. farmers
      b. warriors   d. slaves

14. _____ One Incan ruler unified his empire by making everyone use
      a. Quechua.   c. conch shells.
      b. terraces.   d. a calendar.

15. _____ Besides communication, the main purpose of Incan roads was to
      a. keep workers busy.   c. use up tax money.
      b. remind later people of the Incas.   d. allow the army to travel quickly.

16. _____ The Incas created fortresses and cities out of closely fitted
      a. brick.   c. adobe.
      b. stone.   d. bronze.

17. _____ Where was the large city of Cahokia?
      a. what is now Illinois
      b. Mexico
      c. what is now the Southwest United States
      d. South America

18. _____ The Anasazi altered the environment by building
      a. roadways.   c. canals.
      b. terraces.   d. bridges.

19. _____ Because of the climate of the Southwest, the Pueblos held ceremonies asking spirits to
      a. bring sunny days.   c. build kivas.
      b. plant corn and beans.   d. send rain.

20. _____ Mayan civilization declined when they
      a. were conquered by the Aztecs.   c. invented the calendar.
      b. left their cities.   d. stopped sacrificing humans.

21. _____ The Aztecs gained a huge empire by
      a. warring against others.   c. taking empty land.
      b. making treaties.   d. trading peacefully.

22. ____ The Aztecs grew wealthy because they made conquered people
     a. pay tributes.   c. live in Tenochtitlán.
     b. worship their gods.   d. farm on water.

23. ____ One Incan ruler unified the empire by sending people into newly conquered lands
to
     a. take the population prisoner.   c. carry messages to his army.
     b. search out Aztec priests.   d. teach Incan customs.

24. ____ Incan officials kept records on
     a. Quechua.   c. stone tablets.
     b. quipus.   d. bronze plates.

25. ____ The Incas increased farmland by building
     a. roads and bridges.   c. huge cities on mountainsides.
     b. army supply stations.   d. canals and terraces.

26. ____ The serpent mound of Ohio served as a(n)
     a. city.   c. cemetery.
     b. temple.   d. aqueduct.

27. ____ The Anasazi and Pueblo sometimes built villages on
     a. mesas.   c. floating islands.
     b. kachinas.   d. artificial mounds.

28. ____ The Anasazi used canals to water crops because they
     a. needed to defend their homes. c. needed room for apartments.
     b. wanted to please the spirits.   d. had settled in a dry land.

C. CRITICAL THINKING

Answer the following questions in the space provided, on the back of this paper or on a separate
sheet of paper.

29. Making Comparisons: Compare and contrast the Aztecs and the Anasazi.

30. Identifying Central Issues: What challenges were created by the environment of the Incas?
How did they meet those challenges?

31. Expressing Problems Clearly: Why was it a challenge for the Aztecs to build a city in the middle of Lake Texcoco?

32. Drawing Conclusions: Why do you think the Mound Builders put jewelry, statues, and other works of art in the serpent mound?

D. SKILL: RECOGNIZING CAUSE AND EFFECT

Read the paragraphs below and answer the following questions. Write your answers on the lines provided.

Although Tenochtitlán was a peaceful place, the Aztecs themselves were a warlike people. In the 1400s, Aztec warriors began conquering the other people in the region. Soon, the Aztecs controlled a huge empire. One ruler, the emperor, ruled over all the Aztec lands.

The Aztecs forced the people they conquered to pay tributes, or taxes, in the form of food, gold, or slaves. They also took thousands of prisoners of war to serve as human sacrifices. The Aztecs believed that they had to sacrifice humans to the gods so that the sun would have enough strength to rise every day. Human blood was what gave the sun strength. If the sun did not rise, crops could not grow, and the people would starve. Priests made the offerings to the gods daily. In very bad times, members of noble Aztec families were sometimes sacrificed to please the sun god.

33. What might have caused the Aztecs to conquer the other people in the region? _____
    _____

34. What was the effect of the Aztecs conquering the other people in the region?_____
    _____

35. What is the reason that the Aztecs sacrificed prisoners? _____
    _____

36. What effect does the sun have on crops? _____
    _____

37. What was the reason that the Aztecs would sometimes sacrifice members of noble families?
    _____

Read the paragraphs below and answer the following questions. Write your answers on the lines provided.

To control the empire, the emperor and his officials had to know what was going on. To accomplish this, they needed a communication system—the runners. But these messengers needed roads to travel on. The Incas, therefore, built a large system of highways and bridges.

The roads served another purpose besides communication. In times of trouble, they allowed the army to travel quickly. As the soldiers traveled, they picked up supplies at stations along the way. Thus, the emperor could keep control of every part of the empire.

38. Why did the emperor and his officials have to know what was going on in the empire? _____

_____

39. Why did messengers reach the emperor quickly? _____

_____

40. What was one reason that Incan soldiers could move quickly across the land? _____

_____

41. What was another reason that the soldiers could move quickly? _____

_____

42. What caused the Incas to build such a good road system? _____

_____

ANSWER KEY

1. c	2. b	3. e	4. g	5. d
6. b	7. c	8. e	9. f	10. d
11. c	12. b	13. d	14. a	15. d
16. b	17. a	18. c	19. d	20. b
21. a	22. a	23. d	24. b	25. d
26. c	27. a	28. d		

29. Answers will vary, but might mention the contrast between the warlike Aztecs and the efforts the Anasazi made to defend themselves, and between the sacrifices of the Aztecs and the more peaceful ceremonies of the Anasazi, as well as the similarities between the crops they grew and between their efforts at agricultural engineering.

30. Answers will vary, but should mention that the mountainous terrain caused difficulties for communication and agriculture, and that the Incas met these challenges by extensive road building projects and by terracing slopes to create farmland.

31. Answers will vary, but might mention the problems of creating farmland to feed city dwellers and supplying fresh water.

32. Answers will vary, but might mention that the mounds may have helped preserve or protect the items which were precious to the Mound Builders.

33. They were warlike people.

34. The Aztecs controlled a huge empire.

35. They sacrificed them so that the sun would rise.

36. The sun causes crops to grow.

37. In very bad times, they thought that sacrificing prisoners was not enough to please the sun god.

38. to control it

39. The road system was excellent.

40. The roads and bridges allowed them to move quickly.

41. They could easily pick up supplies.

42. The emperor and his officials needed to know what was going on.

A. KEY TERMS

Match the definitions with the terms. Write the correct letter in each blank. You will not use all the terms.

    a. bushido
    b. caste system
    c. feudal system
    d. Hinduism
    e. merit system
    f. movable type
    g. shogun
    h. sultan
    i. samurai

1. _____ a system in which government officials are chosen based on how well they can do their job

2. _____ separate, reusable characters used for printing

3. _____ Japanese warriors who swear an oath to serve

4. _____ a system of government in which less powerful people give loyalty to more powerful ones

5. _____ a strict system of social classes among Hindus

Complete each sentence by writing the letter of the correct term in the blank. You will not use all the terms.

    a. bushido
    b. dynasty
    c. feudal system
    d. Hinduism
    e. merit system
    f. porcelain
    g. shogun
    h. sultan
    i. samurai

6. _____ A series of rulers from one family is a _____ .

7. _____ A strong and beautiful type of ceramic, called _____ , was a prized product of China.

8. _____ Japanese warriors followed a set of rules called _____ .

9. _____ The most powerful lord in Japan was the _____ , or great general.

10. _____ Muslim empires were ruled by a _____ .

B. KEY CONCEPTS

Write the letter of the correct answer in each blank.

11. _____ Which Chinese thinker taught that if a ruler was virtuous and set a good example then no one would commit crimes?
    a. Taizong
    b. Tokugawa Ieyasu
    c. Confucius
    d. Tamerlane

12. _____ What is one achievement of the Tang dynasty?
    a. the unification of the Chinese people into a great empire
    b. the granting of more power to landowners
    c. the building of the Taj Mahal and other great structures
    d. the isolation of China from the rest of the world

13. _____ Some important Chinese trade products were
    a. books, movable type, and grain.
    b. wood blocks, spices, and salt.
    c. silk, porcelain, and tea.
    d. jewels, spices, and cotton.

14. _____ Japanese warriors pledged their utmost loyalty to their
    a. emperor.
    b. lord.
    c. family.
    d. religion.

15. _____ From 1192 to 1868, Japan had a period of
    a. democratic rule.
    b. military rule.
    c. foreign rule.
    d. violent warfare.

16. _____ What is one reason that Japan has such a distinctive culture?
    a. The division of social classes affects all aspects of daily life.
    b. Japanese culture has combined with the culture of Mongol invaders.
    c. There has been little contact among the people of Japan.
    d. Japan was isolated from the rest of the world for 250 years.

17. _____ The belief in many gods who are all different aspects of one supreme being is a part of the
    a. Hindu religion.
    b. Muslim religion.
    c. feudal system.
    d. merit system.

18. _____ Akbar realized that the best way to make his empire peaceful was to
    a. forbid anyone to practice religion.
    b. grant Hindus more power than Muslims.
    c. grant Muslims more power than Hindus.
    d. be fair to people of different religions.

19. _____ What is one lasting result of the early Muslim invasions of India?
    a. India is still ruled by a Muslim king.
    b. India is a Muslim country.
    c. Religious differences still divide Hindus and Muslims.
    d. All Indians read and write in the same language.

20. _____ During China's golden age, the government improved because of
    a. the new merit system.   c. the invention of porcelain.
    b. rich officials.   d. a revolution.

21. _____ Which one of the following rulers practiced the teachings of Confucius?
    a. Tamerlane   c. Babur
    b. Shah Jahan   d. Taizong

22. _____ What is one reason that China had its golden ages during the Tang and Song dynasties?
    a. Its less powerful people gave loyalty to its more powerful people.
    b. Its strict system of social classes controlled all life.
    c. It developed many trade products and trade routes.
    d. Its officials came only from rich and powerful families.

23. _____ One positive affect of the caste system in India was that
    a. it introduced social equality. c. it stimulated the economy.
    b. it brought stability.   d. it led to democracy.

24. _____ Japanese estate owners became more independent when the Japanese emperor
    a. signed a treaty.   c. lost power.
    b. gave the estate owners more land. d. hired bands of samurai.

25. _____ From 1192 to 1868, Japan had an emperor but was actually ruled by
    a. generals.   c. landowners.
    b. congress.   d. priests.

26. _____ How did the shogun Ieyasu prevent Europeans from conquering Japan?
    a. He invaded China.
    b. He closed Japan to the outside world.
    c. He reestablished the emperor's power.
    d. He built great naval and trading fleets.

27. _____ Unlike earlier Muslim rulers, Akbar allowed the Hindus of India to
    a. end their caste system.   c. practice their religion freely.
    b. reclaim their gold and jewels. d. work as teachers and craftspeople.

28. _____ What is one reason that the Mughal empire declined?
    a. The rulers forbade anyone to practice religion.
    b. Building projects and wars drained the empire of money.
    c. People revolted against the policies of Akbar.
    d. The emperors isolated India from the rest of the world.

CHAPTER 4

C. CRITICAL THINKING

Answer the following questions in the space provided, on the back of this paper or on a separate sheet of paper.

29. Identifying Central Issues: More than 100 years after Akbar's death, the Mughal empire began to fall apart. What were two of the reasons that caused this to happen?

30. Drawing Conclusions: Both Taizong of China and Akbar of India were considered to be great rulers. What made these two men so great?

31. Making Comparisons: Compare the achievements of China's Tang and Song rulers to those of the Mughal ruler Akbar.

32. Recognizing Cause and Effect: What caused the rise of the feudal system in Japan? In your answer, explain what a feudal system is.

D. SKILL: ASSESSING YOUR UNDERSTANDING

Study the following reading assignment. Then assess your understanding of the assignment by answering the questions below on the lines provided.

Li Bo was a famous Chinese writer who served for a time as a court poet to an emperor in the Tang dynasty. Li Bo eventually left the court to roam China's mountains. His poetry reflects his love of these grand mountains, as well as his spiritual journeys and his many friendships. Today, Li Bo is still considered one of China's most brilliant poets.

33. Why was Li Bo famous? _____

_____

34. What clue in this passage tells you when Li Bo wrote? _____

_____

35. What are some of the subjects of Li Bo's poems? _____

_____

36. How could you use the information from this assignment in the future?_____

_____

37. If you are not sure about any of the answers you've written above, what should you do? ____

_____

Study the following reading assignment. Then assess your understanding of the assignment by answering the questions below on the lines provided.

Du Fu was a great Chinese poet who wrote his poems during the Tang dynasty. One of Du Fu's ancestors was a famous Confucian scholar, and his father worked as a scholar-official. However, Du Fu himself failed his government examinations. After spending some time at the emperor's court, and later in a small hut of his own, Du Fu traveled around China. He wrote a large number of poems, and 1,457 of them survived to this day. Many critics consider him China's greatest poet.

38. Who was Du Fu?_____

_____

39. Why wasn't Du Fu a government official like his father? _____

_____

40. What are the main ideas in this passage?_____

_____

41. How could you use the information from this assignment in the future?_____

_____

42. If you are not sure about any of the answers you've written above, what should you do? ____

_____

CHAPTER 4

ANSWER KEY

1. e	2. f	3. i	4. c	5. b
6. b	7. f	8. a	9. g	10. h
11. c	12. a	13. c	14. b	15. b
16. d	17. a	18. d	19. c	20. a
21. d	22. c	23. b	24. c	25. a
26. b	27. c	28. b		

29. Answers may vary. Students should give two of the following three reasons: (1) The empire fell apart because rulers began to spend too much money on expensive building projects. For example, Shah Jahan spent 22 years building the Taj Mahal. (2) Rulers spent too much money on expensive wars. (3) One ruler tried to force Hindus to covert to Islam, which caused the Hindus to rebel. Fighting the rebels took even more money.

30. Answers may vary. Possible answer: Taizong was a great military leader. He also tried to bring peace and stability to China. Akbar of India was also a talented soldier, and he believed in bringing peace to India. He was fair to people of all religions, ended unfair taxes on non-Muslims, and listened to differing viewpoints.

31. Answers may vary. A possible answer: Although the Tang and Song rulers followed the teachings of Confucius while Akbar practiced the Muslim religion, these leaders both achieved good things for their countries. The Chinese rulers and the Indian ruler gave government jobs to the people who were the most qualified for them. This made their governments stronger. They also each encouraged the arts.

32. Answers may vary. A possible answer: A feudal system is a system of government in which less powerful people give loyalty to more powerful people. In Japan, the feudal system arose when the emperor lost power and the daimyo gained independence. The daimyo hired samurai to protect them and their peasants from other daimyo. The samurai pledged loyalty to the daimyo.

33. He was famous for his writing.

34. He was a court poet during the Tang dynasty.

35. his love of the mountains, his friendships, and his spiritual journeys

36. If I wrote a report on the Tang dynasty, I could use Li Bo as an example of one of the great writers of that period.

37. Review the assignment with the questions in mind.

38. Du Fu was a poet during the Tang dynasty.

39. He failed his government examinations.

40. Du Fu was a Tang dynasty poet who couldn't get a government job. Many critics think he is China's greatest poet.

41. If I wrote a report on the Tang dynasty, I could use Du Fu as an example of the great writers of that period.

42. Review the assignment with the questions in mind.

Chapter 5 ■ *Europe in the Middle Ages*

A. KEY TERMS

Complete each sentence by writing the letter of the correct term in the blank. You will not use all the terms.

          a. apprentice
          b. chivalry
          c. Crusades
          d. manor
          e. Middle Ages
          f. nation
          g. Parliament
          h. troubadour
          i. vassal

1. _____ The period between ancient times and modern times is called the _____ .

2. _____ A lord ruled over a(n) _____ , which was a large estate that often included a village and farmlands.

3. _____ A boy who worked as a(n) _____ didn't get paid but did learn a craft.

4. _____ The military expeditions that the Church carried out against the Turks are called the _____ .

5. _____ The council that advised the English king in government matters was called _____ .

Match the definitions with the terms Write the correct letter in each blank. You will not use all the terms.

          a. apprentice
          b. clergy
          c. Crusades
          d. the Magna Carta
          e. medieval
          f. nation
          g. Parliament
          h. serf
          i. self-sufficient

6. _____ from the Middle Ages

7. _____ able to supply one's own needs

8. _____ people who perform the services of the Church

9. _____ military expeditions that the Church carried out against the Turks

10. _____ a community that shares a government

CHAPTER 5

B. KEY CONCEPTS

Write the letter of the correct answer in each blank.

11. _____ A lord's main duty toward the people who pledged loyalty to him was to
    a. educate them.
    c. bring them to God.
    b. take care of their livestock and lands.
    d. protect them and their lands.

12. _____ Most peasants needed a lord's permission to
    a. have children.
    c. farm the lord's fields.
    b. marry or leave the manor.
    d. supply their own needs.

13. _____ What is one reason that the Church was so powerful during medieval times?
    a. It did not allow governments to adopt a national religion.
    b. It made laws and set up courts to uphold them.
    c. It encouraged warfare among feudal lords.
    d. It encouraged serfs to leave the manor.

14. _____ What happened to many of the peasants who left the manor to work in towns?
    a. They made more money than they had on the manor.
    b. They made less money than they had on the manor.
    c. They gained enough property to start their own manors.
    d. They fought against the lords.

15. _____ How was life in the towns different from life on the manor?
    a. In the towns, people were self-sufficient.
    b. In the towns, the Church had no authority.
    c. In the towns, people exchanged goods and services for money.
    d. In the towns, people no longer belonged to guilds.

16. _____ Why is the Holy Land important?
    a. It is the center of Europe.
    b. The Catholic Church is located there.
    c. It is sacred to all of the world's great religions.
    d. It is sacred to three of the world's great religions.

17. _____ The first Christians to fight the Muslims for the Holy Land were
    a. lords and their knights.
    b. common people led by Peter the Hermit.
    c. kings led by Peter the Hermit.
    d. members of the clergy.

18. _____ Kings and popes often disagreed over who should pick
    a. lords.
    c. Church officials called bishops.
    b. a king's vassals.
    d. city mayors.

19. _____ As feudalism weakened, one way kings gained power was by supporting
    a. the Crusades.
    c. the lords in their kingdoms.
    b. new towns.
    d. the Roman Catholic Church.

20. ____ Under the system of feudalism, each person was loyal to those who
   a. had more land and wealth.   c. controlled the whole kingdom.
   b. worked on their lands.   d. had been knighted by a lord.

21. ____ In feudal sociaty, noblewomen
   a. were treated like peasants.
   b. were equal to men.
   c. played important roles in the household.
   d. could become knights.

22. ____ During the Middle Ages, the largest and most powerful religion in Western Europe was the
   a. Roman Catholic Church.   c. Protestant Church.
   b. Eastern Orthodox Church.   d. Church of England.

23. ____ Peasants were often able to improve their standard of living by
   a. staying on the manor for generations.   c. farming the lord's fields.
   b. fighting in the Crusades.   d. moving to towns.

24. ____ What was one problem medieval cities faced?
   a. a lack of guilds
   b. no clergy
   c. invaders from other cities
   d. crowded and unhealthy conditions, which led to disease

25. ____ Guilds were important to medieval society because
   a. they improved sanitation in cities.
   b. they were open even to unskilled workers.
   c. they employed most serfs.
   d. they set prices and standards of equality.

26. ____ Christians fought the Muslim Turks in order to
   a. force them out of Italy.
   b. spread the feudal system of government.
   c. reopen the Holy Land to Christian pilgrims.
   d. convert the Muslims to Christianity.

27. ____ One thing that helped trade grow during the Middle Ages was
   a. the Crusades.
   b. the feudal system.
   c. the growth of the peasant class.
   d. the opening of routes between France and England.

28. ____ The Hundred Years' War was fought between
   a. Christians and Muslims.   c. France and Spain.
   b. kings and clergy.   d. France and England.

CHAPTER 5

C. CRITICAL THINKING

Answer the following questions in the space provided, on the back of this paper or on a separate sheet of paper.

29. Identifying Central Issues: Why was the Roman Catholic Church so powerful during the Middle Ages?

30. Identifying Cause and Effect: What were two causes of the Crusades? In your answer, tell what the Crusades were.

31. Making Comparisons: How was life in a town during the Middle Ages different from life on the manor?

32. Recognizing Cause and Effect: What were two effects of the Crusades? In your answer, tell what the Crusades were.

D. SKILL: USING ROUTE MAPS

Use the route map below to answer the following questions. Write your answers on the lines provided.

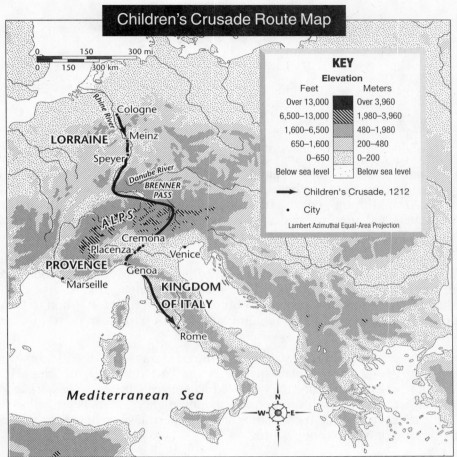

Children's Crusade Route Map

KEY

Elevation

Feet	Meters
Over 13,000	Over 3,960
6,500–13,000	1,980–3,960
1,600–6,500	480–1,980
650–1,600	200–480
0–650	0–200
Below sea level	Below sea level

→ Children's Crusade, 1212

• City

Lambert Azimuthal Equal-Area Projection

33. What title would you give this map? _____

34. How is the route shown? _____

35. Where did the Children's Crusade start? Where did it end? _____

36. About how far was the journey from start to finish? _____

37. What elevation was the highest point of the journey? _____

38. Where did the Children's Crusade take place? _____

39. How is the route shown? _____

40. Where did the journey start? Where did it finish? _____

41. What landform lay along the route? _____

42. About how far did the crusaders travel? _____

ANSWER KEY

1. e	2. d	3. a	4. c	5. g
6. e	7. i	8. b	9. c	10. f
11. d	12. b	13. b	14. a	15. c
16. d	17. b	18. c	19. b	20. a
21. c	22. a	23. d	24. d	25. d
26. c	27. a	28. d		

29. Answers may vary. A possible answer: One reason that the Church was so powerful was that life for many people was short and hard. The Church comforted people with the belief that they would be rewarded in heaven after their death. Also, the Church made laws and enforced their laws through courts. If lords or kings disobeyed the Church, they could be excommunicated and then no one would want to associate with them. In addition, the Church helped keep the peace among the many feudal lords.

30. Answers may vary. A possible answer: The Crusades were the military expeditions that the Church carried out against the Turks who controlled the Holy Land. When Muslim Turks took over the Holy Land, Christian pilgrims were no longer able to visit the area safely. Pope Urban II called for the Crusades in order to reopen the Holy Land to these pilgrims. The Crusades were also fought to regain control of important trade routes that had been taken over by Muslims.

31. Answers may vary. A possible answer: One difference was that since manors were often far from towns or villages, the people who lived there had to be self-sufficient. In the towns, people did not make everything they needed to survive. Instead, they traded money for goods and services. Another difference was that on manors, serfs belonged to the land and were not free to leave or to marry without the lord's permission. In the towns, people didn't belong to the land or have to obey a lord.

32. Answers may vary. A possible answer: The Crusades were the military expeditions that the Church carried out against the Turks who controlled the Holy Land. One effect of the Crusades was to increase trade during the later Middle Ages. This happened because when ships carried armies and supplies to the Holy Land, they came back with goods that Europeans began to want. Another effect of the Crusades was to weaken the nobles and strengthen the kings. Nobles sold land to raise money for the Crusades, and kings took over the land of nobles who died in the Crusades, so kings grew more powerful.

33. Children's Crusade

34. with a line and arrows showing direction of the route

35. Cologne

36. about 900 miles

37. The Brenner Pass in the Alps

38. in Europe, between Cologne and Rome

39. A line shows the route. Arrows show the directions.

40. Cologne; Rome

41. They traveled through the Alps.

42. about 900 miles

Chapter 6 ▪ A New Age in Europe

A. KEY TERMS

Match the definitions with the terms. Write the correct letter in each blank. You will not use all the terms.

a. absolute monarch
b. astrolabe
c. caravel
d. conquistador
e. divine right
f. encomienda
g. perspective
h. indulgence
i. Reformation

1. _____ the change of religious customs caused by Martin Luther

2. _____ an official pardon given by the pope

3. _____ an instrument used to measure latitude

4. _____ the belief that a king's right to rule comes directly from God

5. _____ Spanish conqueror

Complete each sentence by writing the letter of the correct term in the blank. You will not use all the terms.

a. absolute monarchy
b. circumnavigate
c. democracy
d. encomienda
e. indulgence
f. navigator
g. perspective
h. Protestant
i. Reformation

6. _____ People paid money to receive a(n) _____ , or an official pardon given by the pope.

7. _____ In the 1400s, if you were an expert Portuguese sailor, or _____ , you may have attended Prince Henry's school.

8. _____ The Spanish king backed the first people to _____ , or sail around, the world.

9. _____ The people elect representatives to govern them in a(n) _____ .

10. _____ Cortés introduced a new economic system, the _____ , to Mexico.

B. KEY CONCEPTS

Write the letter of the correct answer in each blank.

11. _____ During the Middle Ages, why was life in northern Italy different than life in the rest of Europe?
    a. The lives of Italians were threatened by Muslim invaders.
    b. Italian merchants controlled European trade with Asia.
    c. The lives of Italians were controlled by popes and kings.
    d. Italians were more threatened by war and disease.

12. _____ Luther believed that the key to getting into heaven was
    a. belief in God.
    b. obedience to the Church.
    c. fighting in the Crusades.
    d. giving money to the Church.

13. _____ What was one reason that Portugal led Europe's exploration of the world?
    a. Portugal controlled European trade with Asia.
    b. Portugal supported Magellan's trip around the world.
    c. Prince Henry was the first person to explore Cape Bojador.
    d. Prince Henry opened a school for mapmakers, shipbuilders, and navigators.

14. _____ Christopher Columbus believed that he could reach India by
    a. sailing around Africa.
    b. sailing east.
    c. sailing west.
    d. sailing through the Mediterranean.

15. _____ The first European countries to carve empires in the Americas were
    a. Portugal and Spain.
    b. England and France.
    c. France and Spain.
    d. Italy and England.

16. _____ As an absolute monarch, King Louis XIV shared power with
    a. a council.
    b. no one.
    c. his nobles.
    d. the citizens of France.

17. _____ Which European country had a monarch who had to share power with Parliament?
    a. England
    b. France
    c. Spain
    d. Russia

18. _____ In order for Spain to take over Mexico, Cortés had to conquer the
    a. French navy.
    b. English settlers.
    c. Aztec empire.
    d. Incan empire.

19. _____ Why didn't most people in Europe buy African slaves?
    a. It was against their religion.
    b. They had enough cheap labor.
    c. They had Native American slaves.
    d. European explorers didn't go to Africa.

20. ____ Compared to people in the rest of Europe, the lives of people in northern Italy were not as closely controlled by
   a. the middle class.
   b. trade with Asia.
   c. popes and kings.
   d. the ideas of Greece and Rome.

21. ____ Painters like Michelangelo used perspective, light, and shadow to create paintings that looked
   a. flat.
   b. real.
   c. magical.
   d. the same.

22. ____ The goal of the Reformation was to
   a. improve religious customs.
   b. further the ideas of the Renaissance.
   c. blend Protestantism and Roman Catholicism.
   d. emphasize music and art.

23. ____ Why were European countries looking for a new route to Asia?
   a. They were tired of buying Asian goods from Italian merchants.
   b. They wanted to take back the Holy Land.
   c. They didn't trust Muslim merchants.
   d. They were tired of buying Asian goods from Spanish merchants.

24. ____ Queen Isabella and King Ferdinand of Spain supported Columbus's voyage because they thought
   a. Native Americans should learn about Christianity.
   b. the world was flat.
   c. territories could be gained in the New World.
   d. great riches could be gained from a new route to Asia.

25. ____ In order for the monarchy in France to gain absolute power, it first had to
   a. give the people more rights.
   b. build a strong group of nobles.
   c. convince the people to vote for divine right.
   d. destroy the power of the nobles.

26. ____ Which ruler lived in incredible luxury at Versailles?
   a. Louis XIV
   b. King Ferdinand
   c. Charles I
   d. Moctezuma

27. ____ Why were enslaved Africans brought to the Americas?
   a. Because the Portuguese needed new settlers.
   b. To work on plantations and in mines.
   c. To become American citizens.
   d. Because conditions in Africa were bad.

28. ____ The Aztecs finally surrendered to Cortés after
   a. Quetzalcoatl returned.
   b. Pizarro's army joined the fight.
   c. Cortés promised them their rights.
   d. a fierce and bloody war.

C. CRITICAL THINKING

Answer the following questions in the space provided, on the back of this paper or on a separate sheet of paper.

29. Drawing Conclusions: Why was northern Italy a natural birthplace for the Renaissance? In your answer, explain what the Renaissance was.

30. Expressing Problems Clearly: What problems did Africa face as a result of trade with Europe?

31. Identifying Central Issues: Why did Martin Luther criticize the Roman Catholic Church?

32. Expressing Problems Clearly: How did Louis XIV's absolute rule eventually cause problems for France?

D. SKILL: DISTINGUISHING FACT FROM OPINION

Read the passage below. Then answer the following questions on the lines provided.

Louis XIV began his rule in 1643. He was an absolute monarch, which meant that he could rule France however he wanted to. He built Versailles, which is the world's most beautiful building. All French people loved having such a glamorous and powerful king. They gladly paid high taxes because they would rather see the king living well than live well themselves.

33. What is one fact contained in the passage? _____

_____

34. How can you tell that it is a fact? _____

_____

35. What is one opinion contained in the passage? _____

_____

36. How can you tell that it is an opinion? _____

_____

37. Which sentence from the passage contains both a fact and an opinion? _____

_____

Read the passage below. Then answer the following questions on the lines provided.

In 1519, Cortés arrived in Mexico. Eventually, he would show the native people of Mexico a new religion. Before this could happen, however, Cortés had to bravely battle the Aztec empire. He defeated them in 1521 and ushered in a better age.

38. What is one fact contained in the passage? _____

_____

39. How can you tell that it is a fact? _____

_____

40. What is one opinion contained in the passage? _____

_____

41. How can you tell that it is an opinion? _____

_____

42. Which sentence from the passage contains both a fact and an opinion? _____

_____

CHAPTER 6

ANSWER KEY

1. i	2. h	3. b	4. e	5. d
6. e	7. f	8. b	9. c	10. d
11. b	12. a	13. d	14. c	15. a
16. b	17. a	18. c	19. b	20. c
21. b	22. a	23. a	24. d	25. d
26. a	27. b	28. d		

29. Answers may vary. A possible answer: The Renaissance was a period after the Middle Ages when a love of learning was reborn. It made sense that the Renaissance started in northern Italy, because life was easier here than it was in the rest of Europe. There was less warfare and disease. People's lives weren't as controlled by popes and kings. Also, Italian merchants were growing rich from their trade with Asia. These conditions gave some Italians enough time to think, read, and create and enjoy art. Wealthy people bought art to celebrate their families, their cities, and their religion. Artists competed for fame and money.

30. Answers may vary. A possible answer: When the Portuguese first arrived on the coast of Africa, they wanted to trade for products like gold, ivory, and pepper. However, when Spanish and Portuguese settlers in the Americas needed more workers, the Europeans began importing slaves from Africa. This was a disaster for Africa. Although some Africans grew rich from the slave trade, the region suffered from losing its healthiest, most capable workers. In addition, the people sold as slaves suffered brutality and sometimes death on the journey to the Americas.

31. Answers may vary. A possible answer: Luther criticized the Roman Catholic Church because he didn't think that people needed bishops and popes to tell them what God wanted them to do. He also thought that the Church did not have the power to sell indulgences to people who had sinned.

32. Answers may vary. A possible answer: Louis lived in a luxurious palace called Versailles. He gave large parties for the nobles and didn't make them pay taxes. Keeping the nobles happy in this way was very expensive, and only the poorest people in France were paying the taxes to support this lifestyle. Louis also waged war to gain new territories. These wars added to France's debts. By the time Louis died, France had huge debts.

33. Louis XIV began his rule in 1643.

34. It can be proved true.

35. All French people loved having such a glamorous and powerful king.

36. You cannot prove how all the people in France felt.

37. He built Versailles, which is the world's most beautiful building.

38. In 1519, Cortés arrived in Mexico.

39. It can be proved true.

40. Cortés had to bravely battle the Aztec empire.

41. You cannot prove that Cortés was brave.

42. He defeated them in 1521, and ushered in a better age.

A. KEY TERMS

Complete each sentence by writing the letter of the correct term in the blank. You will not use all the terms.

        a. civil war
        b. Enlightenment
        c. imperialism
        d. Industrial Revolution
        e. natural laws
        f. Reign of Terror
        g. revolution
        h. scientific method
        i. Napoleonic Code

1. _____ A battle for power between two groups within one country is called a(n) _____ .

2. _____ People began to have great faith in the power of reason during the _____ .

3. _____ Forces that rule the behavior of the universe are called _____ .

4. _____ The period of time during which the production of goods shifted from simple tools to complex machines is called the _____ .

5. _____ When European countries set up empires of colonies in Africa and Asia, they were practicing _____ .

Match the definitions with the terms. Write the correct letter in each blank. You will not use all the terms.

        a. bill of rights
        b. colony
        c. constitutional monarchy
        d. imperialism
        e. labor union
        f. nationalism
        g. natural law
        h. revolution
        i. textile

6. _____ a sudden change in the way people think or in the way they are ruled

7. _____ a summary of all the rights held by a people under their government

8. _____ a territory ruled by another nation

9. _____ an organization that helps workers improve their pay and working conditions

10. _____ a desire for independence and pride in one's country

CHAPTER 7

B. KEY CONCEPTS

Write the letter of the correct answer in each blank.

11. _____ How did Queen Elizabeth I strengthen England?
   a. She took power away from the nobles and gave it to the people.
   b. She unified the country by bringing back the Catholic religion.
   c. She stopped war with France and fought a civil war.
   d. She prevented war at home and went to war with Spain.

12. _____ In return for offering the British throne to William and Mary, Parliament demanded that all laws had to be approved by
   a. Parliament.   c. the Catholic Church.
   b. King James.   d. the Protestant Church.

13. _____ After the Scientific Revolution, scientists no longer made their ideas about science fit
   a. the results of their experiments.   c. their observations in nature.
   b. their religious beliefs.   d. their political beliefs.

14. _____ John Locke said that government was based on an agreement between rulers and
   a. the people.   c. the Church.
   b. God.   d. science.

15. _____ What was one positive result of the Industrial Revolution?
   a. People were able to stay home with their children.
   b. Women only had to work in the summer and fall.
   c. More people were able to have comfortable lives.
   d. Poor farmers could afford to buy large machinery.

16. _____ What was one negative result of the Industrial Revolution?
   a. Parents sometimes had to put their children to work in factories.
   b. Fewer people could afford to buy textiles.
   c. Many merchants went out of business.
   d. The size of the middle class decreased.

17. _____ After Louis XVI was executed, Maximilien Robespierre led the Committee of Public Safety in carrying out what became known as the
   a. Scientific Revolution.   c. Reign of Terror.
   b. Industrial Revolution.   d. Hundred Years' War.

18. _____ Under Napoleon, the laws of France became
   a. different for the rich and the poor.
   b. the same as those of the Catholic Church.
   c. more complicated.
   d. clearer and easier to understand.

19. ____ The major countries of Europe set up colonies in Africa and Asia in order to
   a. spread the ideas of the Enlightenment.
   b. get raw materials and sell goods.
   c. spread the ideas of the Reformation.
   d. prevent the loss of monarchs' power.

20. ____ Because Queen Elizabeth I prevented war at home and went to war with Spain, she
   a. strengthened England.   c. weakened the English navy.
   b. lost the support of the people.   d. gained absolute power.

21. ____ Britain became a constitutional monarchy when William and Mary agreed to accept
   a. the laws of the Catholic Church.
   b. the laws of the Protestant Church.
   c. a written summary of the rights of the people.
   d. the Declaration of Independence.

22. ____ During the Renaissance, scientists began to draw conclusions about the universe based on
   a. experiments that they could not control.
   b. ideas that they read in books.
   c. what they had seen.
   d. their faith in God.

23. ____ John Locke said that if a ruler takes away people's rights, then people have a right to
   a. move to another country.   c. appeal to God.
   b. own property.   d. change the government.

24. ____ Among the group of people who agreed with John Locke's ideas were
   a. the rulers of Germany.   c. the Spanish imperialists.
   b. the colonists in North America.   d. the clergy.

25. ____ What was one reason that the Industrial Revolution started in England?
   a. Wealthy business people had money to invest in new factories.
   b. The constitutional monarchy forced people to work.
   c. Small farmers demanded new jobs.
   d. England wanted to compete with Spain's industry.

26. ____ Factory workers eventually improved their working conditions by
   a. revolting against the Industrial Revolution.
   b. joining labor unions that fought for workers' rights.
   c. rioting at the king's palace.
   d. executing those who did not agree with them.

27. ____ One important outcome of England's Glorious Revolution was
   a. social equality.
   b. the bill of rights.
   c. that Catholicism became the national religion.
   d. the power of Parliament was weakened.

28. _____ Why did the countries of Europe set up colonies in Africa and Asia?
   a. to get raw materials and sell goods
   b. to spread the ideas of the Enlightenment
   c. to spread the ideas of John Locke
   d. to prevent the loss of Parliament's power

C. CRITICAL THINKING

Answer the following questions in the space provided, on the back of this paper or on a separate sheet of paper.

29. Identifying Cause and Effect: What were two causes of the English civil war?

30. Making Comparisons: How was life before the Industrial Revolution different from life after it?

31. Distinguishing Fact From Opinion: Give two facts and two opinions about European imperialism.

32. Drawing Conclusions: How do you think that the ideas of John Locke affected the history of the United States? In your answer, explain John Locke's ideas.

D. SKILL: INTERPRETING LINE GRAPHS

Use the line graph below to answer the following questions. Write your answers on the lines provided.

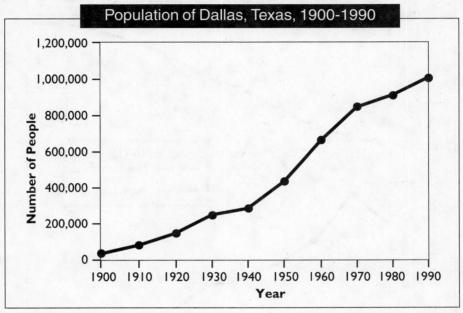

33. What information does this graph provide? _____
_____

34. What does the vertical axis of this graph show? _____
_____

35. What does the horizontal axis of this graph show? _____
_____

36. What general change is shown by the line? _____
_____

37. Did the number of people increase more between 1940 and 1950 or between 1970 and 1980? _____
_____

CHAPTER 7

Use the line graph below to answer the following questions. Write your answers on the lines provided.

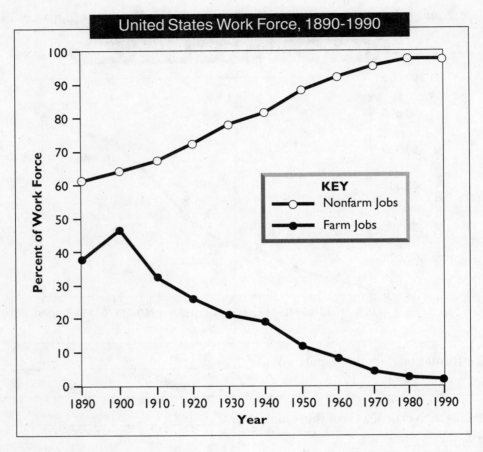

38. What information does this graph provide? _____

_____

39. What does the horizontal axis of this graph show? _____

_____

40. What does the vertical axis of this graph show? _____

_____

41. What general change is shown by the line? _____

_____

42. During what ten-year period did the percentage of workers in farm jobs increase?_____

_____

ANSWER KEY

1. a	2. b	3. e	4. d	5. c
6. h	7. a	8. b	9. e	10. f
11. d	12. a	13. b	14. a	15. c
16. a	17. c	18. d	19. b	20. a
21. c	22. c	23. d	24. b	25. a
26. b	27. b	28. a		

29. Answers may vary. A possible answer: One cause of the English civil war was that King James believed in absolute monarchy and governed without Parliament for long periods of time. His son, Charles I, also governed without Parliament. Parliament didn't like this, and finally passed laws to limit Charles's power. Another cause of the civil war was that Charles tried to arrest Parliament's leaders after those laws were passed.

30. Answers may vary. A possible answer: Before the Industrial Revolution, most people worked in or near their homes at their own pace. This meant that workers could be near their families, but it took a long time to make products such as textiles. Few people could afford more than one change of clothes. After the Industrial Revolution, people who wanted to work had to leave their homes and go to factories. Often, families had to move to cities where the factories were located. Goods were made more quickly, and businesses needed merchants to sell these goods. Because of these business opportunities, more people moved into the middle class.

31. Answers may vary. A possible answer: Fact: By 1914, the British empire covered about one fifth of the Earth's land surface. Fact: France, Germany, Italy, the Netherlands, Portugal, and Belgium were all imperialists. Opinion: British imperialism improved the cultures of people around the world. Opinion: People who didn't agree with imperialism were foolish.

32. Answers may vary. A possible answer: Locke said that government was based on an agreement between rulers and the people. He thought that if a ruler broke that agreement by taking away people's rights, then the people had a right to change the government. The American colonists thought that the British government was taking away their rights when that government taxed them without representation. Therefore, they thought that they had a right to govern themselves, and they fought for that right.

33. population size of Dallas, Texas between 1900–1990

34. number of people

35. years

36. Population grew between 1900–1990.

37. 1940 and 1950

38. the percent of the workforce in farm and nonfarm jobs

39. years in 10-year intervals

40. Percentage of workforce in 10 percent intervals

41. Farm jobs decreased and nonfarm jobs increased.

42. 1890–1900

CHAPTER 7

A. KEY TERMS

Complete each sentence by writing the letter of the correct term in the blank. You will not use all the terms.

        a. racism
        b. reunification
        c. genocide
        d. serf
        e. interdependent
        f. armistice

1. _____ A peasant worker who is considered the property of a wealthy noble is known as a(n) _____ .

2. _____ World War I ended with a(n) _____ , or cease-fire.

3. _____ Some African countries struggled with _____ , or the prejudiced belief that one race is better than another.

4. _____ Germany has had problems since _____ , or the rejoining of its parts.

5. _____ The nations of the world are _____ , or dependent on one another.

Match the definitions with the terms. Write the correct letter in each blank. You will not use all the terms.

        a. alliance
        b. czar
        c. reunification
        d. racism
        e. armistice
        f. civil disobedience

6. _____ the title of a Russian emperor

7. _____ a cease-fire

8. _____ the act of breaking a law on purpose in order to protest it

9. _____ the prejudiced belief that one race is better than another

10. _____ the rejoining of two parts, or countries

CHAPTER 8

B. KEY CONCEPTS

Write the letter of the correct answer in each blank.

11. _____ An event that helped to turn Russians against the czar was
       a. the freeing of the serfs.   c. World War II.
       b. World War I.   d. the birth of Alexis.

12. _____ The spark that brought the European alliances to war was
       a. a murder.   c. a revolution.
       b. an armistice.   d. an atomic bomb.

13. _____ World War I left Germans feeling
       a. content with the cease-fire.   c. good about their economy.
       b. unfairly punished.   d. eager to make friends.

14. _____ Ghana is an example of a nation that gained its independence through
       a. Nazi interference.   c. promises to its rulers.
       b. challenges to the United States.   d. peaceful methods.

15. _____ One of the problems faced by many newly independent nations was
       a. nationalism.
       b. radiation from the atomic bomb.
       c. pollution from highly developed industries.
       d. violence between ethnic groups.

16. _____ The main difference between a developing nation and a developed nation is
       a. civil disobedience.   c. industry.
       b. religion.   d. strikes.

17. _____ During the Cold War, the two superpowers were the United States and
       a. Great Britain.   c. North Vietnam.
       b. West Germany.   d. the Soviet Union.

18. _____ When the Communists lost power in Eastern Europe and the Soviet Union, the Cold War
       a. became a "hot" war.   c. came to an end.
       b. became an arms race.   d. began all over again.

19. _____ The problem of pollution has been growing since
       a. the beginning of the Industrial Revolution.
       b. the beginning of the Cold War.
       c. the end of the Cold War.
       d. North Vietnam defeated South Vietnam.

20. _____ Many Russians under the czar were dissatisfied with their government because they were
       a. nobles.   c. middle class.
       b. disorganized.   d. poor.

21. _____ World War I was caused in part by
    a. alliances.
    b. an armistice.
    c. reunification.
    d. the United States.

22. _____ World War II was caused in part by
    a. England's invasion of France.
    b. Poland's invasion of Serbia.
    c. the atomic bomb.
    d. Germany's invasion of Poland.

23. _____ Gandhi won independence for India through
    a. violent revolt.
    b. civil disobedience.
    c. racist slogans.
    d. communism.

24. _____ India and Pakistan split apart because the two regions had different
    a. economies.
    b. industries.
    c. religions.
    d. types of government.

25. _____ Most of the world's poorer nations are
    a. racist countries.
    b. developed countries.
    c. former rulers of colonies.
    d. former colonies.

26. _____ The Cold War was a struggle between
    a. communist and capitalist countries.
    b. ethnic groups.
    c. the North and the South.
    d. colonies and their rulers.

27. _____ The Cold War ended when
    a. China lost the arms race.
    b. the Holocaust was over.
    c. North Vietnam won.
    d. European communism collapsed.

28. _____ The biggest obstacle to protecting the environment is
    a. the need for economic growth.
    b. world interdependence.
    c. endangered animals.
    d. the domino theory.

CHAPTER 8

C. CRITICAL THINKING

Answer the following questions in the space provided, on the back of this paper or on a separate sheet of paper.

29. **Distinguishing Fact From Opinion:** Explain whether the following statement is a fact or an opinion: "Capitalism is a better system of government than communism." Give reasons for your answer.

30. **Expressing Problems Clearly:** Do you think that the nations of the world could end pollution? Why or why not?

31. **Identifying Central Issues:** It is sometimes said that World War II was just a continuation of World War I. Give reasons to support this statement.

32. **Recognizing Cause and Effect:** How did World War II help bring an end to colonialism?

CHAPTER 8

D. SKILL: EXPRESSING PROBLEMS CLEARLY

Read the following passage and answer the following questions. Write your answers on the lines provided.

Many positive changes have occurred in the twentieth century. The end of the system of apartheid in South Africa, international cooperation in space exploration, and the civil rights movement in the United States are just a few achievements. However, many of the changes made during the last century have caused problems. Around the world, the movement of large numbers of people from the country to urban areas has resulted in cities becoming overcrowded. It is hard for many people to find education, health care, and other services. Some people cannot find places to live. An increase in the population has put a strain on worldwide natural resources. Some experts predict that humans will run out of resources such as fuels, good soil for growing food, and water. Burning fossil fuels and using water for growing populations and new industries have sometimes caused population problems. The modern world faces many challenges.

33. How can the movement of large numbers of people to urban areas cause problems? _____

_____

34. What problems might be caused by an increase in population?_____

_____

35. What could be one cause of pollution? _____

_____

36. Are there any changes mentioned in this passage that are not problems? _____

_____

37. How would you express one of the problems described in this passage clearly?_____

_____

CHAPTER 8

Read the passage below and answer the following questions. Write your answers on the lines provided.

For centuries, people have used devices such as dams, flood basins, and canals to control natural water sources. Recently, people have questioned whether or not they should build dams in particular areas. Although farmers living downstream from a dam might have water for irrigation, they would lose the silt deposits left by a moving river. Rivers might no longer support living organisms, including fish. People along the river would lose a source of food and fertilizer. There is some evidence that building dams contributes to erosion in some areas. These are a few of the reasons why many people are thinking carefully before they build dams.

38. Describe the subject of this passage. _____

_____

39. What is one problem that can result from building a dam? _____

_____

40. How could building a dam on a river affect the food supply of people living along the river?

_____

41. What is one benefit of dams? _____

_____

42. What problems can dams cause to the quality of farmland? _____

_____

ANSWER KEY

1. d	2. f	3. a	4. b	5. e
6. b	7. e	8. f	9. d	10. c
11. b	12. a	13. b	14. d	15. d
16. c	17. d	18. c	19. a	20. d
21. a	22. d	23. b	24. c	25. d
26. a	27. d	28. a		

29. The statement is an opinion. The reasoning given may vary, but may point out that the criterion "better" is too vague, and many arguments could be advanced for or against the truth of the statement.

30. Answers will vary.Students may mention the economic pressures that force nations to continue to pollute the environment, even though they know that pollution is harmful.

31. Answers will vary, but should show an awareness of the fact that parts of the alliances persisted through both wars and that the discontent over the settlement of World War I helped bring about World War II—that in a sense, World War I was never "settled."

32. Answers will vary, but might mention war weariness on the part of colonial powers and cite raised expectations on the part of colonies, including promises from the allies that nations would be independent after the war.

33. Urban areas become overcrowded. There are not enough places to live. Services, including education and health care, are sometimes not adequate.

34. Natural resources might be used up.

35. the use of water and fuels by so many people

36. the end of apartheid, space exploration, and the civil rights movement in the United States

37. Sample response: Large numbers of people have moved from the countryside to urban areas. Sometimes this movement results in overcrowding and poor living conditions.

38. how dams can affect areas surrounding them

39. Possible answers: Rivers would no longer deposit silt along their banks. Small organisms would die. Fish in a river could disappear. Land erosion could become a problem.

40. Rivers might no longer support living organisms. People would not have fish to eat.

41. Farmers living downstream from a dam would have their crops irrigated.

42. Soil wouldn't get silt deposits. Erosion might occur.

CHAPTER 8

Chapter 9 ■ *Final Exam*

A. KEY TERMS

Match the definitions with the terms. Write the correct letter in each blank. You will not use all the terms.

    a. caliph
    b. clan
    c. colony
    d. communism
    e. feudal system
    f. guild
    g. merit system
    h. mosque
    i. pueblo

1. _____ a Muslim place of worship

2. _____ a group of families who trace their roots back to the same ancestor

3. _____ an apartment-type village built by Native Americans

4. _____ a type of government in which less powerful people promise loyalty to more powerful people

5. _____ a theory of government that says all people should share work equally and receive equal parts of the rewards

Complete each sentence by writing the letter of the correct term in the blank. You will not use all the terms.

    a. artisan
    b. conquistador
    c. dynasty
    d. genocide
    e. labor union
    f. oasis
    g. patriarch
    h. prophet
    i. vassal

6. _____ Muslims believe that Muhammad is a(n) _____ , or messenger of God.

7. _____ A person who practices a trade is a(n) _____ .

8. _____ Someone who promised loyalty to a lord was called a(n) _____ .

9. _____ The leader of the Church in Constantinople was called the _____ .

10. _____ The systematic killing of an entire group of people is called _____ .

B. KEY CONCEPTS

Write the letter of the correct answer in each blank.

11. _____ Muslim beliefs are expressed in the Five Pillars of Islam, which include
   a. faith, prayer, sharing, fasting, and pilgrimage.
   b. bishops, cardinals, popes, priests, and nuns.
   c. loyalty, bravery, chivalry, honor, and victory.
   d. worship, confession, marriage, baptism, and burial.

12. _____ The largest desert in the world, the Sahara, stretches across most of
   a. the Arabian Peninsula.   c. North Africa.
   b. Southeast Asia.   d. South Africa.

13. _____ Two great civilizations from Central America were
   a. the Mayas and the Aztecs.   c. the Anasazi and the Pueblos.
   b. the Incas and the Peruvians.   d. the Aztecs and the Mound Builders.

14. _____ During the Tang and Song dynasties, China was one of the most
   a. violent regions in the world.
   b. advanced and powerful empires in the world.
   c. democratic countries in the world.
   d. isolated empires in the world.

15. _____ The system of government in which local lords ruled the land but had ties to higher lords was
   a. the merit system.   c. the guild system.
   b. chivalry.   d. feudalism.

16. _____ One reason the Church was so powerful during the Middle Ages was that it
   a. had the largest army in Europe.
   b. waged warfare against powerful lords.
   c. made laws and set up courts to enforce them.
   d. gave the serfs more rights than the lords did.

17. _____ During the Reformation, kings and nobles who disliked the power of the pope quickly
   a. arrested Luther.   c. put down Catholic uprisings.
   b. punished Protestants.   d. accepted Luther's ideas.

18. _____ What was one benefit resulting from the Industrial Revolution?
   a. Workers could stay home with their children.
   b. Small farmers began to earn more money.
   c. More people could move into the middle class of society.
   d. People could work at their own pace.

19. _____ What was the immediate cause of World War II?
    a. religious differences between European nations
    b. Germany's invasion of Poland
    c. the growth of communism in Russia
    d. the death of Archduke Franz Ferdinand

20. _____ What is one thing that Jews, Christians, and Muslims have in common?
    a. They all worship in mosques.
    b. They all strive to make a pilgrimage to Mecca.
    c. They all believe in one God alone.
    d. They all prohibit the eating of pork.

21. _____ What makes the Bantu migrations so amazing?
    a. They were the first migrations to be recorded in writing.
    b. They are among the largest population movements in human history.
    c. They spread African culture to Europe.
    d. They happened over a period of 10 years.

22. _____ One of the great achievements of the Incas was their
    a. organized legal code.   c. writing system.
    b. strict system of social classes.   d. system of roads and bridges.

23. _____ What did the shogun Ieyasu Tokugawa do to prevent Europe from conquering Japan?
    a. He isolated Japan from the West.
    b. He traded for European weapons.
    c. He launched an attack on the British navy.
    d. He encouraged Japanese people to convert to Christianity.

24. _____ Why was Akbar considered India's greatest Mughal emperor?
    a. He abolished the caste system.
    b. He spread Islam throughout India.
    c. He was fair to people of different religions.
    d. He filled all government positions with wise Hindus.

25. _____ Why did the Crusades take place?
    a. to reopen the Holy Land to Christian pilgrims
    b. to stop the Viking attacks on Europe
    c. to force Italy to open its trade routes
    d. to protect the Italians and Spanish from the Muslims

26. _____ By reducing the power of the nobles and the Church, Louis XIV gained
    a. more power for the people.   c. power for himself.
    b. control over Spain.   d. control over England.

27. _____ Britain is considered a constitutional monarchy because the monarch's power is
    a. granted by the Church of England.   c. given by God.
    b. voted on each year.   d. limited by a set of laws.

28. ____ One of the main causes of World War I was
   a. the increase in nationalism throughout Europe.
   b. religious differences between European nations.
   c. the growth of communism in Russia.
   d. Germany's invasion of Poland.

C. CRITICAL THINKING

Answer the following questions in the space provided, on the back of this paper or on a separate sheet of paper.

29. Drawing Conclusions: Why do you think the Byzantine empire lasted so long? In your answer, give at least three reasons.

30. Making Comparisons: Compare the golden ages of China with the Renaissance in Europe.

31. Expressing Problems Clearly: Why were the early Middle Ages a dangerous time in European history?

32. Recognizing Cause and Effect: What are some global effects of the Industrial Revolution? In your answer, describe two effects that concern people around the world.

D. SKILL: DISTINGUISHING FACT FROM OPINION

Read the passage below. Then answer the following questions on the lines provided.

The Industrial Revolution began in Great Britain in the late 1700s. All English people rejoiced at its coming because it was the greatest thing to happen in Britain's history. Spinning and weaving machines were among the first inventions of the Industrial Revolution, and clothmakers were happy to leave their homes to work in factories. All in all, the industrial revolution improved the lives of many people.

33. What is one fact contained in the passage? _____

_____

34. How can you tell that it is a fact? _____

_____

35. What is one opinion contained in the passage? _____

_____

36. How can you tell that it is an opinion?_____

_____

37. Which sentence from the passage contains both a fact and an opinion? _____

_____

Study the following reading assignment. Then assess your understanding of the assignment by answering the questions below on the lines provided.

Although the Mayas suffered under Spanish rule, their culture survived. Today, the modern Mayas live near where their ancestors did, in Mexico, Belize, Guatemala, and Honduras. Many age-old traditions continue in these communities. For example, ways of naming children, celebrating marriages, and marking deaths are similar to what they were hundreds of years ago. In some places, Mayan clothing has also remained traditional. The Mayan language continues to be spoken throughout Central America.

38. What is the point of this assignment? _____

_____

39. What are some Mayan traditions that continue today? _____

_____

40. What are the main ideas in this paragraph? _____

_____

41. How could you use the information from this assignment in the future?_____

_____

42. If you are not sure about any of the answers you've written above, what should you do? ____

_____

ANSWER KEY

1. h	2. b	3. i	4. e	5. d
6. h	7. a	8. i	9. g	10. d
11. a	12. c	13. a	14. b	15. d
16. c	17. d	18. c	19. b	20. c
21. b	22. d	23. a	24. c	25. a
26. c	27. d	28. a		

29. Answers may vary. A possible answer: One reason that the Byzantine empire lasted so long was that it was located at a great trading crossroads. The Byzantines grew rich from the taxes they charged on goods that went through their territory. Another reason was that it had the best army in the world and used many advanced weapons, including "Greek fire," to defeat enemies. The empire also had a series of good rulers, including Justinian.

30. Answers may vary. A possible answer: The golden ages of China, which occurred under the Tang and Song dynasties, were similar to the Renaissance in Europe. In China, new trade routes and trade products helped to make the country rich. In Italy, merchants grew rich from trading with Asia. This trade wealth helped encourage creativity and the arts in both countries. In addition, there was a love of knowledge during both time periods. The invention of printing helped to spread knowledge throughout China, while during the Renaissance, some people had more time to think and to read.

31. Answers may vary. A possible answer: The early Middle Ages were a dangerous time because the Roman Empire was no longer strong enough to defend its borders. Invaders like the Vikings attacked Western Europe. With no strong force to prevent them, these fierce warriors murdered people and looted villages. They destroyed towns and cut off trade routes, so Europeans became isolated from one another. Eventually, Europeans worked out a new system of government, feudalism, to protect themselves.

32. Answers may vary. A possible answer: One effect of the Industrial Revolution was imperialism. Factories needed a lot of raw materials and made a lot of goods, so European countries set up colonies in Africa and Asia to get raw materials and to sell goods. Another lasting effect of the Industrial Revolution is pollution. Factories pollute the water and air, and getting raw materials to feed the factories has destroyed much of the environment around those resources. Today, controlling pollution is one of the world's greatest challenges.

33. The Industrial Revolution began in Great Britain in the late 1700s.

34. It can be proved true.

35. The Industrial Revolution was the greatest thing to happen in Britain's history.

36. You cannot measure the single greatest thing in a country's history.

37. Spinning and weaving machines were among the first inventions of the Industrial Revolution, and clothmakers were happy to leave their homes to work in factories.

38. to assess understanding

39. ways of naming children, celebrating marriages, and marking deaths

40. Many of the traditions of Mayan culture are practiced by modern Mayas.

41. If I wrote a report on the Mayan civilization, I could include information about the Mayas today.

42. Review the assignment with the questions in mind.